CONTEMPORARY'S

GED

LANGUAGE ARTS, READING

John M. Reier

Reviewers

Pamela A. Blundell, Coordinator
Oklahoma State Dept. of Education
Lifelong Learning Section
Oklahoma City, Oklahoma

Dom Gagliardi, Assistant Principal
Escondido Adult School
Escondido, CA

Rosalie Kavadlo
Office of Adult and Continuing Education
New York City Board of Education
Long Island City, New York

Sandra Koehler, Consultant
Adult Learning Resource Center
Des Plaines, IL

Judy Voth, ABE/GED Instructor
Portland Community College
Portland, Oregon

Paula Wood, Adult Basic Ed Coordinator
Region 16 Education Service Center
Amarillo, Texas

 **Wright Group**

3 4 5 6 7 8 9 0   QPD/QPD   1 0 9 8 7

ISBN 0-07-140710-3

McGraw-Hill books are available at special quantity discounts to use as premiums and sales promotions, or for use in corporate training programs. For more information, please write to the Director of Special Sales, Professional Publishing, McGraw-Hill, Two Penn Plaza, New York, NY 10121-2298. Or contact your local bookstore.

This book is printed on acid-free paper.

Table of Contents

PART II: UNDERSTANDING LANGUAGE ARTS, READING

Acknowledgments

Excerpt on page 2 from "The Cultures of Illness", *U.S. News & World Report*, February 15, 1993.

Excerpt on page 6 from *West Side Story* by Arthur Laurents and Stephen Sondheim, music by Leonard Bernstein. Copyright © 1956, 1958 by Arthur Laurents, Leonard Bernstein, Stephen Sondheim and Jerome Robbins. Used by permission of Random House, Inc.

Excerpt on page 8 from "The Joys of Having a Mom With a Job" by Reed Karaim, as appeared in *Washington Post*, July 30, 2000. Reed Karaim is the author of the novel *If Men Were Angels*. Reprinted with his permission.

Poem on page 10, "We Alone", from *Horses Make a Landscape Look More Beautiful*. Copyright © 1984 by Alice Walker, reprinted by permission of Harcourt, Inc.

Excerpt on page 18 reprinted from *Black Elk Speaks* by John G. Niehardt, by permission of the University of Nebraska Press. Copyright 1932, 1959, 1972, by John G. Niehardt. Copyright © 1961 by the John G. Niehardt Trust.

Excerpt on page 21 reprinted from *Blue-Collar Journal*, © 1974 by John R. Coleman, by permission of Collier Associates, P.O. Box 20149, West Palm Beach, FL 33416 USA.

Excerpt on page 25 from *Long Lance* by Chief Buffalo Child Long-Lance. Copyright 1928 by Cosmopolitan Book Corporation. Copyright © 1956 by Holt, Rinehart and Winston. Reprinted by permission of Henry Holt and Company, LLC.

Excerpt on page 28, "About the Author," from *Modern Black Stories*, Martin Mirer, ed. Copyright © 1971 by Barrons Educational Series, Inc., Hauppage, NY. Reprinted by permission.

Excerpt on page 30 from "Vietnam, Vietnam," by Pete Hamill, as appeared in *Vanity Fair*, April 1985. Reprinted by permission of International Creative Management, Inc. Copyright © 1985 by Pete Hamill.

Excerpt on page 32 from "Just a Housewife" from *Working: People Talk About What They Do All Day and How They Feel About What They Do*, by Studs Terkel. Reprinted by permission of Donadio & Olson, Inc. Copyright 1972 by Studs Terkel.

Excerpt on page 34 from "The Puck Stops Here" by Elizabeth Kaufmann, as appeared in *Women's Sports and Fitness*, January/February 1993. Reprinted with permission from Elizabeth Kaufmann.

Excerpt on page 36 from "Barrio Boy" by Ernesto Galarza. © 1971 by University of Notre Dame Press. Reprinted by permission of the publisher.

Excerpt on page 37 from *The Road to Wigan Pier* by George Orwell, copyright © 1958 and renewed 1986 by the Estate of Sonia B. Orwell, reprinted by permission of Harcourt, Inc. Also, (Copyright © George Orwell, 1937) reproduced by permission of A.M. Heath & Co. Ltd. on behalf of William Hamilton as the Literary Executor of the Estate of the Late Sonia Brownell Orwell and Secker & Warburg Ltd.

Exerpt on page 42 from *Driving Miss Daisy* by Alfred Uhry. Copyright © 1986 by Alfred Uhry. Used by permission of Flora Roberts, Inc.

Exerpt on page 44 from "The Bridge" by Gay Talese.

Excerpt on page 46 from "On Form, Not Plot, In the Short Story," from *A Storyteller's Story*, by Sherwood Anderson. Reprinted by permission of Harold Ober Associates. Copyright © 1924 by Sherwood Anderson.

Excerpt on page 55 from "The Five-Forty-Eight" by John Cheever. Copyright © 1958 by John Cheever. Reprinted by permission.

Excerpt on page 56 from "Two Kinds", from *The Joy Luck Club* by Amy Tan. Copyright © 1989 by Amy Tan. Used by permission of G.P. Putnam's Sons, a division of Penguin Putnam Inc.

Excerpt on page 59 from *A Sense of Where You Are* by John McPhee. Copyright © 1965, 1978 by John McPhee. Reprinted by permission of Farrar, Straus and Giroux, LLC.

Excerpt on pages 62–63 reprinted with permission, from "Giving Power to Words" by Philip W. Swain, *American Journal of Physics*, 13, p. 318. Copyright 1947, American Association of Physics Teachers.

Excerpt on page 65 from "Puritanism Revisited: An Analysis of the Contemporary Screen-Image Western" by Peter Homans. Reprinted by permission of Peter Homans, Professor Emeritus at the University of Chicago.

Excerpts on pages 66 and 67 from *In Search of the Present: Nobel Lecture 1990* by Octavio Paz and Anthony Stanton. © The Nobel Foundation,1990.

Excerpt on pages 69–70 from *Small Comforts* by Tom Bodett. Copyright © 1987 by Tom Bodett. Reprinted by permission of Perseus Books Publishers, a member of Perseus Books, L.L.C.

Excerpt on page 70 from the radio show "The Shadow." The Shadow character, copyrights, and trademarks are owned by The Condé Nast Publications. Used with permission.

Excerpt on page 71 from "Fifteen" by Bob Greene, 1982. Reprinted with permission.

Excerpt on page 71 reprinted with permission of Scribner, a Division of Simon & Schuster, Inc., from *The Great Gatsby* (Authorized Text) by F. Scott Fitzgerald. Copyright 1925 by Charles Scribner's Sons. Copyright renewed 1953 by Frances Scott Fitzgerald Lanahan. Copyright © 1991, 1992 by Eleanor Lanahan, Matthew J. Bruccoli and Samuel J. Lanahan as Trustees under Agreement dated July 3, 1975 created by Frances Scott Fitzgerald Smith.

Excerpt on page 73 from "The Assassination" by Tom Wicker, from *The New York Times* "Times Talk," December 19, 1963. Copyright © 1963 by the New York Times Co. Reprinted by permission.

Excerpt on page 73 from "Kennedy Is Killed by Snipers as He Rides in Car in Dallas" by Tom Wicker, from *The New York Times*, November 23, 1963. Copyright © 1963 by the New York Times Co. Reprinted by permission.

Excerpt on page 74 from "Big Two-Hearted River, Part II." Reprinted with permission of Scribner, a Division of Simon & Schuster, Inc., from *In Our Time* by Ernest Hemingway. Copyright 1925 by Charles Scribner's Sons. Copyright renewed 1953 by Ernest Hemingway.

Excerpt on page 75 from *Down These Mean Streets* by Piri Thomas. Copyright © 1967 by Piri Thomas. Reprinted by permission of Alfred A. Knopf, a Division of Random House, Inc.

Excerpt on page 81 from "The Rocking-Horse Winner," copyright 1933 by the Estate of D.H. Lawrence, renewed © 1961 by Angelo Ravagli and C.M. Weekley, Executors of the Estate of Frieda Lawrence, from *Complete Short Stories of D.H. Lawrence* by D.H. Lawrence. Used by permission of Viking Penguin, a division of Penguin Putnam Inc.

Excerpt on page 84 from "How to Kick a Machine," by Mike Royko. Reprinted with special permission from the Chicago Sun-Times, Inc. © 1986.

Excerpt on page 86 from "English Gets a Pro-Active Downsizing," January 1, 1993. Copyright Reuters Limited 1993. Reprinted by permission.

Excerpt on page 87 from Hisaye Yamamoto, *Seventeen Syllables and Other Stories*, copyright © 1988 by Hisaye Yamamoto DeSoto. Reprinted by permission of Rutgers University Press.

Excerpt on page 91 from "The Unreality of TV," from *The Buchwald Stops Here* by Art Buchwald, copyright © 1978 by Art Buchwald. Used by permission of Putnam Berkley, a division of Penguin Putnam Inc.

Excerpt on page 92 from "A Quarter-Century Later, The Myth Endures," by Lance Morrow in *Time*, August 25, 1986. © 1986 Time Inc. Reprinted by permission.

Excerpt on page 92–93 from "Slouching Toward Washington" by Darryl Pinckney, from *The New York Review of Books*, 1995. Reprinted with permission from The New York Review of Books. Copyright © 1995 NYREV, Inc.

Excerpt on page 243 from "Ex-Basketball Player," from *The Carpentered Hen and Other Tame Creatures* by John Updike, copyright © 1982 by John Updike. Used by permission of Alfred A. Knopf, a division of Random House, Inc.

Poem on page 246, "Daybreak" from *New and Selected Poems* by Gary Soto © 1995. Reprinted by permission of Chronicle Books, San Francisco.

Excerpts on pages 249–251 from *Of Mice and Men* by John Steinbeck, copyright 1937, renewed © 1965 by John Steinbeck. Used by permission of Viking Penguin, a division of Penguin Putnam Inc.

Excerpt on page 258 from "I Remember Mama—A Play in 2 Acts," copyright 1945 by John Van Druten and reviewed 1972 by Carter Lodge, reprinted by permission of Harcourt, Inc.

Excerpt on page 259 from *The Odd Couple*, © 1966 by Neil Simon. Professionals and amateurs are hereby warned that *The Odd Couple* is fully protected under the Berne Convention and the Universal Copyright Convention and is subject to royalty. All rights, including without limitation professional, amateur, motion picture, television, radio, recitation, lecturing, public reading and and foreign translation rights, computer media rights, and the right of reproduction, and electronic storage or retrieval, in whole or in part and in any form, are strictly reserved and none of these rights can be exercised or used without written permission from the copyright owner. Inquiries for stock and amateur performances should be addressed to Samuel French, Inc., 45 West 25th Street, New York, NY 10010. All other inquires should be addressed to Gary N. DaSilva, 11 N. Sepulveda Blvd., Suite 250, Manhattan Beach, CA 90266-6850.

Excerpt on pages 261–262 from *The Tumult and the Shouting*, Act One, Scene Five by Thomas Pawley. Reprinted by permission.

Excerpt on pages 263–265 from "A Doll's House," from *The Complete Major Prose Plays of Henrik Ibsen* by Henrik Ibsen, translated by Rolf Fjelde. Copyright © 1965, 1970, 1978 by Rolf Fjelde. Used by permission of Dutton Signet, a division of Penguin Putnam Inc.

Excerpt on pages 267–274 from *Death of a Salesman* by Arthur Miller, copyright 1949, renewed © 1977 by Arthur Miller. Used by permission of Viking Penguin, a division of Penguin Putnam Inc.

Excerpt on page 277 from "Fool for Love," copyright © 1983 by Sam Shepard, from *Fool For Love and Other Plays* by Sam Shepard. Used by permission of Bantam Books, a division of Random House, Inc.

Excerpt on page 278 from *Cat on a Hot Tin Roof* by Tennessee Williams, copyright © 1954, 1955, 1971, 1975 by the University of the South. Reprinted by permission of New Directions Publishing Corp.

Excerpt on page 280 from *A Raisin in the Sun* by Lorraine Hansberry, copyright © 1958 by Robert Nemiroff as an unpublished work. Copyright © 1959, 1966, 1984 by Robert Nemiroff. Used by permission of Random House, Inc.

Excerpt on page 284 from "The Jockey," from *The Ballad of the Sad Cafe and Collected Short Stories* by Carson McCullers. Copyright 1936, 1941, 1942, 1950, © 1955 by Carson McCullers, © renewed 1979 by Floria V. Lasky. Reprinted by permission of Houghton Mifflin Co. All rights reserved.

Excerpt on page 286 from *On Golden Pond* by Earnest Thompson, 1979. Reprinted with permission of the Graham Agency.

Excerpt on page 288 from "The Forest and the Trees," by John Lahr. Copyright © 1993 by John Lahr. Originally published in *The New Yorker*. Reprinted by permission of Georges Borchardt, Inc. for the author.

Excerpt on page 290 from *Snow in August* by Pete Hamill. Copyright © 1997 by Deidre Enterprises, Inc. By permission of Little, Brown and Company (Inc.).

Excerpt on page 292 reprinted from www.hrnext.com with permission of the publisher, HRnext.com, a division of Business & Legal Reports, Inc. Copyright © 2001.

PHOTO CREDITS

To the Student

If you're studying to pass the GED Tests, you're in good company. In 1999, the most recent year for which figures are available, the American Council on Education GED Testing Service reported that over 750,700 adults took the GED Test battery worldwide. Of this number, more than 526,400 (70 percent) actually received their certificates. About 14 percent of those with high school credentials, or about one in seven, have a GED diploma. One in twenty (5 percent) of the students in their first year of college study is a GED graduate.

The average age of GED test-takers in the United States was over 24 in 1999, but nearly three quarters (70 percent) of GED test-takers were 19 years of age or older. Two out of three GED test-takers report having completed the tenth grade or higher, and more than a third report having completed the eleventh grade before leaving high school.

Why do so many people choose to take the GED Tests? Some do so to get a job, to advance to a better job, to attend college, or to qualify for military service. More than two out of every three GED graduates work toward college degrees or attend trade, technical, or business schools. Still others pursue their GED diplomas to feel better about themselves or to set good examples for their children.

More than 14 million adults earned the GED diploma between 1942 and 1999. Some well-known graduates include country music singers Waylon Jennings and John Michael Montgomery, comedian Bill Cosby, Olympic gold medalist Mary Lou Retton, Delaware Lieutenant Governor Ruth Ann Minner, Colorado's U.S. Senator Ben Nighthorse Campbell, Wendy's founder Dave Thomas, Famous Amos Cookies creator Wally Amos, and Triple Crown winning jockey Ron Turcotte.

This book has been designed to help you, too, succeed on the test. It will provide you with instruction in the skills you need to pass and plenty of practice with the kinds of test items you will find on the real test.

What Does GED Stand For?

GED stands for the Tests of **General Educational Development.** The GED Test Battery is a national examination developed by the GED Testing Service of the American Council on Education. The certificate earned for passing the test is widely recognized by colleges, training schools, and employers as equivalent to a high school diploma. The American Council reports that almost all (more than 95 percent) of employers in the nation employ GED graduates and offer them the same salaries and opportunities for advancement as high school graduates.

The GED Test reflects the major and lasting outcomes normally acquired in a high school program. Since the passing rate for the GED is based on the performance of graduating high school seniors, you can be sure your skills are comparable. In fact, those who pass the GED Test actually do better than one-third of those graduating seniors. Your skills in communication, information processing, critical thinking, and problem solving are keys to success. The test also places special emphasis on questions that prepare you for entering the workplace or higher education. Much that you have learned informally or through other types of training can help you pass the test.

Special editions of the GED Test will include the Spanish language, Braille, large print, and audiocasette formats. If you need special accomodations because of a learning or physical disability, your adult education program and testing center can assist you.

What Should You Know to Pass the Test?

The GED Test consists of five examinations called Language Arts, Writing; Social Studies; Science; Language Arts, Reading; and Mathematics. On all five tests, you are expected to demonstrate the ability to think about many issues. You are tested on knowledge and skills you have acquired from life experiences, television, radio, books and newspapers, consumer products, and advertising. Your work or business experiences may be helpful during the test. You can expect the subjects to be interrelated. This is called *interdisciplinary* material. For example, a mathematics problem may include a scientific diagram. Or a social studies question may require some mathematical skills.

Keep these facts in mind about specific tests:

1. The **Language Arts, Writing Test** requires you in Part 1 to recognize or correct errors, revise sentences or passages, and shift constructions in the four areas of organization, sentence structure, usage, and mechanics (capitalization and punctuation). Letters, memos, and business-related documents are likely to be included.

In Part 2 you will write an essay of 200 to 250 words presenting an opinion or an explanation on a topic familiar to most adults. You should plan and organize your ideas before you write, and revise and edit your essay before you are finished.

2. Three of the five tests—**Social Studies, Science,** and **Mathematics**—require you to answer questions based on reading passages or interpreting graphs, charts, maps, cartoons, diagrams, or photographs. Developing strong reading and critical thinking skills is the key to succeeding on these tests. Being able to interpret information from graphic sources, such as a map or cartoon, is essential.

3. The **Language Arts, Reading Test** asks you to read literary text and show that you can comprehend, apply, analyze, synthesize, and evaluate concepts. You will also read nonfiction and show that you can understand the main points of what you are reading.

4. The **Mathematics Test** consists mainly of word problems to be solved. Therefore, you must be able to combine your ability to perform computations with problem-solving skills.

Part 1 of the Mathematics Test will permit the use of the Casio fx-260 calculator, which will be provided at the test site. The calculator will eliminate the tediousness of making complex calculations. Part 2 will not permit the use of the calculator. Both parts of the test will include problems without multiple-choice answers. These problems will require you to mark your answers on bubble-in number grids or on coordinate plane graphs.

Who May Take the Tests?

About 3,500 GED Testing Centers are available in the fifty United States, the District of Columbia, eleven Canadian provinces and territories, U.S. and overseas military bases, correctional institutions, Veterans Administration hospitals, and certain learning centers. People who have not graduated from high school and who meet specific eligibility requirements (age, residency, etc.) may take the tests. Since eligibility requirements vary, you should contact your local GED testing center or the director of adult education in your state, province, or territory for specific information.

What Is a Passing Score on the GED Test?

A passing score varies from area to area. To find out what you need to pass the test, contact your local GED testing center. However, you should keep two scores in mind. One score represents the minimum score you must get on each test. The other is the minimum average score on all five tests. Both of these scores will be set by your state, province, or territory and must be met in order to pass the GED Test.

Can You Retake the Test?

You are allowed to retake some or all of the tests. The regulations governing the number of times that you may retake the tests and the time you must wait before retaking them are set by your state, province, or territory. Some states require you to take a review class or to study on your own for a certain amount of time before retaking the test.

THE GED TESTS

Tests	Minutes	Questions	Content/Percentages
Language Arts, Writing			
Part 1: Editing (multiple choice)	75	50	Organization 15% Sentence Structure 30% Usage 30% Mechanics 25%
Part 2: Essay	45	1 topic: approx. 250 words	
Social Studies	70	50	World History 15% U.S. History 25% Civics and Government 25% Economics 20% Geography 15%
Science	80	50	Earth and Space Science 20% Life Science 45% Physical Science 35% (Physics and Chemistry)

Language Arts, Reading	65	40	Literary Text 75%
			   Poetry 15%
			   Drama 15%
			   Fiction 45%
			Nonfiction 25%
			   Informational Text
			   Literary Nonfiction
			   Reviews of Fine and Performing Arts
			   Business Documents

Mathematics			
Part 1: Calculator	45	25	Number Operations and Number Sense 20–30% Measurement and Geometry 20–30%
Part 2: No Calculator	45	25	Data Analysis, Statistics, and Probability 20–30% Algebra, Functions, and Patterns 20–30%
	Total: 7 1/4 hours	Total: 240 questions and one essay	

How Can You Best Prepare for the Test?

Many community colleges, public schools, adult education centers, libraries, churches, community-based organizations, and other institutions offer GED preparation classes. While your state, province, or territory may not require you to take part in a preparation program, it's a good idea if you've been out of school for some time, if you had academic difficulty when you were in school, or if you left before completing the eleventh grade. Some television stations broadcast classes to prepare people for the test. If you cannot find a GED preparation class locally, contact the director of adult education in your state, province, or territory.

What Are Some Test-Taking Tips?

1. Prepare physically. Get plenty of rest and eat a well-balanced meal before the test so that you will have energy and will be able to think clearly. Intense studying at the last minute probably will not help as much as having a relaxed and rested mind.

2. Arrive early. Be at the testing center at least 15 to 20 minutes before the starting time. Make sure you have time to find the room and to get situated. Keep in mind that many testing centers refuse to admit latecomers. Some testing centers operate on a first come, first served basis; so you want to be sure that there is an available seat for you on the day that you're ready to test.

3. Think positively. Tell yourself you will do well. If you have studied and prepared for the test, you should succeed.

4. Relax during the test. Take half a minute several times during the test to stretch and breathe deeply, especially if you are feeling anxious or confused.

5. Read the test directions carefully. Be sure you understand how to answer the questions. If you have any questions about the test or about filling in the answer form, ask before the test begins.

6. Know the time limit for each test. The Language Arts, Reading Test has a time limit of 65 minutes (1 hour 5 minutes). Work at a steady pace; if you have extra time, go back and check your answers.

7. Have a strategy for answering questions. You should read through the reading passages or look over the materials once and then answer the questions that follow. Read each question two or three times to make sure you understand it. It is best to refer back to the passage or graphic in order to confirm your answer choice. Don't try to depend on your memory of what you have just read or seen. Some people like to guide their reading by skimming the questions before reading a passage. Use the method that works best for you.

8. Don't spend a lot of time on difficult questions. If you're not sure of an answer, go on to the next question. Answer easier questions first and then go back to the harder questions. However, when you skip a question, be sure that you have skipped the same number on your answer sheet. Although skipping difficult questions is a good strategy for making the most of your time, it is very easy to get confused and throw off your whole answer key.

Lightly mark the margin of your answer sheet next to the numbers of the questions you did not answer so that you know what to go back to. To prevent confusion when your test is graded, be sure to erase these marks completely after you answer the questions.

9. Answer every question on the test. If you're not sure of an answer, take an educated guess. When you leave a question unanswered, you will always lose points, but you can possibly gain points if you make a correct guess.

If you must guess, try to eliminate one or more answers that you are sure are not correct. Then choose from the remaining answers. Remember that you greatly increase your chances if you can eliminate one or two answers before guessing. Of course, guessing should be used only when all else has failed.

10. Clearly fill in the circle for each answer choice. If you erase something, erase it completely. Be sure that you give only one answer per question; otherwise, no answer will count.

11. Practice test-taking. Use the exercises, reviews, and especially the Posttest and Practice Test in this book to better understand your test-taking habits and weaknesses. Use them to practice different strategies such as skimming questions first or skipping hard questions until the end. Knowing your own personal test-taking style is important to your success on the GED Test.

How to Use This Book

This book will guide you through the types of questions you can expect to find on the Language Arts, Reading Test. To answer the questions successfully, you will need to focus on getting the meaning from what you have read. You will be reading literary fiction pieces as well as nonfiction from books, magazines, newspapers, and workplace materials. If you do not read very much, now is the time to start. Not only will you improve your reading skills but you will also set a pattern for lifelong learning.

Before beginning this book, you should take the Pretest. This will give you a preview of what the Language Arts, Reading Test includes but, more important, it will help you identify which areas you need to concentrate on most. Use the chart at the end of the Pretest to pinpoint the types of questions you have answered incorrectly and to determine which skills you need the most work in. You may decide to concentrate on specific areas or to work through the entire book. We strongly suggest you do work through the whole book to best prepare yourself for the GED Test.

This book has a number of features designed to help make the task of test preparation easier and more effective.

- The first four chapters isolate the four **thinking skills** covered on the Language Arts, Reading Test—comprehension, application, analysis, and synthesis. **Comprehension** refers to the ability to understand and draw conclusions about a passage. **Application** is the ability to take information or knowledge gained from one situation and use it to answer questions about another, similar situation. **Analysis** consists of breaking a passage into logical parts and thinking about how the parts fit together. **Synthesis** involves taking information from two different sources and combining that information to create a new idea or understanding. The first four chapters isolate these skills and give plenty of practice exercises to help you understand and develop your abilities.

- Chapter 5, **Nonfiction Prose**, helps develop techniques for reading nonfiction. This chapter includes excerpts from recent magazine articles, including articles about visual communication, editorials, essays, and biographies. You will also practice reading business-related documents of types that might be included on the Language Arts, Reading Test, such as excerpts from employee handbooks, information from training manuals, and legal workplace documents. Approximately 25% of the passages on the Language Arts, Reading Test will be nonfiction text.

- Chapters 6, 7, and 8 cover literary text—**Prose Fiction, Poetry,** and **Drama**. Literary excerpts have been chosen from the three time periods covered on the Language Arts, Reading Test—before 1920, from 1920 to 1960, and after 1960. As you read these excerpts, you will strengthen your thinking and reading skills with GED practice questions. Approximately 75% of the passages on the Language Arts, Reading Test will be literary text.

- The literary selections feature popular and classic authors with **diverse ethnic and cultural backgrounds** to reflect our world today.

- **Writing activities** provide an opportunity to practice and form a deeper understanding of specific literary concepts immediately after their lessons.

- The **Answer Key** explains the correct answers for the exercises. If you make a mistake, you can learn from it by reading the explanation that follows the answer and then reviewing the question to analyze the error.

- Throughout the chapters you'll see references to **www.GEDReading.com**. This Web site has been designed to accompany this book. Check it out for additional instruction and practice.

After you have worked through the eight chapters in this book, you should take the Posttest. The Posttest is a simulated GED Test that presents questions in the format, at the level of difficulty, and in the percentages found on the actual GED Test. The Posttest will help you determine whether you are ready for the GED Language Arts, Reading Test. The evaluation chart at the end of the test will help you locate the areas of the book you need to review.

After you have reviewed, the Practice Test can be used as a final indicator of your readiness for the GED Test. This test has the same format, level of difficulty, and percentages as the Posttest and the GED Language Arts, Reading Test.

Language Arts, Reading

Directions: Before you begin to work with this book, take this pretest. The purpose of the pretest is to help you determine which skills you need to develop to pass the GED Language Arts, Reading Test.

The pretest consists of twenty multiple-choice questions. These questions are based on passages of fiction, nonfiction, poetry, and drama.

Answer each question as carefully as possible, choosing the best of five answer choices and blackening in the grid for that answer. If you find a question too difficult, do not waste time on it. Work ahead and come back to it later when you can think it through carefully.

When you have completed the test, check your work with the answers and explanations at the end of the section.

Use the evaluation chart on page 12 to determine the areas you need to review most. However, for the best preparation for the GED Language Arts, Reading Test, we advise you to work through this entire book.

Pretest Answer Grid

1	① ② ③ ④ ⑤	8	① ② ③ ④ ⑤	15	① ② ③ ④ ⑤
2	① ② ③ ④ ⑤	9	① ② ③ ④ ⑤	16	① ② ③ ④ ⑤
3	① ② ③ ④ ⑤	10	① ② ③ ④ ⑤	17	① ② ③ ④ ⑤
4	① ② ③ ④ ⑤	11	① ② ③ ④ ⑤	18	① ② ③ ④ ⑤
5	① ② ③ ④ ⑤	12	① ② ③ ④ ⑤	19	① ② ③ ④ ⑤
6	① ② ③ ④ ⑤	13	① ② ③ ④ ⑤	20	① ② ③ ④ ⑤
7	① ② ③ ④ ⑤	14	① ② ③ ④ ⑤		

Directions: Read each passage and choose the best answer to the questions that follow.

Questions 1–4 refer to the following excerpt from an article.

HOW DOES IT FEEL TO BE SICK IN A FOREIGN COUNTRY?

Shotsy Faust walks into the examining room wearing casual clothes and her best bedside manner, and introduces herself to a Russian patient recently arrived in San
5 Francisco. She smiles. "Hi, nice to meet you. I'm a nurse practitioner. How are you today?" The man looks uncomfortable. He scowls and mutters to the interpreter in Russian, "Who is this fool?" Later, the
10 interpreter explains: "He thought you were a ninny because you were so friendly. Next time you have a Russian patient, try wearing a white coat and acting more formal."

It is one of the twists and turns Faust
15 has become accustomed to as director of San Francisco General Hospital's bustling refugee clinic; one of the hazards of stepping into a different world each time she greets a new patient, moving seamlessly
20 from Saigon to Ethiopia to Baghdad to Cuba to a small village in the hills of Laos. A Haitian man refuses a blood test, fearing that the blood, which holds part of the soul, might be used for sorcery. A
25 Vietnamese patient cuts his medication in half, convinced that American drugs, meant for large people, will be too strong. A Cambodian woman's family does not want her to die at home: her spirit, they insist, will
30 linger in the apartment after her death.

In clinics and emergency rooms across the country, Western medical science is colliding headlong with the beliefs and practices of other cultures as a new wave
35 of migration turns even many a suburban hospital into a small United Nations. In 1992, more than 1 million legal immigrants and refugees entered the United States. Most of the newcomers speak little or
40 no English. Many regard doctors with exaggerated awe, distrust or a mixture of the two. And more than a few carry the scars of horrifying experiences—rape, torture, imprisonment, slaughter of family
45 members—experiences making them prime candidates for both physical and psychological illness.

This multicultural flood is changing the way health workers practice
50 their profession, creating a surge of interest in cross-cultural research and challenging American medicine's traditional ethnocentrism. In Boston and Fresno, Minneapolis and Miami, a growing number
55 of hospitals are hiring full-time interpreters for significant patient minorities, providing training for staff in cultural differences and even adding ethnic foods to their menus.

—Excerpted from "The Cultures of Illness,"
U.S. News & World Report, February 15, 1993

1. According to the passage, which choice best identifies Shotsy Faust?

   (1) representative to the United Nations
   (2) director of a hospital refugee clinic
   (3) foreign-language expert specializing in Russian
   (4) Cambodian woman who is dying
   (5) Russian doctor who understands her patients

2. What is the main idea of the passage?

(1) U.S. hospitals try to meet the special needs of immigrant patients.

(2) Patients from other countries travel to the United States for health care.

(3) U.S. doctors struggle to get along with their immigrant patients.

(4) Patients from other countries dislike and distrust U.S. doctors.

(5) Immigrant patients tend to ignore U.S. doctors' orders and prescriptions.

3. What does the author mean when she says in lines 34–36 that ". . . a new wave of migration [is] turn[ing] even many a suburban hospital into a small United Nations?"

(1) Small suburban hospitals are becoming more like big-city hospitals.

(2) Suburban hospital workers are learning to solve problems in democratic ways.

(3) Suburban hospitals are treating increasing numbers of newcomers to the United States.

(4) Suburban hospitals are not equipped to treat patients who do not speak English.

(5) Hospitalized suburbanites are forming close relationships with patients from other nations.

4. What advice might Shotsy Faust give to health care workers who treat minority patients?

(1) Make patients feel comfortable by acting casual and friendly.

(2) Write instructions clearly to make them easy for patients to follow.

(3) Speak loudly and carefully to ensure that the patients understand you.

(4) Improve communication by showing respect for the beliefs of the patients.

(5) Dress in white clothing to inform the patients that you are a medical doctor.

PRETEST

Questions 5–8 refer to the following excerpt from a novel.

WHAT DO YOU NOTICE ABOUT HUCK'S RELATIONSHIP WITH HIS FATHER?

As for his clothes—just rags, that was all. He had one ankle resting on t'other knee; the boot on that foot was busted, and two of his toes stuck through, and he worked
5 them now and then. His hat was laying on the floor—an old black slouch with the top caved in, like a lid.

I stood a-looking at him; he set there a-looking at me, with his chair tilted back a
10 little. I set the candle down. I noticed the window was up; so he had clumb in by the shed. He kept a-looking me all over. By and by he says:

"Starchy clothes—very. You think you're
15 a good deal of a big-bug, *don't* you?"

"Maybe I am, maybe I ain't," I says.

"Don't you give me none o' your lip," says he. "You've put on considerable many frills since I been away. I'll take you down a
20 peg before I get done with you. You're educated, too, they say—can read and write. You think you're better'n your father, now, don't you, because he can't? *I'll* take it out of you. Who told you you might meddle
25 with such hifalut'n foolishness, hey?—who told you you could?"

"The widow. She told me."

"The widow, hey?—and who told the widow she could put in her shovel about a
30 thing that ain't none of her business?"

"Nobody never told her."

"Well, I'll learn her how to meddle. And looky here—you drop that school, you hear? I'll learn people to bring up a boy to put on
35 airs over his own father and let on to be

better'n what he is. You lemme catch you fooling around that school again, you hear? Your mother couldn't read, and she couldn't write, nuther, before she died. None of the
40 family couldn't before they died. I can't; and here you're a-swelling yourself up like this. I ain't the man to stand it—you hear?"

—Excerpted from *The Adventures of Huckleberry Finn*
by Mark Twain, 1884

5. What do the phrases "a-looking" (lines 8 and 12) and "clumb in" (line 10) tell you about the narrator of the story?

   (1) He doesn't get along with his father.
   (2) He speaks a foreign language.
   (3) He speaks standard English.
   (4) He cannot read or write.
   (5) He speaks a dialect of English.

6. What is the main topic of conversation between Huck and his father?

   (1) the widow's meddling
   (2) Huck's education
   (3) Huck's mother's death
   (4) Huck's family's background
   (5) Huck's father's behavior

7. What is the purpose of the dialogue in the passage?

   (1) to explain why sons should obey their fathers
   (2) to reveal some of the problems of a single parent
   (3) to imply that Huck and his father should study grammar
   (4) to dramatize the conflict between Huck and his father
   (5) to make fun of Huck's and his father's upbringing

8. What social problem discussed in this
   excerpt is also being addressed today?

   (1) illiteracy
   (2) child abuse
   (3) alcoholism
   (4) juvenile delinquency
   (5) kidnapping

Questions 9–12 refer to the following excerpt from a drama.

HOW DO TONY AND RIFF FEEL ABOUT A GANG CALLED THE JETS?

TONY: Now go play nice with the Jets.

RIFF: The Jets are the greatest!

TONY: Were.

RIFF: Are. You found somethin' better?

5 **TONY:** No. But—

RIFF: But what?

TONY: You won't dig it.

RIFF: Try me.

TONY: O.K. . . . Every single damn night for
10 the last month, I wake up—and I'm
reachin' out.

RIFF: For what?

TONY: I don't know. It's right outside the
door, around the corner. But it's
15 comin'!

RIFF: What is? Tell me!

TONY: I don't know! It's—like the kick I
used to get from bein' a Jet.

RIFF: . . . Or from bein' buddies.

20 **TONY:** We're still buddies.

RIFF: The kick comes from people, buddy
boy.

TONY: Yeah, but not from being a Jet.

RIFF: No? Without a gang you're an
25 orphan. With a gang you walk in
twos, threes, fours. And when your
gang is the best, when you're a Jet,
buddy boy, you're out in the sun and
home free home!

30 **TONY:** Riff, I've had it. [Pause]

RIFF: Tony, the trouble is large: the Sharks
bite hard! We got to stop them now,
and we need you! [Pause. Quietly] I
never asked the time of day from a
35 clock, but I'm askin' you: Come to
the dance tonight . . . [TONY turns
away] . . . I already told the gang
you'd be there.

TONY: [After a moment, turns to him with a
40 grin] What time?

RIFF: Ten?

TONY: Ten, it is.

—Excerpted from *West Side Story* by Arthur Laurents and
Leonard Bernstein, 1957

9. According to the excerpt, what does the
word *kick* (lines 17 and 21) mean?

   (1) a football punt
   (2) a drug-induced sensation
   (3) a thrilling experience
   (4) a sum of money
   (5) a leg movement

10. Why does Riff say, "Without a gang you're
an orphan" (lines 24–25)?

   (1) to suggest that Tony's parents are dead
   (2) to analyze why city kids feel abandoned
   (3) to imply that Tony's parents ignore him
   (4) to compare a gang to a family
   (5) to show that the gangs recruit orphans

11. What is Riff's tone of voice when he asks
Tony to go to the dance?

   (1) unfriendly
   (2) pleading
   (3) angry
   (4) bossy
   (5) sad

12. Why does Tony decide to attend the dance?

Because he
(1) is excited about being in a gang
(2) hasn't gone out for the last month
(3) wants to find a girlfriend
(4) doesn't have anything better to do
(5) values his friendship with Riff

Questions 13–16 refer to the following passage from a newspaper article.

HOW DOES THE AUTHOR FEEL ABOUT WORKING MOTHERS?

According to Department of Labor statistics from 1999, 72 percent of all women with children under 18 work. Even most moms with infants work: 61 percent of
5 all mothers with children under the age of 3. This isn't going to change. We are eight years into an economic boom of historic proportions; if ever there was a time working mothers were going to retire from
10 the job force, this would be it. Yet the percentage of working mothers continued to climb throughout the '90s. The Beaver's mom has left a casserole in the refrigerator and gone off to work. She'll try to be home
15 by 6.

What is her family getting in return? For starters, quite often the answer is the groceries and a roof over their heads. The money working mothers make is
20 tremendously important to their families. Two-parent families where the mother works have an annual average income of $63,751, $26,000 more a year than households where only the father works. In most of America,
25 this extra income may not seem extravagant, but it helps boost many families onto the verdant green lawns of the middle class, with all the comforts, chances for education and opportunity that provides
30 to children.

Somehow this gets neglected in the various academic studies that seek to determine whether the children of working mothers do worse than their peers, either
35 socially or academically. The studies disagree. But there's one thing we can be sure of—the money matters.

Something else that matters is the example we set for our children. And one
40 important example is a willingness to work. There's no one who doesn't need to learn this sooner or later, and it's a lesson taught best by example.

—Excerpted from "The Joys of Having a Mom with a Job" by Reed Karaim, *Washington Post*, 2000

13. Based on the passage, what is the major benefit a family gets from a mother working?

   (1) higher social status
   (2) increased job opportunities
   (3) more time together
   (4) more chances for education
   (5) debt reduction

14. Which of the following additional benefits does the excerpt discuss?

   (1) Children learn to be more self-sufficient.
   (2) Fathers spend more time with their children
   (3) Parents instill a positive work ethic in their children.
   (4) Families appreciate their time together more.
   (5) Management positions are open to working mothers.

15. How will the trend discussed in the passage most likely affect communities?

Communities will
   (1) experience a sharp rise in the number of stay-at-home fathers
   (2) increase the average class size in elementary schools
   (3) insist that businesses offer more training to mothers
   (4) need more playground facilities
   (5) need more child-care facilities

16. On the basis of this excerpt, which of the following words or phrases best describes the nation's attitude toward working mothers?

    (1) positive because of the high employment created

    (2) critical of the effects on children

    (3) critical of the effects on business

    (4) mixed in positive and negative attitudes

    (5) indifferent and unconcerned

PRETEST

Questions 17–20 refer to the following poem.

WHAT DOES THE SPEAKER VALUE?

We Alone

We alone can devalue gold
by not caring
if it falls or rises
in the marketplace.

5 Wherever there is gold
there is a chain, you know,
and if your chain
is gold
so much the worse
10 for you.

Feathers, shells
and sea-shaped stones
are all as rare.

This could be our revolution:
15 To love what is plentiful
as much as
what's scarce.

—"We Alone" by Alice Walker

17. According to the poem, what does gold
represent for the speaker?

   (1) escape
   (2) captivity
   (3) learning
   (4) wealth
   (5) poverty

18. What is meant by the lines, "Wherever there
is gold/there is a chain"?

   (1) Many wear chains that are made of gold.
   (2) Gold can blind one to life's simple joys.
   (3) Slavery's chains can be broken by gold.
   (4) A person's value is determined by gold.
   (5) Gold must be earned by hard work.

19. What is the purpose of the third stanza (lines
11–13)?

   To list
   (1) objects of similar value
   (2) treasures from the sea
   (3) items that are very rare
   (4) scraps without value
   (5) simple objects to treasure

20. What is the purpose of the poem?

   (1) to stress the importance of gold to our
   economy
   (2) to suggest the wealth found in life's
   simple things
   (3) to convey the sense of power that
   wealth gives
   (4) to revolt so that everyone shares in the
   wealth
   (5) to praise those who have risen from
   poverty

Answer Key

1. (2) Lines 15–17 say that Faust is director of San Francisco General Hospital's refugee clinic.

2. (1) Throughout the excerpt statements point out the main idea that 'Western medical science is colliding headlong with the beliefs and practices of other cultures" (lines 32–34) and that "this multicultural flood is changing the way health workers practice their profession" (lines 48–50).

3. (3) The entire excerpt describes how hospitals are dealing with the increasing need to understand people of cultural backgrounds as diverse as the member countries of the United Nations.

4. (4) As director of a refugee clinic, Faust is sensitive to the needs of people of other cultures.

5. (5) Huck, the narrator, speaks a regional English dialect that differs from standard English. You know from the passage that Huck and his father do not get along, yet that is unrelated to Huck's manner of speech. Lines 20–22 clearly state that Huck knows how to read and write.

6. (2) The focus of their discussion is the father's reaction to Huck's education.

7. (4) The dialogue dramatizes the conflict between Huck and his father. Huck's father is strongly opposed to Huck's schooling.

8. (1) In the concluding paragraph the father states that no one in the family could read or write. Today many Americans are also illiterate.

9. (3) Tony and Riff use the word *kick* figuratively, not literally. The kick from belonging to a gang or being with people refers to a thrilling experience.

10. (4) Riff is indirectly comparing a gang to a family. He is suggesting that the bond among gang members is similar to the bond among blood relatives. He is saying that not belonging to a gang is like being an orphan.

11. (2) Riff's request that Tony attend the dance is urgent.

12. (5) In line 20 Tony says to Riff, "We're still buddies." You can conclude that Tony's decision to attend the dance is a personal favor to Riff.

13. (4) Paragraph 2 states that the income earned by working mothers helps to improve the families' lifestyles.

14. (3) In paragraph 4, the topic is the example parents set for their children of a "willingness to work."

15. (5) With 61 percent of all mothers with children under 3 working, and this figure expected to climb, more day-care or child-care centers will be needed to care for the children during working hours.

16. (4) The Labor Department statistics and the academic studies mentioned indicate that the issue is a concern to the nation, but the figures about the number of families involved and the listing of benefits suggests approval.

17. (4) Gold, which is a precious metal, represents wealth and material satisfaction.

18. (2) The speaker says, "We can devalue gold/by not caring/if it falls or rises." An obsession with wealth ignores the simple beauties of life. Those who pursue gold chain themselves to the accumulation of wealth.

19. (5) The objects have no financial value but are objects of treasure valued by the eye for their natural beauty.

20. (2) The speaker urges a revolution to care about those simple things in everyday life that are so abundant.

Evaluation Chart

Use the following chart to determine the skill areas in which you need the most work. For the GED Language Arts, Reading Test, you are required to answer the following types of questions: comprehension, application, analysis, and synthesis. These reading skills, covered in

Chapters 1–4 of this book (pages 15–105), are absolutely essential for success on the test. Circle any items that you got wrong and pay particular attention to areas where you missed half or more of the questions.

Skill Area/Content Area	Comprehension (pages 15–37)	Application (pages 39–46)	Analysis (pages 47–88)	Synthesis (pages 89–105)
Nonfiction Prose (pages 109–164)	1, 2, 3, 13, 14	4	15	16
Prose Fiction (pages 165–215)	6	8	5, 7	
Poetry (pages 217–247)	17		18, 19	20
Drama (pages 249–281)	9, 10		11, 12	

Critical Thinking Skills in Reading

CHAPTER 1

Comprehension

In their writing, authors sometimes directly state ideas, facts, and details. Understanding what the author has told you directly is called **comprehension**. This chapter will help you build your reading comprehension skills. You will learn how to

- identify the main idea

- summarize and restate information

- recognize supporting details

- understand a term in context

Identifying the Main Idea

When you are reading the newspaper, you immediately notice the headlines:

Police Crack Down on Drug Ring

Blizzard Paralyzes City

Funding for Day-care Centers Slashed

Baseball Players Threaten to Strike

Lottery Winner Takes All: A Cool Million

Headlines attract your attention. They also serve a more important purpose. They alert you to the content of the news story that follows. A headline tells you, in brief, what a story is mainly about. You expect newspaper articles to explain the headlines in more detail. The following example demonstrates this relationship between a headline and a news story. Read the story and answer the questions that follow.

Woman Lifts Car off Son

CALIFORNIA—Cynthia Burgess, a five-foot-three, 110-pound woman, lifted a Toyota weighing nearly a ton off her son, who was trapped under the car when the emergency brake was accidentally released. She described her show of strength as "no big deal."

1. According to the headline, what is the story about?

   _____

2. What is the woman's name? What are her height and weight?

   _____

3. How much did the car weigh?

   _____

4. Why did she lift the car?

   _____

5. What was her reaction to this show of strength?

   _____

These are the answers to the questions: 1. a woman who lifts a car off her son; 2. Cynthia Burgess, five-foot-three, 110 pounds; 3. nearly a ton; 4. to free her son who was trapped under it; 5. She said that it was "no big deal."

If you answered number 1 correctly, you understood that the headline announced the major point of the story. If you answered the remaining questions correctly, you grasped the basic facts relating to this amazing event.

The major point of a passage is the **main idea**. Like a newspaper headline, the main idea expresses the central message—what the passage is about. On the GED Language Arts, Reading Test, you will have to understand the main idea of the passages presented. To develop your skill in identifying the main idea, you will begin with paragraph exercises. Then you will apply this skill to longer reading selections.

Identifying the Main Idea in Paragraphs

Understanding the structure of a paragraph will help you identify the main idea. A paragraph usually consists of a **topic sentence** and several other sentences that explain or give details about the topic. Often the topic sentence is the first sentence in a paragraph. However, the topic sentence may appear in the middle or at the end of a paragraph. Sometimes the topic sentence is not stated but suggested. All of the other sentences within the paragraph focus on, or relate to, the topic sentence.

Suppose you were reading a paragraph on the topic of missing children. Within the paragraph the author would focus on a single issue concerning the topic—one point about missing children. The following sentences are examples of topic sentences, each of which could be expanded into a paragraph.

The largest reported group of missing children is runaways.

A large number of children are kidnapped by relatives or friends rather than strangers.

Stricter laws should be passed to punish people who abduct children.

Fingerprinting and videotaping are two ways to help identify missing children.

Grace Hechinger's book, *How to Raise Street Smart Children,* offers advice to families about facing the problems of child abduction.

Notice how each sentence makes a clear, definite statement about the topic of missing children. Authors often directly state the main idea when they are presenting information.

Now look at how the last topic sentence can be developed into a paragraph:

Grace Hechinger's book, *How to Raise Street Smart Children,* offers advice to families about facing the problems of child abduction. The author urges parents to discuss the subject of missing children openly. By honestly telling children about kidnappers, parents can teach their children how to avoid dangerous situations and to feel more secure. The author also suggests that parents establish rules to ensure their children's safety. Parents who want to protect their children from kidnappers will find this book invaluable.

As you can see, all of the sentences in the paragraph relate to the main idea expressed in the topic sentence. They explain the author's purpose and highlight what makes the book worth reading.

Recognizing the main idea helps you organize your reading. Once you understand the major point of a paragraph, you can better understand how the remaining sentences are linked to the main idea.

To find the topic sentence of a paragraph, follow this procedure:

1. Read the entire paragraph.

2. Ask yourself, "What is the author writing about?" This is the topic.

3. Ask yourself, "What is the author saying about the topic?" This is the main idea.

4. Look for a sentence that generally states the main idea. This is the topic sentence.

Use this procedure to read and answer questions regarding the following paragraph about Marvel comic books:

> For a while everybody was laughing at Marvel because we were going after the college crowd. But I've always felt comics were a very valid form of entertainment. There's no reason to look down on telling a good story in the comic book medium. It's just a dialogue and illustrations, after all, like film, except it's harder than film because our action is frozen. If Ernest Hemingway had written comic books, they would have been just as good as his novels.
>
> —Stan Lee of Marvel Comics

1. What is the topic of the preceding paragraph?

_____

2. Which sentence generally states the author's attitude toward the topic?

_____

The topic of the paragraph is comic books. The author summarizes his attitude about the value of comic books in the second sentence: "But I've always felt comics were a very valid form of entertainment." This topic sentence directly tells you the main idea of the paragraph. The other sentences support the main idea. By comparing comic books to films and novels, the supporting sentences explain the merits of telling a story through comic books.

EXERCISE 1

Directions: Read the following paragraph. What pattern does the writer, a Native American, observe in the world? The answer to this question is summarized in the topic sentence. Underline the topic sentence. Then, on the lines provided, write the main idea in your own words.

Everything the Power of the World does is done in a circle. The sky is round, and I have heard that the earth is round like a ball, and so are all the stars. The wind, in its greatest power, whirls. Birds make their nests in circles, for theirs is the same religion as ours. The sun comes forth and goes down again in a circle. The moon does the same, and both are round. Even the seasons form a great circle in their changing, and always come back again to where they were. The life of a man is a circle from childhood to childhood, and so it is in everything where power moves. Our tepees were round like the nests of birds, and these were always set in a circle, the nation's hoop, a nest of many nests, where the Great Spirit meant for us to hatch our children.

—Excerpted from *Black Elk Speaks* by John G. Neihardt, 1932

Your restatement of the main idea:

_____

_____

_____

The first sentence, "Everything the Power of the World does is done in a circle," states the main idea. In writing the main idea in your own words, did you preserve the meaning of the original sentence? Your version should have explained that movements and objects in the world are based on the shape of a circle. Reread the paragraph and pay close attention to the examples that illustrate this observation. Then list six examples of circular objects or movements mentioned in the paragraph.

1. _____

2. _____

3. _____

4. _____

5. _____

6. _____

Answers are on page 319.

Identifying the Main Idea in Passages

A passage, like a paragraph, often centers around one main idea. This main idea may be stated directly in one or more **main-idea sentences.** The main idea provides the overall focus of the passage. Just as a topic sentence states in general terms what a paragraph is about, so a main-idea sentence states in general terms what a passage is about. Every other sentence in the passage, including topic sentences, relates to the main-idea sentence.

To find the main idea sentence of a passage, follow this procedure:

1. Read the entire passage.

2. Ask yourself, "What is the author writing about?" This is the topic.

3. Ask yourself, "What general statement about the topic is expanded in the passage?" This is the main idea.

4. Look for a sentence or sentences that generally state the main idea. They are the main idea sentences.

Apply this procedure as you read the following passage:

> It is strange that many people think ballet is a difficult thing to enjoy. Ballet isn't any harder to enjoy than a novel, a play, or a poem—it's as simple to like as a baseball game.
>
> Yet imagine a person who goes to a baseball game for the first time. He hasn't played the game, he doesn't know the rules, and he gets confused trying to watch everything at once. He feels out of place and annoyed because he isn't sure why everyone else is so excited.
>
> If he had played baseball himself, he wouldn't have this problem. But he doesn't have to play to enjoy. Once he knows what it's all about, once he understands why the players run and slide and leap and catch as they do, he begins to appreciate the game. He becomes familiar with its elements, he enjoys it. The same thing is true of ballet.
>
> —Excerpted from *Balanchine's Complete Stories of the Great Ballets* by George Balanchine and Francis Mason, 1954

Now answer the following multiple-choice question:

Which statement best summarizes this passage?

(1) A person at a baseball game for the first time feels uncomfortable.

(2) People appreciate baseball more if they understand the game.

(3) Reading a novel, a play, or a poem is an enjoyable experience.

(4) Ballet is as easy to like as a baseball game.

(5) Ballerinas are excellent athletes.

The second sentence of the first paragraph states the main idea as summarized in answer (4). Review the other choices to see why they are not main ideas:

(1) This sentence restates the main idea of the second paragraph only. It is not broad enough to be the central point of the entire selection.

(2) This statement is also too specific to be the main idea.

(3) This statement is mentioned in the first paragraph but is not developed in the rest of the passage.

(5) Although this statement is true, the author never discusses the athletic ability of ballerinas.

Main ideas of magazine articles are sometimes summarized in the titles. What would be an effective title for the passage you just read? On the following lines, write two descriptive titles that would tell the reader what the passage is about.

_____

_____

EXERCISE 2

Directions: The following passage is from the journal of John Coleman, a college president who left his position for a year and took blue-collar, or manual labor, jobs. In this excerpt he describes his experience as a kitchen helper. As you read the passage, notice how he builds to the main idea. Then choose the best answer to each question.

WHAT MAKES A MAN?

Tuesday, March 27

One of the waitresses I find hard to take asked me at one point today, "Are you the boy who cuts the lemons?"

"I'm the man who does," I replied.

5 "Well, there are none cut." There wasn't a hint that she heard my point.

Dana, who has cooked here for twelve years or so, heard that exchange.

"It's no use, Jack," he said when she
10 was gone. "If she doesn't know now, she never will." There was a trace of a smile on his face, but it was a sad look all the same.

In that moment I learned the full thrust of those billboard ads of a few years ago
15 that said, "BOY. Drop out of school and that's what they'll call you the rest of your life." I had read those ads before with a certain feeling of pride; education matters, they said and that gave a lift to my field.
20 Today I saw them saying something else. They were untrue in part; it turns out that you get called "boy" if you do work that others don't respect even if you have a Ph.D. It isn't education that counts, but the
25 job in which you land. And the ads spoke too of a sad resignation about the world. They assumed that some people just won't learn respect for others, so you should adapt yourself to them. Don't try to change
30 them. Get the right job and they won't

call you boy any more. They'll save it for the next man.

—Excerpted from *Blue-Collar Journal*
by John R. Coleman, 1974

1. Which of the following was one of Coleman's jobs in the kitchen?
   (1) cleaning the grill
   (2) cooking short orders
   (3) helping the waitresses
   (4) washing the dishes
   (5) slicing the lemons

2. What does the waitress do that angers Coleman?
   (1) criticizes him for not doing his work
   (2) calls him *boy* instead of *man*
   (3) makes fun of his college education
   (4) asks him if he cuts the lemons
   (5) makes more money than he does

3. What is the main idea of this passage?
   (1) You should adapt yourself to people who don't have respect for others.
   (2) Respect is based on the kind of job you hold, not your education.
   (3) People who do not respect you will call you boy.
   (4) Billboard ads make fun of the less educated.
   (5) Education is essential if others are to respect you.

Answers are on page 319.

Writing Activity 1

Building your skills in comprehension relies on your ability to restate or summarize the information you read. To develop this skill, write a one-paragraph summary of the excerpt from *Blue-Collar Journal* on a separate sheet of paper. Your summary should contain the most essential points, including the main idea and important facts and details. Use your answers from Exercise 2 to help you select and organize your information. Write your summary as though you were explaining the passage to a friend.

Answers will vary.

Using the Entire Passage to Find the Main Idea

Sometimes an author does not directly tell you the main idea in one or two sentences. If this is the case, how can you identify the main idea? Add up the key points and see how they are related. Then form a general statement that ties all this information together.

Use this process as you read the next passage, which describes school teacher Ichabod Crane.

In this by-place of nature, there abode, in a remote period of American history, that is to say, some thirty years since, a worthy wight of the name of Ichabod Crane; who sojourned, or as he expressed it, "tarried," in Sleepy Hollow, for the purpose of instructing the children of the vicinity. He was a native of Connecticut; a State which supplies the Union with pioneers for the mind as well as for the forest, and sends forth yearly its legions of frontier woodsmen and country schoolmasters. The cognomen of Crane was not inapplicable to his person. He was tall, but exceedingly lank, with narrow shoulders, long arms and legs, hands that dangled a mile out of his sleeves, feet that might have served for shovels, and his whole frame most loosely hung together. His head was small, and flat at top, with huge ears, large green glassy eyes, and a large snipe nose, so that it looked like a weather-cock perched upon his spindle neck, to tell which way the wind blew. To see him striding along the profile of a hill on a windy day, with his clothes bagging and fluttering about him, one might have mistaken him for the genius of famine descending upon the earth, or some scarecrow eloped from a cornfield.

—Excerpted from "The Legend of Sleepy Hollow" by Washington Irving

From the sentences listed below, choose the four statements that present the most important information in the passage.

(1) Crane "tarried" in Sleepy Hollow.

(2) Crane was tall and skinny.

(3) Connecticut provided frontiersmen and school teachers.

(4) Crane had long arms and legs, and hands that dangled "a mile out of his sleeves."

(5) The story happened in a remote period of American history.

(6) Crane had a small head with green glassy eyes, a large snipe nose, and a spindle neck.

Sentences (3) and (5) are not central to the story's purpose. Sentences (1), (2), (4), and (6) are the most important. Write the main idea of this passage in a statement combining the information in the four sentences:

_____

_____

_____

_____

Check to see if your words convey a message similar to the following statement:

The main idea of the passage is that Ichabod Crane comically resembled the bird called a crane.

The entire passage describes Ichabod Crane. The main idea could be expressed in many ways.

Recognizing Supporting Details

As you have already read, identifying the main idea focuses your attention on the most important point expressed in a passage. You have also observed that authors develop the main idea by including additional information. Specific statements relating to the passage's central message provide you with a more complete picture of what the author is saying. These specific statements are called **supporting details**.

In your conversations with friends, you often use supporting details to explain or clarify a general comment. If you were telling someone that you enjoyed watching a certain TV show, you might give an example of your favorite episode. You could also describe the major characters, offer reasons why the show is so entertaining, or report facts about the actors. Similarly, examples, reasons, facts, and descriptions are ways in which an author supports the main idea.

The GED Language Arts, Reading Test will help measure your ability to understand information that is stated directly in supporting details. In this section, you will improve your skill in comprehending the types of specific statements that back up the main idea.

Supporting Examples

Authors use specific **examples** to illustrate the main idea. You can more clearly understand the meaning of a general statement when you are shown an example. As you read the following paragraph, notice how the examples explain the main idea:

> Many of Charles Dickens's novels portray social problems in Victorian England. In *Oliver Twist,* Dickens conveys the abuses of the workhouses. The character of Micawber in *David Copperfield* depicts the cruel treatment people in debt were subjected to. In *Great Expectations,* Dickens shows the inequities based on distinctions in social class.

The first sentence introduces the main idea. The rest of the paragraph names three examples of social problems in Victorian England. Using your own words, restate the information given in each example. Write your responses under the titles of the Dickens novels.

1. *Oliver Twist*:

_____

_____

2. *David Copperfield*:

_____

_____

3. *Great Expectations*:

_____

_____

EXERCISE 3

Directions: Read the passage below and answer the questions that follow.

In the civilization in which we live, a man may be one thing and appear to be another. But this is not possible in the social structure of the Indian, because an Indian's name tells the world what he is: a coward, a liar, a thief, or a brave.

When I was a youngster, every Indian had at least three names during his lifetime. His first name, which he received at birth and retained until he was old enough to go on the war-path, was descriptive of some circumstance surrounding his birth. As an instance, we have a man among the Blackfeet whose name is Howling-in-the-Middle-of-the-Night. When he was born along the banks of the Belly River in southern Alberta, the Indian woman who was assisting his mother went out to the river to get some water with which to wash him. When she returned to the teepee she remarked: "I heard a wolf howling across the river." "Then," said the baby's mother, "I shall call my son 'Howling-in-the-Middle-of-the-Night.'"

—Excerpted from *Long Lance: An Autobiography of an Indian Chief*
by Chief Buffalo Child Long-Lance

1. What does the passage say about the meaning of Indian names?

   _____

   _____

2. According to paragraph 2, what is the significance of an Indian's first name?

   _____

   _____

3. According to the passage, why was one man named "Howling-in-the-Middle-of-the-Night"?

   _____

   _____

Answers are on page 319.

Go to **www.GEDReading.com** for additional practice and instruction!

Writing Activity 2

Some people have nicknames that describe their appearance or personality. For instance, Al Capone, a notorious Chicago gangster, was called "Scarface" because his face was severely scarred.

On a separate sheet of paper, write a brief paragraph in which you explain how someone received a nickname. You may write about a friend, a relative, or a famous person.

Answers will vary.

Supporting Reasons

Imagine you are watching a TV commercial about a computer training school. To persuade you to enroll, the TV announcer makes these statements:

> **Excellent job opportunities exist for both men and women in the computer industry.**

> **Since most businesses use computers, a variety of interesting positions is available.**

> **Computer professionals receive high salaries.**

> **Working with computers can be a rewarding career.**

Each statement explains why you should attend computer training school. Statements that answer the question "Why?" are called **reasons**. Main ideas that describe a viewpoint, an opinion, or an action may be supported by reasons.

The following passage gives one person's point of view about the risks of laser eye surgery. As you read the passage, identify the main idea and the reasons that the author gives to support it.

> **For anyone who has fussed with eyeglasses or suffered through the cleaning procedures of contact lenses, the option to correct one's vision to 20/20 seems to be a dream come true. Laser surgery offers patients this possibility in a painless 15-minute procedure that surgically reshapes the cornea of the eye. For approximately $1,000 per eye, hundreds of thousands of individuals have been lured to the possibility of freeing themselves from the lifetime burden of glasses and contact lenses. However, this wonder surgery is not without risks of irreparable eye damage, and before consenting to the operation, a candidate needs to consider the risks.**

First of all, laser eye surgery is relatively new; in fact, the lasers used in the LASIK (laser-assisted in situ keratomileusis) procedure were not approved by the Food and Drug Administration until 1998. Research has continued and improvements are taking place in the technology, but because this procedure is relatively new, no one can say for sure what problems will show up 10, 20, or 30 years later.

Second, procedures are becoming so routine that shoppers in malls can view through a plate glass window ophthalmologists performing the operation. This frequency of the operations brings up a second issue—the experience of the doctor performing laser eye surgery. Individuals who are considering laser eye surgery need to research the credentials of the surgeon in whose hands they trust their future eyesight. Some eye doctors are conducting operations after brief training courses while others have one to two years of additional preparation. Studies have shown that patient complications drop after a doctor has performed 300 procedures and then drop again after 600 procedures. Candidates for laser eye surgery need to search for a doctor who has patient complications fewer than 3 patients per 1,000 procedures.

Finally, the procedure does correct vision to 20/20, but does 20/20 mean perfect vision? Practitioners of laser eye surgery will tell patients that the surgery works well in most cases. However, the laser is really a hi-tech scalpel, and any surgery has its risks: the risk of infection and accidents with the laser. Also, following surgery, most patients have experienced some glare and halos, usually at night. In some more severe cases, patients have suffered from double vision and lost their night vision, making it impossible to operate an automobile after dark. Some patients required a second round of laser surgery.

All of these factors need to be carefully weighed before consenting to surgery on a person's one pair of eyes.

—Based on "R U Ready to Dump Your Glasses? Laser Surgery Can Work Wonders But There Are Risks" by Christine Gorman, Time, October 11, 1999

Go back and underline the main-idea sentence. Then circle the reasons that the author gives to support the main idea.

You should have underlined the last sentence in the first paragraph: "However, this wonder surgery is not without risks of irreparable eye damage, and before consenting to the operation, the candidate needs to consider the risks." The author lists three risks involved in the eye surgery: the fact that it is relatively new, the fact that some doctors do not have much experience, and the fact that there can be complications.

Writing Activity 3

Support one of your own opinions with reasons. Choose one of the following issues to write about. Take a stand on the issue, either pro (in favor of) or con (against). On another piece of paper, write down your opinion and support it with at least three reasons. Use the preceding passage on laser eye surgery as a model.

- higher gasoline prices

- censorship of videos and music CDs

- universal medical insurance

Supporting Facts

Newspapers report the facts of daily events. Encyclopedias are filled with facts about thousands of topics. The *Guinness Book of World Records* states amazing facts: the longest sentence, the tallest man, the thinnest woman.

Facts are statements that can be proved. Authors develop their main ideas with facts when their purpose is to explain by conveying detailed and accurate information. Authors may also present facts to persuade readers to agree with them or to take a particular action.

EXERCISE 4

Directions: To build your skill in locating specific facts within a passage, read the following biographical sketch and answer the questions that follow.

Ralph Ellison was born in Oklahoma City in 1914 and attended segregated schools where he developed a special interest in jazz and classical music. To further his ambition to become a composer of symphonic music, he went to Tuskegee Institute in Alabama, majoring in music and composing. Becoming interested in sculpture, he left Tuskegee after three years and went to New York City in 1936 to develop his talent. Then he became attracted to literature and came under the influence of Richard Wright, the noted novelist.

In the 1940's Ellison had a number of short stories and articles published in which he expressed again and again his belief that white America had to recognize the blacks as human beings. In 1952 his *Invisible Man* was published and recognized as a work of major importance. It won the National Book Award for Fiction in 1953. He is also the author of *Shadow and Act*, a collection of essays.

—Excerpted from *Modern Black Stories* edited by Martin Mirer

1. What is the significance of the following dates in Ralph Ellison's life?

   1. **1914** _____

   2. **1936** _____

   3. **1952** _____

   4. **1953** _____

2. What were Ellison's major subjects when he attended Tuskegee Institute?

   _____

3. What novelist influenced Ellison?

   _____

4. What belief did Ellison repeatedly express in his short stories and articles?

   _____

   _____

   _____

5. What is the title of Ellison's collection of essays?

   _____

Answers are on page 319.

Supporting Descriptions

Police ask an eyewitness to a robbery questions about the thief's appearance. For example, they ask about height and weight, age, hair color, facial features, and clothing. Then the police jot down notes like these:

> The thief was about six feet tall. Husky build. Probably weighs close to 200 pounds. In his late twenties, maybe thirty. Reddish brown hair. Fair complexion, freckles. Last seen wearing a wool plaid jacket and faded blue jeans. Bony face. Sharp features. Thin-lipped.

Based on the eyewitness's **description**, an artist sketches the suspect.

Similarly, when you read a description, you should try to create a mental picture based on the details that the author includes. The author's purpose in developing a main idea through descriptive details is to help you visualize a person, place, object, or event.

In the following paragraph, a southern writer describes a photograph of her grandfather. As you read the description, try to imagine a black-and-white snapshot of her grandfather.

In our picture of Grandpa Carlen, his long beard and side whiskers are pure white, and seem to be stirred by some mountain wind. His large black hat is resting upside-down on his knee and he sits in a straight-back bench. His right hand is holding, straight-up-and-down and thin as a rod, his staff; it looks four or five feet tall. The photograph is inscribed across the back in a strict hand, "To Chessie, if she will have it."

—Excerpted from "Learning to See" in *One Writer's Beginnings* by Eudora Welty

Can you see an image of Grandpa Carlen? What does he look like? What was his pose in the photograph? What objects are described? Reread the paragraph and underline specific phrases that answer these questions.

Observe in the following passage how the author, a Vietnam veteran, uses descriptive detail to support the main idea:

Sometimes, in odd places, it all comes back. You are walking a summer beach, stepping around oiled bodies, hearing only the steady growl of the sea. Suddenly, from over the horizon, you hear the *phwuk-phwuk-phwuk* of rotor blades and for a frozen instant you prepare to fall to the sand. Then the Coast Guard chopper moves by, its pilot peering down at the swimmers, but your mind is stained with old images. Or you are strolling the sidewalks of a northern city, heading toward the theater or a parking lot or some dismal appointment, eyes glazed by the anonymous motion of the street. A door opens, an odor drifts from a restaurant; it's ngoc nam sauce, surely, and yes, the sign tells you this is a Vietnamese restaurant, and you hurry on, pursued by a ghost. Don't come back, the ghost whispers: I'll be crouched against the wall, grinning, my teeth stained black from betel root.

Vietnam.

—Excerpted from "Vietnam, Vietnam" by Pete Hamill

You can identify the main idea by combining the first sentence with the last word of the passage: "Sometimes, in odd places, it all comes back. . . . Vietnam." In other words, certain situations remind the author of his experience in Vietnam. When he is "walking a summer beach" or "strolling the sidewalks of a northern city," he sees, hears, or smells something that makes him recall Vietnam. On the following lines, identify a specific phrase that appeals to each one of these senses.

Sight:_____

Sound:_____

Smell:_____

Your responses might include seeing and hearing a Coast Guard chopper and smelling an odor coming from a Vietnamese restaurant. Notice how all the descriptive details in this passage contribute to your understanding of the main idea of the author's memories of Vietnam.

Understanding a Word in Context

In your everyday conversations, you sometimes repeat in your own words what another person is telling you. Perhaps you are unsure about the way the person is using a word or a phrase. Restating the definition in your own words helps you understand the meaning.

The following dialogue between an interviewer and a job applicant illustrates this process of defining a term.

Interviewer: Are you a cooperative person?

Job Applicant: By *cooperative*, do you mean "getting along with my coworkers and boss?"

Interviewer: Well, that's part of it. Cooperation also means doing your share of the work and supporting the efforts of other employees.

Job Applicant: In that case, I'm sure you'll find me to be a cooperative person. I've always related well to the people I've worked with, and I believe in carrying my own weight. I learned the importance of cooperation when I played high school football. The guys respected me because I was a team player.

Interviewer: I like that example. Team players know the importance of cooperation in doing a job well.

Did you notice that both the interviewer and the job applicant explain in their own words the meaning of *cooperative*? Although they each use different language in defining the term, they eventually agree about what cooperation means on the job. For example, the interviewer says, "Cooperation also means doing your share of the work and supporting the efforts of other employees."

On the lines, write the job applicant's restatement of that definition.

_____

_____

Your restatement was correct if you included the phrases "getting along with my coworkers," "carrying my own weight," and "team player."

Imagine that you were the job applicant. What words would you use to show the interviewer that you understood the meaning of *cooperation*? Write your version here:

_____

_____

An accurate restatement would use different language, but the meaning would remain the same. For example, you might say something like this: Cooperation means "working well with others."

Using Context Clues

Studying the context of a word means looking at the way it is used in a sentence or passage. The **context,** or surrounding phrases and sentences, will sometimes give you direct clues about the meaning of a word. The following passage shows how an author gives examples to make sure that readers understand what *networking* means.

> If you are looking for a job, employment counselors have a suggestion: start networking. Tell everyone you know—friends, relatives, neighbors, teachers—that you are eager to get back to work. Telephone local businesspeople and ask for their advice. Be sure to describe your qualifications and tell them what kind of job you'd like.
>
> Visit the kinds of places that are related to your job interests and find out as much as you can about them. Ask questions. In addition, be prepared to answer some. Sign up for classes or workshops with people in your field of interest and exchange information with them. The more people who know that you're out there looking for a job, the better your chances of finding one that's right for you.

In the passage above, the word *networking* refers to a good strategy for job hunting. Each sentence illustrates a type of networking. The last sentence sums up the concept of networking. On the lines, put into your own words what is meant by *networking* to find a job.

_____

_____

In the following paragraph, Nancy Rogers, a bank teller, describes her job:

> What I do is say hello to people when they come up to my window. "Can I help?" And transact their business, which amounts to taking money from them and putting it into their account.

—Excerpted from *Working* by Studs Terkel

As used in this example, what does *transact their business* mean?

(1) telling customers about the bank's services

(2) depositing money in the customers' accounts

(3) balancing customers' checkbooks

(4) selling stocks and savings bonds

(5) cashing customers' paychecks

The correct answer is (2). *Depositing* is another way of saying putting it (money) into their account. The other answers describe ways of transacting business but do not define the term according to the teller's explanation.

On the GED Language Arts, Reading Test, you will be asked multiple-choice questions about the meaning of a word or phrase that appears in the reading selection. Derive the meaning of unfamiliar words or phrases from the way they are used in relation to other words in the sentence or paragraph. Context clues can help you figure out a definition when taking the GED Tests and in other situations in which you can't look up words in a dictionary.

EXERCISE 5

Directions: Look for the context clues that help you define the word in **bold face type.** Pay close attention to words or phrases that restate the meaning or give an example. Then write the meaning of the word.

1. Many characters in Charles Dickens's novels are **waifs,** homeless children who must fend for themselves.

   _____

2. John F. Kennedy had **charisma.** Old films of press conferences illustrate his magnetic, charming personality.

   _____

3. Leon received a **subpoena,** a legal document requiring him to testify in court.

   _____

4. The **extraterrestrial**—a creature from another planet—had three eyes, an oversized head, and green skin.

   _____

5. Isabel had a hard time following the **convoluted** plot of the murder mystery. The complicated story had numerous twists and turns in the action.

   _____

6. The Environmental Protection Agency found **toxic** chemicals in the city's water supply. Because these poisonous chemicals posed a health hazard, the agency advised residents to boil their drinking water.

   _____

7. XYZ Company provides **tuition reimbursement** for courses relating to the employee's job. If a clerical assistant wants to take a bookkeeping class, the company will pay for the cost.

   _____

8. During the Great Depression, thousands of Americans resorted to **panhandling.** Unemployed and poverty-stricken, they would walk the streets begging for money. This practice was expressed in the popular song "Brother, Can You Spare a Dime?"

   _____

Answers are on page 319.

Chapter Review

Directions: Read each passage and choose the best answer to the questions that follow.

Questions 1–5 refer to the following excerpt from a sports article.

DOES SHE DESERVE TO BE DUBBED A KNIGHT?

Maybe it's understandable that nobody noticed the girl until she played against the boys. There are others out there, too, certainly, who skate, score, make diving
5 saves—yes, even deliver body-slamming checks—and never get any recognition.

But younger girls now have a new role model, because Manon Rheaume (Man-ohn Ray-oom) has broken a gender barrier
10 at the national level, shattered another misconception about the limits of female athletes and demanded that all hockey players be taken seriously.

The 20-year-old French Canadian goalie
15 from Lac Beauport, Quebec, made history last September when she became the first woman to play in a National Hockey League game—infiltrating one of the roughest of the men's big four sports. Minding the
20 net for the Tampa Bay Lightning, she gave up two goals and made seven saves in the first period of an exhibition contest. Afterward, Tampa Bay general manager Phil Esposito signed her to a three-year
25 contract with the club's minor-league affiliate, the Atlanta Knights.

Her detractors say she didn't deserve the NHL tryout, that she's just the victim of a cheap publicity stunt engineered by
30 Esposito to sell tickets. They say she wouldn't have been there if she weren't attractive (the first thing you notice about any goalie wearing full head gear and pounds of padding) and that she's too
35 small—5'6", 135 pounds—to play against men. Finally, they say she'll never play in the NHL—and may not even play in a game for Atlanta all year, since she's just the third-string goalie.

40 All these knocks, legitimate or not, have their roots in the *F* word: *female.* No young man at her level of play would ever have suffered this manner or degree of scrutiny. What the critics seem to have largely
45 overlooked is her performance. "She earned the chance to go to Atlanta," says Esposito. "She did well during the preseason, and she earned a spot on the roster."

Rheaume isn't complaining, and she's
50 working hard. The way she sees it, stopping 100-mile-per-hour slap shots on a minor-league team, even if it's just in practice, is better than not playing at all. Where else could she be paid to improve her game?

55 "Yes, I'm happy to be with Atlanta because I have a good chance to get experience, to learn more," she says. "I didn't try to be the first woman to do this, I just want to play. I never before had the
60 chance to practice every day. It's normal to be the number three goalie, because I'm just 20 years old. The two other goaltenders are 24 and 25, and they have a lot more experience than me."

65 "If you didn't know she was a woman, then you wouldn't have known by watching her play," wrote *Tampa Tribune* hockey writer Tom Jones. "She did a respectable job. She played as well as any goaltender
70 would have. She doesn't have a problem reacting to shots or making saves. She has a good glove hand."

—Excerpted from "The Puck Stops Here" by Elizabeth Kaufmann, *Women's Sports & Fitness,* January/February 1993

1. Why is Manon Rheaume satisfied, for now, to be a third-string goalie?

   (1) She has been told that she will never play well enough to play first string.
   (2) She thinks that she can't compete seriously against the men on the team.
   (3) She fears that she is too short and too lightweight to succeed.
   (4) She believes that being in the minor leagues is enough achievement for a woman.
   (5) She knows that goaltenders are usually older and more experienced than she is.

2. How has Rheaume reacted to all of the criticism?

   (1) She has hired a public relations person to improve her image.
   (2) She angrily demands her right to be taken seriously as an athlete.
   (3) She decided to stay with the Tampa Bay Lightning.
   (4) She has become the best goaltender on the team.
   (5) She works hard and tries to enjoy the experience of playing.

3. What is the meaning of the expression *gender barrier* (line 9)?

   (1) the goaltender's job of minding the net
   (2) the tradition of excluding women from "men's" sports
   (3) the difference between the major and minor leagues
   (4) the full head gear and padding worn by hockey players
   (5) an exhibition contest as opposed to a regular game

4. What is the purpose of this passage?

   To show how
   (1) a female hockey player is helping to change people's attitudes toward women in sports
   (2) sportswriters tend to ignore female professional athletes in the big four sports
   (3) a National Hockey League team has generated publicity by hiring a female goalie
   (4) the manager of a hockey team has had to defend his decision to hire women
   (5) a female hockey player is being banned from playing on the national level

5. What is the purpose of paragraph four?

   (1) to explain why Rheaume cannot play in the National Hockey League
   (2) to illustrate Rheaume's weaknesses as a hockey player
   (3) to describe how Rheaume was hired as a publicity stunt
   (4) to give reasons why some people object to Rheaume's being hired
   (5) to present facts about Rheaume's physical appearance and skills

Questions 6–9 refer to the following excerpt from an autobiography.

HOW DO YOUNG BOYS PRETEND TO BE BULLFIGHTERS?

Once in a great while the older boys would also allow us to join them in the bullfights they organized in one corner of the pasture. The bulls, the *matadores*, and
5 the *picadores* were the ten- to twelve-year-olds, and the master of the fight was the oldest of the gang. We were permitted to take part only as fans or *aficionados*, to provide the yelling, the catcalls and the
10 cheers. The master of the *corrida* directed us to sit on the ground on the upper slope of the bullring, which was entirely imaginary.

From behind a tree a trumpeter stepped to the edge of the ring. Blowing on a make-
15 believe bugle he sounded a call and the bull rushed in—a boy with a plain sarape over his shoulders, holding with both hands in front of his chest the bleached skull of a steer complete with horns. Between the horns a
20 large, thick cactus leaf from which the thorns had been removed, was tied. It was at the cactus pad that the *matadores* and *picadores* aimed their wooden swords and bamboo spears.

25 If the fight went according to the rules, the master declared the bull dead after a few rushes, by counting the stabs into the cactus, and the dead bull was replaced by a live one. Sometimes a sword or a spear missed the
30 cactus pad and poked the bull in the stomach or some more sensitive spot. If the bull suspected that the miss was on purpose and dropped his skull to charge the *torero* with his fists, there was a free-for-all. We
35 *aficionados* fell on one another with grunts and kicks, wrestling on the ground to increase the bedlam. If the commotion got out of the hands of the master of the *corrida*, there was always an adult watching from the
40 village across the *arroyo*, who would walk over to the ring to scatter the rioters and send them home.

—Excerpted from *Barrio Boy* by Ernesto Galarza, 1971

6. Which of the following titles best describes this passage?

(1) Games Children Play
(2) Imitating a Bullfight
(3) Becoming a Man
(4) A Childhood Memory
(5) How Fights Start

7. According to the passage, what does the word *aficionado* in line 8 mean?

(1) steers
(2) wrestlers
(3) fans
(4) yells
(5) troublemakers

8. What is the topic of the second paragraph?

(1) the reaction of the younger observers
(2) the purpose of the bullfight
(3) the rules for playing the game
(4) how a boy disguised himself as the bull
(5) how the game prepared the boys for adulthood

9. What happened when the "bull" thought he had been poked intentionally in a sensitive spot?

(1) An adult sent everyone home.
(2) All the boys started fighting.
(3) The fans started booing.
(4) The master declared the bull dead.
(5) The bull rolled over in pain.

Questions 10–13 refer to the following excerpt from a book about workers.

WHAT DO YOU NOTICE ABOUT COAL MINERS?

When the miner comes up from the pit his face is so pale that it is noticeable even through the mask of coal dust. This is due to the foul air that he has been breathing, and
5   will wear off presently. To a Southerner, new to the mining districts, the spectacle of a shift of several hundred miners streaming out of the pit is strange and slightly sinister. Their exhausted faces, with the grime
10 clinging in all the hollows, have a fierce, wild look. At other times, when their faces are clean, there is not much to distinguish them from the rest of the population. They have a very upright square-shouldered walk, a
15 reaction from the constant bending underground, but most of them are shortish men and their thick ill fitting clothes hide the splendor of their bodies. The most definitely distinctive thing about them is the blue scars
20 on their noses. Every miner has blue scars on his nose and forehead, and will carry them to his death. The coal dust of which the air underground is full enters every cut, and then the skin grows over it and forms a
25 blue stain like tattooing, which in fact it is. Some of the older men have their foreheads veined like Roquefort cheeses from this cause.

—Excerpted from *The Road to Wigan Pier*
by George Orwell, 1937

10. What is the purpose of the passage?

(1) to explain the dangers of coal mining
(2) to tell why miners are exhausted after work
(3) to describe how a coal miner looks
(4) to detail the way a coal miner walks
(5) to warn miners to watch their health

11. According to the passage, why are the miners' faces pale when they leave the coal pit?

Because the men
(1) are tired from working hard
(2) have been breathing foul air
(3) aren't exposed to enough sunlight
(4) want to look strange and sinister
(5) feel faint from the heat

12. Why do miners have permanent scars on their noses and foreheads?

(1) They often bang their heads against the low ceiling of the coal pit.
(2) They all tattoo their noses and foreheads with blue ink.
(3) Their noses and foreheads are covered with bluish-black coal dust.
(4) They bruise themselves when they are shoveling coal.
(5) Blue-stained skin forms over the coal miners' cuts.

13. According to the passage, to what does the word *Roquefort* in line 27 refer?

(1) a growth on the skin
(2) the medical term for a wound
(3) the name of a coal-mining town
(4) a type of cheese
(5) a muscular pain

Answers are on pages 319–320.

CHAPTER 2

Application

You use comprehension skills when you reveal your understanding of details stated directly by the author. You use different skills when you show understanding of ideas not directly stated by the author. **Application** is the skill of transferring your understanding of a concept in a passage to a different situation. This chapter will help you build the reading skill of making applications.

Making Applications

What do you learn about Ted from this paragraph?

> Although Ted excelled in his university studies and earned recognition for his keen intellect, he was not a person who freely engaged in discussion. He was not unfriendly; any person who met him would receive a warm smile, a firm handshake, and a pleasant greeting. But Ted felt more at ease reading and writing by himself than he did interacting with others. He reluctantly kept a telephone in his apartment, not for speaking with others but solely for retrieving messages, which he could screen on his answering machine. At social gatherings, Ted would not mingle and join in a conversation; he would go off to admire the host's library or garden.

The paragraph describes Ted's reluctance to interact freely with others. It provides examples of his attitude in two situations: how he used the phone, and how he behaved at parties. Now use what you know to predict how Ted would behave in a new situation:

How would Ted most likely wish to share information with others?

    (1) in a one-on-one conversation

    (2) in a lecture to a class

    (3) in a panel discussion

    (4) in an e-mail message

    (5) on a television talk show

None of the answer choices is directly stated in the passage. Therefore, you need to make your choice by applying what you know about Ted from the passage to this new context, "share information." Only choice (4), "in an e-mail message", would permit Ted to communicate information without face-to-face contact. It is the best choice.

The skill of application requires two steps:

1. understanding the main idea or supporting details of a passage

2. applying this information to a new context or setting

Use this approach as you read the following paragraph:

> When you interview for a job, you want to make a good first impression. Dressing neatly and professionally shows the interviewer that you take pride in your appearance. Therefore, use good judgment in selecting the clothes you wear on a job interview. Don't wear outfits that are too casual or flashy.

Which of the following behaviors should a job applicant display during an interview?

(1) respond directly to the interviewer's questions, sticking to the issues the interviewer raises

(2) interrupt the interviewer to show how you can take command of a situation

(3) laugh loud and long if the interviewer says something funny

(4) answer every question with a joke or story about yourself

(5) use difficult words whenever possible

The correct answer is choice (1). A direct response is businesslike and professional, like appropriate office clothing. Acting rude, overly amused, self-centered, or intent on showing off are all flashy, inappropriate behavior.

Here is a second passage with which you can practice the skill of application.

> When Maria returns home after her job at the law office, she is welcomed by the retreat she has made. Maria enjoys working outdoors, and her home reflects this interest. The flower beds are artistically planted with flowers that bloom three seasons of the year. Maria carefully maintains the beds and looks for new additions. Crushed stone walkways lead visitors to her house along scenic paths. In her yard she has built a water pond filled with water plants, live fish, and a small fountain. She has planted trees and shrubs selected for their colors, flowers, and fruit. All of her neighbors envy the beautiful garden home she has created.

Based on the information in the passage, if Maria were looking to change jobs, what other type of employment might she seek?

(1) tour guide

(2) home builder

(3) portrait artist

(4) software designer

(5) landscaper

The answer is (5). Applying the information from the passage, you understand Maria as a person who enjoys gardening, planting, and caring for the grounds of her home. All of those interests are suited to the job of a landscaper who designs, selects plants, and constructs the beds and gardens.

Another way of applying ideas is to see a concept or a situation in a different historical context. For example, Shakespeare's play *Romeo and Juliet*, written in the 16th century, takes place in an Italian city. The story is about two feuding families—the Montagues and the Capulets. Romeo and Juliet, who are on opposite sides of the feud, fall in love with each other. Despite their families' disapproval, they secretly marry. However, Romeo and Juliet's love is not strong enough to overcome the hatred between their families. Their relationship is doomed to end tragically.

The musical *West Side Story* applies the story of Romeo and Juliet to a modern-day situation. The story takes place in New York City. Instead of feuding families, *West Side Story* is about two feuding gangs of teenagers— the Sharks and the Jets. Like Romeo and Juliet, Tony and Maria fall in love, although each associates with a rival gang. Caught in the middle of the conflict, they, too, face tragedy in the end.

The point to remember in recognizing and responding to an application question is the question, not the passage. The question tells you the new idea, new information, or new situation to which you must transfer your understanding of the passage.

Go to **www.GEDReading.com** for additional practice and instruction!

Chapter Review

Directions: Read each passage and choose the best answer to the questions that follow.

Questions 1–5 refer to the following excerpt from a play.

WHY DOESN'T MISS DAISY WANT A DRIVER?

Hoke: How yo' Temple this mornin', Miz Daisy?

Daisy: Why are you here?

Hoke: I bring you to de Temple like you tell
5   me. *(He is helping her into the car.)*

Daisy: I can get myself in. Just go. *(She makes a tight little social smile and a wave out the window.)* Hurry up out of here! *(Hoke starts up the car.)*

10 **Hoke:** Yassum.

Daisy: I didn't say speed. I said get me away from here.

Hoke: Somethin' wrong back yonder?

Daisy: No.

15 **Hoke:** Somethin' I done?

Daisy: No. *(a beat)* Yes.

Hoke: I ain' done nothin'!

Daisy: You had the car right in front of the front door of the Temple! Like I was
20   Queen of Romania! Everybody saw you! Didn't I tell you to wait for me in the back?

Hoke: I jes tryin' to be nice. They two other chauffeurs right behind me.

25 **Daisy:** You made me look like a fool.

Hoke: Lawd knows you ain't no fool, Miz Daisy.

Daisy: Slow down. Miriam and Beulah and them, I could see what they were
30   thinking when we came out of services.

Hoke: What that?

Daisy: That I'm trying to pretend I'm rich.

Hoke: You is rich, Miz Daisy!

35 **Daisy:** No I'm not! And nobody can ever say I put on airs. On Forsyth Street we only had meat once a week. We made a meal off of grits and gravy. I taught the fifth grade at the Crew
40   Street School! I did without plenty of times, I can tell you.

Hoke: And now you doin' with. What so terrible in that?

Daisy: You! Why do I talk to you? You don't
45   understand me.

Hoke: Nome, I don't. I truly don't. Cause if I ever was to get ahold of what you got I be shakin' it around for everybody in the world to see.

50 **Daisy:** That's vulgar. Don't talk to me! *(Hoke mutters something under his breath.)* What? What did you say? I heard that!

Hoke: Miz Daisy, you needs a chauffeur and
55   Lawd know, I needs a job. Let's jes leave it at dat.

—Excerpted from *Driving Miss Daisy* by Alfred Uhry, 1986

1. Considering the opinions Miss Daisy expresses in this passage, how would you expect her to be dressed?

   (1) in the latest style from a world-famous designer
   (2) in flashy, inexpensive clothing from a discount store
   (3) in well-made clothing in a classic style
   (4) in old, worn clothes that she had had for years
   (5) in very casual clothing

2. If the car were stuck in a massive traffic jam, how would Miss Daisy most likely react?

   (1) by fuming and criticizing whatever caused the jam
   (2) by taking a short nap in the back seat
   (3) by starting a conversation with people in nearby stopped cars
   (4) by getting out of the car and walking
   (5) by sitting quietly and reading

3. If the car were stuck in a massive traffic jam, how would Hoke most likely react?

   (1) by fuming and criticizing whatever caused the jam
   (2) by taking a short nap in the front seat
   (3) by starting a conversation with people in nearby stopped cars
   (4) by criticizing Miss Daisy for wanting to go that way
   (5) by sitting quietly and waiting for the jam to end

4. If Hoke won a great deal of money in a lottery, which of the following best describes what he would do with the money?

   (1) hide the cash in a safe place in his house and tell no one about it
   (2) invest the money in stocks, and advise his friends to do the same
   (3) tell everyone about his good fortune, and spend the money on family and friends
   (4) live in the same style he had before
   (5) contribute the money anonymously to a good cause

5. How did students in Miss Daisy's fifth grade class most likely describe her as a teacher?

   (1) "She makes every lesson fun!"
   (2) "She really makes us work."
   (3) "She never knows what to do."
   (4) "She makes a lot of money."
   (5) "She wastes too much class time."

Questions 6–11 refer to the following excerpt from an essay.

WHAT KIND OF PEOPLE ARE THESE CONSTRUCTION WORKERS?

They drive into town in big cars, and live in furnished rooms, and drink whiskey with beer chasers, and chase women they will soon forget. They linger only a little while,
5 only until they have built the bridge; then they are off again to another town, another bridge, linking everything but their lives.

They possess none of the foundation of their bridges. They are part circus, part
10 gypsy—graceful in the air, restless on the ground; it is as if the wide-open road below lacks for them the clear direction of an eight-inch beam stretching across the sky six hundred feet above the sea.

15 When there are no bridges to be built, they will build skyscrapers, or highways, or power dams, or anything that promises a challenge—and overtime. They will go anywhere, will drive a thousand miles all day
20 and night to be part of a new building boom. They find boom towns irresistible. That is why they are called "the boomers."

In appearance, boomers usually are big men, or if not always big, always strong, and
25 their skin is ruddy from all the sun and wind. Some who heat rivets have charred complexions; some who drive rivets are hard of hearing; some who catch rivets in small metal cones have blisters and body burns
30 marking each miss; some who do welding see flashes at night while they sleep. Those who connect steel have deep scars along their shins from climbing columns. Many boomers have mangled hands and fingers
35 sliced off by slipped steel. Most have taken falls and broken a limb or two. All have seen death.

They are cocky men, men of great pride,
30 and at night they brag and build bridges in bars, and sometimes when they are turning to leave, the bartender will yell after them, "Hey, you guys, how's about clearing some steel out of here?"

—Excerpted from "The Bridge" by Gay Talese, 1964

6. What is the author's purpose in this passage?

(1) to explain why construction work is a rewarding career
(2) to describe the physical appearance of construction workers
(3) to illustrate how skyscrapers and bridges are built
(4) to suggest that construction workers are irresponsible
(5) to show the personalities of construction workers

7. Why does the author use the phrase "part circus, part gypsy" (lines 9–10)?

(1) to explain why construction workers like to travel
(2) to show how construction workers are similar to acrobats and roaming people
(3) to contrast the differences between construction workers and entertainers
(4) to show that construction workers are men of great pride
(5) to explain construction workers' outdoor activities

8. Why are construction workers called *boomers*?

   (1) because they are attracted to new building developments
   (2) because they have loud and boisterous personalities
   (3) because their rivets make an exploding sound
   (4) because they earn extra money working overtime
   (5) because their voices sound like thunder

9. Which statement best expresses the main idea of the fourth paragraph?

   (1) Welders and riveters are careless workers.
   (2) Construction workers have strong muscles.
   (3) Construction work is a dangerous job.
   (4) Construction work requires special skills.
   (5) Construction workers fear injuries.

10. What activity can you infer from this passage that construction workers would least likely do?

    (1) go wherever work was available
    (2) settle down and live a safe life
    (3) perform other kinds of physical labor
    (4) party wildly with their coworkers
    (5) seek out adventures and thrilling situations

11. If the construction workers had lived in the late nineteenth century, what type of work might they have done?

    (1) built railroads
    (2) raised cattle
    (3) planted crops
    (4) sold real estate
    (5) worked in factories

Questions 12–15 refer to the following excerpt from an essay.

WHAT DOES A WRITER EXPERIENCE?

Having, from a conversation overheard or in some other way, got the tone of a tale, I was like a woman who has just become impregnated. Something was growing inside
5 me. At night when I lay in bed I could feel the heels of the tale kicking against the walls of my body. Often as I lay thus every word of the tale came to me quite clearly but when I got out of bed to write it down the
10 words would not come.

I had constantly to seek in roads new to me. Other men had felt what I had felt, had seen what I had seen—how had they met the difficulties I faced? My father when he
15 told his tales walked up and down the room before his audience. He pushed out little experimental sentences and watched his audience narrowly. There was a dull-eyed old farmer sitting in a corner of the room.
20 Father had his eyes on the fellow. "I'll get him," he said to himself. He watched the farmer's eyes. When the experimental sentence he had tried did not get anywhere he tried another and kept trying. Besides
25 words he had—to help the telling of his tales—the advantage of being able to act out those parts for which he could find no words. He could frown, shake his fists, smile, let a look of pain or annoyance drift over his
30 face.

These were his advantages that I had to give up if I was to write my tales rather than tell them and how often I had cursed my fate.

—Excerpted from "On Form, Not Plot, in the Short Story" by Sherwood Anderson, 1924

12. In lines 3–4, why does the author compare himself to a pregnant woman?

  (1) to show sympathy for women writers
  (2) to illustrate that writers carry heavy burdens
  (3) to show that a story "grows" inside him
  (4) to imply that he has a large belly
  (5) to show respect for mothers and infants

13. Which statement below best summarizes the main idea of the second paragraph?

  (1) The farmers didn't enjoy listening to the stories of the author's father.
  (2) The author's father could use gestures as well as words to capture his audience's attention.
  (3) The author's father experimented with his sentences.
  (4) The author faced many hardships during his lifetime.
  (5) The author's father should have become a professional actor.

14. From the final sentence, what can you conclude about the author's attitude toward writing?

  (1) He would rather write speeches than stories.
  (2) He frequently struggles over his decision to become a writer.
  (3) He regards writing as predictable.
  (4) He feels that writing offers little personal satisfaction.
  (5) He believes that writing a story has more advantages than telling it.

15. Which of the following would most closely identify with the author's occupation?

  (1) a pediatrician
  (2) a farmer
  (3) a typist
  (4) a painter
  (5) a stagehand

Answers are on page 321.

CHAPTER 3

Analysis

Some of the questions on the GED Language Arts, Reading Test will ask you to do more than demonstrate your understanding of information directly stated by the author or to make applications of that information to a new situation. You will also be asked to identify *how* the author presented the information. You will need to recognize both the methods used and their effects. Breaking a selection down to its parts and examining each part is called **analysis**. The following are important skills used in analysis:

- making inferences and drawing conclusions
- interpreting figurative language
- identifying elements of an author's style, such as word usage and tone
- recognizing techniques used to give structure to a passage, such as time order, classification, and cause-and-effect relationships

Making Inferences

You are driving along a main street. As you near the railroad tracks, you notice two flashing red lights. Bells clang as you watch the crossing gates fall, stopping traffic. You hear a distant whistle.

What can you **infer** about this situation? You have probably concluded that a train is approaching. Why? Certain clues guided your thinking. Flashing red lights, clanging bells, falling crossing gates, a distant whistle—all of these clues hinted that a train was approaching.

From your observations and knowledge, you made an educated guess, or an **inference**. You assumed your inference was correct, although nobody told you so directly. Actually seeing the train speeding by would prove you were right.

In reading, as in real life, the inferences that you make depend largely upon your powers of observation—your ability to spot important details or clues. The following example illustrates how specific clues support an inference.

Observation: A man wearing dark glasses taps his cane against the pavement. His German Shepherd leads him across an alley.

Inference: The man is blind.

Clues: 1. The man wears dark glasses.

2. He walks with a cane.

3. He is directed by a German Shepherd, probably trained as a guide dog.

EXERCISE 1

Directions: Apply your skills in detecting clues that support inferences. Carefully study the observations. Then list the clues that show why the inference for each observation is valid.

1. **Observation:** During the second quarter of a football game, the referee blows his whistle. The tackled quarterback lies motionless on the field. Two men with a stretcher rush from the sidelines and carry him away.

Inference: The quarterback is injured.

Clues: _____

_____

2. **Observation:** A job seeker receives a message asking that she call the Human Resources Department of a company where she interviewed for a job. When she calls, the director says, "Congratulations!"

Inference: The director is extending a job offer.

Clues: _____

_____

3. **Observation:** As a woman walks toward the door of a small clothing store, a high-pitched alarm goes off. The store manager races after the woman and grabs her arm. A sweater, stuffed inside the woman's coat, drops to the floor.

Inference: The manager caught the woman shoplifting.

Clues: _____

_____

4. **Observation:** After a concert, people in the audience loudly clap their hands and cheer. Some stand and yell, "Bravo! Bravo!"

Inference: The audience enjoyed the performance.

Clues: _____

_____

5. **Observation:** A black limousine heads a long line of cars moving steadily through traffic. Although it is early afternoon, all of the car headlights are on.

Inference: These cars are part of a funeral procession.

Clues: _____

_____

Answers are on page 321.

Drawing Valid Inferences

In your own experiences you probably make inferences automatically. You form first impressions about the people you meet. You may make assumptions about what life is like in a city, a suburb, or a small town. However, once you have made an inference, do you check its accuracy? Do you ask yourself, "Is there enough evidence to support the conclusion I have drawn? Have I overlooked any facts?" It is all too easy to draw faulty inferences.

For example, on Halloween Eve in 1938, hundreds of Americans made the same faulty inference. On that evening, the CBS Mercury Theater on Air presented a radio broadcast entitled "War of the Worlds." The script was adapted from an H. G. Wells science fiction novel. The famous actor Orson Welles told the story of an invasion from the planet Mars. Posing as an announcer, he told listeners that he had a "grave announcement." Then he proceeded to say, "Both the observations of science and the evidence of our eyes lead to the inescapable assumption that those strange beings who landed in the Jersey farmlands tonight are the vanguard of an invading army from the planet Mars."

Because the dramatic interpretation sounded real, hundreds of Americans panicked, convinced that Martians were actually destroying the country.

These people mistakenly assumed the truth of the broadcast. They feared that their lives were in danger. Yet they didn't check to find out whether their assumptions were based on fact.

How could they have avoided jumping to a hasty conclusion?

- Listeners heard Orson Welles say, "Within two hours three million people moved out of New York." This statement was an important clue. It is impossible for a city to be cleared out so quickly.

- Reading the newspaper listing of radio programs would have proved that CBS *scheduled* "War of the Worlds" to be broadcast on October 30.

- By turning the radio dial, the listeners would have discovered that the show was not an authentic broadcast. Had it been authentic, they would have heard this "national crisis" reported on other stations.

- During intermissions, the CBS radio announcer reminded the audience that they were listening to a drama.

What can you learn from this example? One important lesson is that you should understand all the facts before you make an inference. The same word of advice applies to your reading skills. You need to build *both* literal and inferential understanding. These two skills are closely connected. Discovering the literal meaning of a passage requires you to identify what the author says directly—ideas, factual content, and supporting details. Once you have grasped the stated ideas and facts, you will want to explore what the author says indirectly—the implied or unstated meaning.

Inferring the Unstated Main Idea

In the first chapter of this book you learned that the main idea expresses the central message of a passage. Sometimes authors will suggest the main idea rather than state it directly. In other words, the main idea is implied, and you must infer the major point based on the information given.

The following suggestions will help you infer an unstated main idea:

1. Read the passage for its literal meaning. What ideas are stated directly?

2. Read between the lines. What do the stated facts and details seem to show? How are they related? Why did the author include these facts and details?

3. Ask yourself, "What is the author suggesting about a person, a place, an event, or a belief?"

Use these guidelines as you read the following passage:

> After the game, the Crushers, a football team, slowly return to the locker room. There are no television camera operators shooting postgame highlights, no photographers popping flash bulbs, no sportscasters conducting exclusive interviews.
>
> The media are all in the opposing team's locker room. The Crushers, too exhausted to shower, sit on wooden benches. They hold their heads down and stare blankly at the floor. No one speaks. The coach bangs his fist against a locker and storms into his office, slamming the door.

Can you infer the main idea of this passage? Although the author does not state it directly, a main idea is clearly implied. To infer the point of the passage, answer the questions below.

1. Why are the camera operators, the photographers, and the sportscasters in the opposing team's locker room?

   _____

   _____

2. Why are the Crushers silent? How do team members' gestures and reactions reveal their emotions?

   _____

   _____

3. From the coach's behavior, what can you infer about his feelings?

   _____

   _____

Here are the details that provide suport for the unstated main idea: 1. The camera operators, photographers, and sportscasters are in the winning team's locker room. 2. The description of the losing players' silence and gestures suggests that they are depressed about their loss. 3. The description of the coach's behavior suggests that he is upset. By adding these clues together, you should be able to make an inference about the main idea. The author is showing you the team's reaction after losing a game. All the details contribute to the main idea. The author does not directly state, "The team is unhappy about the defeat," yet you can infer this meaning from your answers to the preceding questions.

Writing Activity 1

Choose one of the emotions from the list below. Then, on another piece of paper, write a description of a person displaying the emotion you chose. Do *not* directly state what the emotion is. Instead, imply the emotion by using plenty of descriptive details. When you are finished, give your description to someone else and ask the person to guess what emotion is being described.

- terror
- grief
- joy
- excitement

Answers will vary.

EXERCISE 2

Directions: Read each passage below and answer the questions that follow.

PASSAGE 1

Now there were no fish in the river. There were no deep potholes where fish could live. I had not been mistaken as I rode the bus, thinking that the rivers were shallower than I remembered them. The Poor Fork now was not only low; it was apparently the local refuse dump. Tin cans, pop bottles, and discarded automobile tires lined the banks, while the river itself was full of debris which it apparently was too sluggish to move along.

—Excerpted from *My Appalachia: A Reminiscence* by Rebecca Caudill

1. Which of the following statements best expresses the main idea?

   (1) The river moves slowly.
   (2) The trash in the river is an eyesore.
   (3) People no longer go fishing.
   (4) The river is being destroyed by pollution.
   (5) People should dump their trash in garbage cans.

2. What clues in the paragraph support your answer? On the lines list the descriptive details that you used as evidence.

   _____

   _____

   _____

PASSAGE 2

A man stood upon a railroad bridge in northern Alabama, looking down into the swift water twenty feet below. The man's hands were tied behind his back, the wrists bound with a cord. A rope closely encircled his neck. It was attached to a stout cross-timber above his head and the slack fell to the level of his knees.

—Excerpted from "An Occurrence at Owl Creek Bridge" by Ambrose Bierce

3. What is the purpose of this paragraph?

   (1) to show a man about to be hanged
   (2) to describe the scenery of northern Alabama
   (3) to explain the size of a railroad bridge
   (4) to illustrate one of the uses of a rope
   (5) to tell about a man being held hostage

4. What clues in the paragraph support your answer?

   _____

   _____

   _____

Answers are on page 321.

 Go to **www.GEDReading.com** for additional practice and instruction!

Drawing Conclusions from Details

You have already observed how supporting details are clues to discovering the main idea. These details also serve another purpose. Drawing **conclusions** from supporting details enables you to interpret the passage. Certain phrases and sentences hint at information that is not directly stated. From these specific details, you can draw conclusions about a person, a place, or a situation.

What inferences can you make from the details in the following paragraph?

In walks these three girls in nothing but bathing suits. I'm in the third checkout slot, with my back to the door, so I don't see them until they're over by the bread. The one that caught my eye first was the one in the plaid green two-piece. She was a chunky kid, with a good tan and a sweet broad soft-looking can with those two crescents of white just under it, where the sun never seems to hit, at the top of the backs of her legs. I stood there with my hand on a box of HiHo crackers trying to remember if I rang it up or not. I ring it up again and the customer starts giving me hell. She's one of those cash-register watchers, a witch about fifty with rouge on her cheekbones and no eyebrows, and I know it made her day to trip me up.

—Excerpted from "A&P" in *Pigeon Feathers and Other Stories* by John Updike, 1962

Identify the clues that support each of the following inferences:

1. The story takes place in a supermarket.

   Clues: _____

   _____

2. The weather outside is hot.

   Clues: _____

   _____

3. The person telling the story is a teenage boy.

   Clues: _____

   _____

4. The boy is distracted by one of the girls.

   Clues: _____

   _____

5. The checkout boy views the customer as a nasty, ugly-looking woman who enjoys complaining.

   Clues: _____

   _____

Here are supporting details that provide clues for the inferences above:

1. References to "checkout slot," "cash register," "HiHo crackers," and "bread" suggest that the story takes place in a supermarket.

2. The girls are wearing bathing suits.

3. The clerk's speech and his interest in the girls suggest that he is a teenage boy.

4. He has observed every detail of the girl's physical appearance. He is so distracted by her that he makes a mistake ringing up groceries.

5. By saying that the woman is a "witch" and describing her face, the boy implies that she is nasty and ugly. His statement "I know it made her day to trip me up" suggests that the customer enjoys complaining.

Notice how much information you were able to infer from the supporting details. What if the author had decided to report all this information directly? Read the following version:

> I am a teenage boy who works as a cashier in a supermarket. One hot day three girls wearing bathing suits walked into the store. I was so distracted by the girl wearing the two-piece suit that I made a mistake ringing up a customer's groceries. Although the customer started complaining, I didn't really care. She looked and acted like a mean old witch.

This paragraph is obviously less interesting to read. One reason authors suggest rather than state ideas is to get the reader more interested.

EXERCISE 3

Directions: Read the passage below and choose the best answer to each question that follows.

WHAT DOES BLAKE FEEL?

When Blake stepped out of the elevator, he saw her. A few people, mostly men waiting for girls, stood in the lobby watching the elevator doors. She was among them.
5 As he saw her, her face took on a look of such loathing and purpose that he realized she had been waiting for him. He did not approach her. She had no legitimate business with him. They had nothing to say.

10 He turned and walked toward the glass doors at the end of the lobby, feeling that faint guilt and bewilderment we experience when we by-pass some old friend or classmate who seems threadbare, or sick, or
15 miserable in some other way. It was five-eighteen by the clock in the Western Union office. He could catch the express. As he waited his turn at the revolving doors, he saw that it was still raining. It had been
20 raining all day, and he noticed now how much louder the rain made the noises of the street. Outside, he started walking briskly east toward Madison Avenue. Traffic was tied up, and horns were blowing urgently on
25 a crosstown street in the distance. The sidewalk was crowded.

—Excerpted from "The Five-Forty-Eight" by John Cheever, 1958

1. What place is Blake leaving?

   (1) a department store
   (2) an office building
   (3) a train station
   (4) a high-rise apartment
   (5) a movie theater

2. Who could the woman in the lobby be?

   (1) a stranger
   (2) an old classmate
   (3) a casual acquaintance
   (4) Blake's ex-wife
   (5) an elevator operator

3. How does Blake feel about the woman?

   (1) sick
   (2) uneasy
   (3) comfortable
   (4) impatient
   (5) happy

4. Where does the story take place?

   In a
   (1) city
   (2) small town
   (3) suburb
   (4) foreign country
   (5) dangerous neighborhood

Answers are on page 321.

Drawing Conclusions About People

Authors often write about people and their relationships—either real or imagined. Through descriptive details, authors suggest what people are like. One way of revealing a person's character is to show how someone else feels about that person's behavior. As you read the next passage, what can you conclude about the girl and her mother's feelings about her?

EXERCISE 4

Directions: Read the passage below. Then complete the exercise by putting a check mark next to each statement that is a valid conclusion (one that can be supported by details in the passage).

One night I had to look at a page from the Bible for three minutes and then report everything I could remember. "Now Jehoshaphat had riches and honor in abundance and . . . that's all I remember, Ma," I said.

And after seeing my mother's disappointed face once again, something inside of me began to die. I hated the tests, the raised hopes and failed expectations. Before going to bed that night, I looked in the mirror above the bathroom sink and when I saw only my face staring back—and that it would always be this ordinary face—I began to cry. Such a sad, ugly girl! I made high-pitched noises like a crazed animal, trying to scratch out the face in the mirror.

And then I saw what seemed to be the prodigy side of me—because I had never seen that face before. I looked at my reflection, blinking so I could see more clearly. The girl staring back at me was angry, powerful. This girl and I were the same. I had new thoughts, willful thoughts, or rather thoughts filled with lots of won'ts. I won't let her change me, I promised myself. I won't be what I'm not.

—Excerpted from "Two Kinds" in *The Joy Luck Club* by Amy Tan, 1989

_____ 1. The girl knows that her mother accepts her the way she is.

_____ 2. The girl promises herself that she will make every effort to please her mother.

_____ 3. The girl enjoys memorizing passages from the Bible.

_____ 4. The girl changes from feeling sad to feeling powerful.

_____ 5. The girl decides to be true to herself.

Answers are on page 322.

Interpreting Figurative Language

Words can be defined literally: A *graveyard* is a cemetery, a place where dead people are buried. A *bomb* is an exploding weapon that causes destruction. Words can also have figurative meanings: A mail sorter works the *graveyard* shift at the post office. Theater critics say that a certain Broadway musical is a *bomb*.

According to the literal definitions of *graveyard* and *bomb*, the preceding two sentences do not make sense. A mail sorter's shift is unrelated to cemetery work. A musical is not a destructive weapon. However, in these sentences, *graveyard* and *bomb* are used as **figurative language**—words that mean something other than their literal definitions. Here's a translation of both sentences into literal language—words that directly express a factual meaning.

1. A mail sorter assigned to the graveyard shift works from midnight to 8:00 A.M. at the post office.

2. Theater critics who say that a certain Broadway musical is a bomb mean that it is a complete failure.

Did you notice that the figurative language is more colorful and vivid than the literal language? Figurative language appeals to your imagination—your ability to understand the creative power of words. When you search for the figurative meaning of an expression, be aware of what the words suggest. What imaginative associations can you infer from the figurative meaning?

You use figurative language in your everyday speech. Here is an example:

> Statement: "My new car is a lemon."

> Literal meaning: "My new car is a yellow, sour-tasting piece of fruit."

This is not what the speaker means.

> Figurative meaning: "My new car is constantly breaking down."

This is what the speaker really means.

Figures of speech often make comparisons—direct or implied—between different things. Sometimes figurative language intentionally exaggerates or distorts the truth to emphasize a feeling or an idea.

The next two exercises will help you build your skill in understanding the differences between literal and figurative language.

EXERCISE 5

Directions: Match the figurative expression shown on the left with the correct meaning shown on the right by writing the correct letter in the space provided.

Figurative Expressions   **Meanings**

_____ 1. puppy love   a. an outstanding athlete or performer

_____ 2. penny-pincher   b. celebrate wildly

_____ 3. monkey business   c. an easy target

_____ 4. paint the town red   d. a teenage romance

_____ 5. tearjerker   e. votes cast using dead people's names

_____ 6. hothead   f. a sad story or performance that makes you cry

_____ 7. sitting duck   g. a person with a bad temper

_____ 8. ghost ballots   h. a successful song or performance

_____ 9. smash hit   i. a cheap person

_____ 10. star   j. foolish or playful behavior

Answers are on page 322.

EXERCISE 6

Directions: Write *L* if the statement is literal or *F* if it is figurative.

_____ 1. On July 20, 1969, two men walked on the moon.

_____ 2. The prizefighter kissed the canvas.

_____ 3. I've got the blues.

_____ 4. The lion tamer cracked his whip.

_____ 5. A dentist was the first patient to receive an artificial heart.

_____ 6. The horror movie was a hair-raising experience.

_____ 7. He soft-soaped his boss.

_____ 8. Money burns a hole in his pocket.

_____ 9. The firefighters rescued the children from the burning building.

_____ 10. The fly was trapped in the spider web.

Answers are on page 322.

Figurative Language in Literature

Through figurative language, authors invent original ways of describing a subject or expressing emotions. You can experience how authors see and interpret the world by understanding their figurative language.

The figurative language used in poetry, fiction, and drama is more moving than the literal language used in newspaper articles. For example, a part of the weather forecast might say, "mostly cloudy skies." This is a factual report, stated directly.

In William Shakespeare's play *Romeo and Juliet*, a tragic love story, the playwright describes the same weather conditions in figurative language. After Romeo and Juliet have died, Shakespeare writes at the end of the play:

The sun, for sorrow, will not show its head.

Shakespeare gives the sun human qualities. The sun is unhappy and appears to be mourning the deaths of Romeo and Juliet. Because of its grief, "the sun, . . . will not show its head," or, in other words, will not appear in the sky. What can you infer from Shakespeare's description?

The sky is dark and overcast, and the atmosphere is gloomy.

Of course, Shakespeare never tells you this directly. You interpreted the meaning from the figurative language. Compare Shakespeare's description to the newspaper account of the weather presented earlier. Shakespeare's words create an imaginary picture and express strong feelings. In contrast, you probably do not respond emotionally to the literal statement about the sky.

Figurative language often involves comparison or contrast. A writer will often link two things that appear at first to have nothing in common, pointing out at least one way in which the things are the same, or almost the same. By bringing out an unexpected similarity, the figurative language presents each item in the comparison in a new light. The reader's concept of the item is broadened or made clearer.

Look at how another author, John McPhee, uses figurative language. In the following excerpt, he describes a basketball player:

A star is often a point-hungry gunner, whose first instinct when he gets the ball is to fire away, and whose playing creed might be condensed to "When in doubt, shoot." Another, with legs like automobile springs, is part of the group because of an unusual ability to go high for rebounds.

—Excerpted from *A Sense of Where You Are* by John McPhee

In his description McPhee makes two comparisons:

1. "A *star* is often a point-hungry *gunner*, whose first instinct when he gets the ball is to fire away . . ."

2. "*legs* like *automobile springs* . . ."

What do these comparisons show? The first presents an exaggerated image of a star player by comparing how he instinctively shoots baskets to how a gunner instinctively shoots at targets. The second emphasizes the rebounding power of a basketball player's legs.

Here are some suggestions for interpreting figurative language:

- Identify the comparisons—direct or implied.

- Picture in your mind the two images being compared—for example, a basketball player's legs and automobile springs.

- Determine the author's purpose in drawing the comparison. What is the author trying to show?

EXERCISE 7

Directions: For each excerpt, identify the two things being compared. Then interpret the reason for the comparison. Follow the example below.

My father is eighty-six years old and in bed. His heart, that bloody motor, is equally old and will not do certain jobs any more. It still floods his head with brainy light. But it won't let his legs carry the weight of his body around the house.

—Excerpted from "A Conversation with My Father" by Grace Paley

Example: The father's heart is compared to an old motor.

Interpretation (the reason for the comparison): The comparison explains why the father's heart condition has confined him to his bed.

1. "Earlier in the evening it had rained, and now icicles hung along the station-house eaves like some crystal monster's vicious teeth."

—Excerpted from "A Tree of Night" by Truman Capote

_____ are compared to _____

Interpretation: _____

_____

2. "I feel as if I were walking a tight-rope a hundred feet over a circus audience and suddenly the rope is showing signs of breaking."

—Excerpted from _In Dreams Begin Responsibilities_ by Delmore Schwartz

_____ is compared to _____

Interpretation: _____

_____

3. "The lid of the left eye twitched; it fell down and snapped up; it was exactly as though the lid of the eye were a window shade and someone stood inside the doctor's head playing with the cord."

—Excerpted from *Winesburg, Ohio* by Sherwood Anderson

_____ is compared to _____

Interpretation: _____

_____

4. "The heavy noon-day sun hit him directly in the face, beating down on him like a club."

—Excerpted from *The Day of the Locust* by Nathanael West

_____ is compared to _____

Interpretation: _____

_____

5. "Lucy wiped the perspiration-soaked wisp of hair back from her face, and gave that last-minute look around the table to see if anything was missing, like a general inspecting troops."

—Excerpted from *All the King's Men* by Robert Penn Warren

_____ is compared to _____

Interpretation: _____

_____

6. "The high grey-flannel fog of winter closed off Salinas Valley from the sky and from the rest of the world."

—Excerpted from "The Chrysanthemums" by John Steinbeck

_____ is compared to _____

Interpretation: _____

_____

Answers are on page 322.

Style

You have probably heard the term *style* used in various contexts. For instance, clothing designers create styles of fashion—distinctive ways of dressing. Designers believe that a person's choice of clothes makes a fashion statement—a comment about his or her personality and background.

The term style can also be applied to literature and the arts. In this context, style refers to the distinguishing characteristics of an artist's performance and work—his or her unique way of singing or dancing or writing. For example, imagine how three very different singers might perform the same song. Contrast how "Happy Birthday" might sound as sung by Aretha Franklin, Garth Brooks, and Luciano Pavarotti. Each would imprint his or her own way of singing on the song, and it would sound very different as performed by each.

Styles of writing vary as much as styles of fashion and musical performance. Because each author's personality and talents are unique, the **style** of a written passage—the kind of language an author uses to express him or herself—is highly individual. How is this individuality achieved? In this section you will learn to analyze two elements that affect an author's style:

- diction
- tone

Diction: Types

Before authors begin writing, they might ask themselves these questions:

- What is my purpose for writing? to persuade? to inform? to entertain?
- What is my topic?
- Who is my audience?
- What response do I want from my readers?

The answers to these questions affect the author's **diction**—the words used to express ideas. Diction, or word choice, characterizes an author's writing style.

The following paragraph illustrates different types of diction. What do you observe about the ways that the scientist, the engineer, the foreman, and the salesman use language? As you read, notice that their statements are related to the function of levers.

Note the many languages within our language. The college freshman learns that "the moment of force about any specified axis is the product of the force and perpendicular distance from the axis to the line of action of the force." Viewing the same physical principle, the engineer says: "To lift a heavy weight with a lever, a man should apply his strength to the end of a long lever arm and work the weight on a short lever arm." Out on the factory floor the foreman shouts, "Shove that brick up snug under the crowbar and get a good purchase; the crate is heavy." The salesman says: "Why let your men kill themselves heaving those boxes all day long? The job's easy with this new long-handled pinch bar. With today's high wages you'll save the cost the first afternoon."

—Excerpted from "Giving Power to Words" by Philip W. Swain, *American Journal of Physics*, 1947

Examine these four statements and analyze the writing styles.

Statement	Analysis
Scientist: "The moment of force about any specified axis is the product of the force and perpendicular distance from the axis to the line of action of the force."	This style is formal. The scientist explains how a lever works according to the principles of physics. She assumes that the audience has a scientific background and can understand the technical language.
Engineer: "To lift a heavy weight with a lever, a man should apply his strength to the end of a long lever arm and work the weight on a short lever arm."	This style is informal. The engineer uses simpler words to explain how to operate a lever. His message is geared toward a general audience.
Foreman: "Shove that brick up snug under the crowbar and get a good purchase; the crate is heavy."	This style is conversational. The foreman uses words and colorful expressions from everyday speech. The foreman does not scientifically explain that the crowbar is a lever. He directly tells another factory worker how to lift a crate with a crowbar.
Salesman: "Why let your men kill themselves heaving those boxes all day long? The job's easy with this new long-handled pinch bar. With today's high wages you'll save the cost the first afternoon."	This style is also conversational. The salesman's purpose, however, is to persuade factory managers to purchase his product—a crowbar.

You can analyze an author's diction as formal, informal, or conversational. A *formal style* is usually found in scholarly essays, legal documents, and technical articles. The reading level is often very challenging.

An *informal style* generally appears in magazine and newspaper articles. The author's choice of words is directed to the general reading public.

A *conversational style* imitates the way people speak. It may include slang expressions and dialects.

Notice the different language used in each of the following statements:

Formal: Two officers arrested Mr. Bowman for driving his automobile under the influence of alcohol. His blood alcohol content (BAC), the percentage of alcohol in his blood, was higher than .10.

Informal: Two officers arrested Mr. Bowman for drunken driving.

Conversational: Two cops threw Bowman into the slammer for driving his car while he was smashed on booze.

Fiction writers may choose to tell an entire story in one of these three styles. However, sometimes they combine different kinds of diction. For example, they might write a character description in an informal style and a character's dialogue in a conversational style.

EXERCISE 8

Directions: What kinds of writing style—*formal*, *informal*, or *conversational*—would you probably find in each of the following examples? Fill in the blank for each.

1. a letter to a close friend _____

2. a TV commercial starring football players eating snacks _____

3. a doctor's medical report analyzing childhood diseases _____

4. a brochure for parents on taking care of a newborn baby _____

5. a lawyer's movie contract for a film star _____

6. a newspaper article on drug abuse in professional sports _____

7. an advice column written by Ann Landers _____

8. a magazine article about Disneyland _____

Answers are on page 322.

EXERCISE 9

Directions: Identify the style of each excerpt as *formal, informal*, or
conversational.

1. It was Paul's afternoon to appear before the faculty of the
    Pittsburgh High School to account for his various misdemeanors. He
    had been suspended a week ago, and his father had called at the
    Principal's office and confessed his perplexity about his son. Paul
    entered the faculty room suave and smiling.

    —Excerpted from "Paul's Case" by Willa Cather

    Style:_____

2. You see that cat inside the bar with that long fingernail, don't you?
    Well, he uses that nail to mark cards with. Every time I get into a
    game, there is somebody dealing with a long fingernail. It ain't safe!

    —Excerpted from "Conversation on the Corner" by Langston Hughes

    Style:_____

3. Few evils are less accessible to the force of reason, or more
    tenacious of life and power, than long-standing prejudice. It is a
    moral disaster, which creates the conditions necessary to its own
    existence, and fortifies itself by refusing all contradiction. It paints a
    hateful picture according to its own diseased imagination, and
    distorts the features of the fancied original to suit the portrait.

    —Excerpted from "The Color Line" by Frederick Douglass

    Style:_____

4. Jack is wandering around town, not knowing what to do. His
    girlfriend is babysitting at the Tuckers', and later, when she's got the
    kids in bed, maybe he'll drop over there. Sometimes he watches TV
    with her when she's babysitting, it's about the only chance he gets
    to make out a little since he doesn't own wheels, but they have to
    be careful because most people don't like their sitters to have their
    boyfriends over.

    —Excerpted from "The Babysitter" by Robert Coover

    Style:_____

5. The saloon is the most important building in the Western. It is the
    only place in the story where people can be seen together time
    after time. It thereby functions as a meetinghouse, social center,
    church. More important, it is the setting for the climax of the story,
    the gunfight. No matter where the fight ends, it starts in the saloon.

    —Excerpted from "The Western: The Legend and the Cardboard Hero" by Peter Homans

    Style:_____

Answers are on page 322.

Diction: Figurative Language

You have already learned that figures of speech often make direct or implied comparisons between two things. Figurative language suggests a meaning beyond the literal definition of the words.

When you are analyzing the diction of a passage, you should notice if the author uses figurative language. Figurative language characterizes some authors' styles. Through figures of speech, an author can more vividly convey his or her feelings or viewpoints.

For example, Octavio Paz, the winner of the 1990 Nobel Prize for literature, sometimes uses figurative language and images to communicate his beliefs. Read the passage below.

> The consciousness of being separate is a constant feature of our spiritual history. This separation is sometimes experienced as a wound that marks an internal division, an anguished awareness that invites introspection; at other times it appears as a challenge, a spur
> 5 to action, to go forth into the outside world and encounter others. It is true that the feeling of separation is universal and not peculiar to Spanish Americans. It is born at the very moment of our birth: as we are wrenched from the Whole, we fall into a foreign land. This never-healing wound is the unfathomable depth of every man. All our
> 10 ventures and exploits, all our acts and dreams, are bridges designed to overcome the separation and reunite us with the world and our fellow beings. Each man's life and the collective history of humanity can thus be seen as an attempt to reconstruct the original situation, an unfinished and endless cure for our divided condition.

—Excerpted from "In Search of the Present" by Octavio Paz, 1990

In this passage Paz makes these two comparisons:

- The feeling of being separate is like a wound (line 9).

- People's actions and dreams are like bridges designed to overcome the feelings of being separate from the world and "our fellow beings" (lines 10–12).

Why does Paz make these comparisons? The first comparison helps readers understand the intensity of our feelings of separation. The author makes it easier for readers to relate to the loneliness by comparing it to something familiar to everyone—a wound. The second comparison helps readers understand how actions and dreams can overcome the feelings of separation and connect people with one another. Paz helps readers picture the abstract idea of connectedness by comparing it to a familiar object—a bridge.

EXERCISE 10

Directions: Read the following passage and choose the best answer to each question that follows.

HOW DID THE AUTHOR FEEL AS A CHILD?

The feeling of separation is bound up with the oldest and vaguest of my memories: the first cry, the first scare. Like every child, I built emotional bridges in the
5 imagination to link me to the world and to other people. I lived in a town on the outskirts of Mexico City, in an old dilapidated house that had a junglelike garden and a great room full of books. First
10 games and first lessons. The garden soon became the center of my world; the library, an enchanted cave. I read alone but played with my cousins and schoolmates. There was a fig tree, temple of vegetation, four
15 pine trees, three ash trees, a nightshade, a pomegranate tree, wild grass, and prickly plants that produced purple grazes. Adobe walls. Time was elastic; space was a spinning wheel. All time, past or future, real
20 or imaginary, was pure presence, and space transformed itself ceaselessly. The beyond was here, all was here: a valley, a mountain, a distant country, the neighbors' patio. Books with pictures, especially history
25 books, eagerly leafed through, supplied images of deserts and jungles, palaces and hovels, warriors and princesses, beggars and kings.

—Excerpted from "In Search of the Present" by Octavio Paz, 1990

1. What is the author's purpose in this passage?

   To describe how
   (1) poor his family was when he was growing up
   (2) beautiful his family's garden was years ago
   (3) he and his family traveled together to the mountains
   (4) he used his imagination to link up with the world outside
   (5) he taught himself all about the beauty of nature

2. What does Paz mean by the phrase "time was elastic" in line 18?

   (1) His imagination let him stretch time backward into the past or forward into the future.
   (2) He had so much free time that he didn't know what to do with it.
   (3) He had so few responsibilities that he could fill his time however he wished.
   (4) His parents' library had so many books that he couldn't read them all.
   (5) His picture books had many stories of times in the distant past.

3. According to the passage, what was at the center of Paz's childhood world?

   (1) his family's garden
   (2) Mexico City
   (3) a mountain range
   (4) his neighbors' patio
   (5) his parents' library

Answers are on page 322.

Tone

You have probably heard the expression *tone of voice*. If you tell a friend "I don't like your tone of voice," you are annoyed by the person's manner of speaking. You are reacting to the sound of the spoken words.

In your daily conversations, you make inferences about people's attitudes based on their speech—what they say and how they say it.

Imagine that you are observing the following situation. A customer in a restaurant is dissatisfied with his meal. The steak he ordered is too tough to eat. The way he phrases his complaint and the manner in which he expresses it to the waiter reveal his attitude. How would you describe the tone of each of these remarks?

1. "Would you please return the steak to the kitchen? Tell the chef that this cut of beef is a little too tough to eat."

2. "I refuse to pay for this steak dinner! How do you expect me to eat food that I can't chew? Let me see the restaurant manager. Now!"

3. "What animal did this steak come from? Only a power saw could cut through this meat!"

The first statement sounds courteous. The word *please* shows politeness.

The second statement reveals the customer's anger. He refuses to pay for his meal and demands to see the restaurant manager.

The third statement is sarcastic. By making a joke about the food, the customer indirectly conveys his feelings. He does not expect the waiter to interpret the words literally.

A person's tone of voice may be described in several ways. Following are some examples. Add some of your own examples in the spaces provided.

friendly	phony	serious
sincere	sad	happy
understanding	polite	violent
_____	_____	_____
_____	_____	_____

WRITING ACTIVITY 2

Listen to a TV show or recall a recent conversation with a friend. Pay close attention to the person's tone of voice. On a separate sheet of paper, record three statements that you heard and indicate the attitude conveyed by the person's tone of voice.

Answers will vary.

Like tone of voice in speech, tone in writing expresses an attitude. In the study of literature, **tone** refers to an author's attitude toward his or her subject. The author's tone affects the way you respond to the subject.

When analyzing a passage for tone, ask yourself these questions:

• What subject is the author discussing?

• What is my overall reaction after reading the passage?

• How does the author feel about the subject?

• What language or descriptive details reveal the author's attitude?

Answer these questions as you read the following passage from a newspaper column:

Machinery and I have an understanding: we hate each other. I just have a hard time when it comes to fixing things. This, along with my inability to spit very far, is the most disappointing aspect of my life as a man. I do have some mechanical inclination. It's an attribute of my gender. There's a certain amount of knowledge about things mechanical that is passed on genetically from man to boy. Even my little son, when presented with a toy tractor, knew that blowing air through his flapping lips is what a tractor sounds like. He'd never seen a tractor until that day, but innately knew as much about them as I do. When tractors don't sound like flapping lips, they're broken. Of course, knowing when something is broken and knowing how to fix it are two separate fruits altogether.

It is something of a tribal custom among the males of our species to hold forth on what we know about twirly things with gears and springs. If you want to entertain the menfolk on a slow Sunday, throw a broken lawnmower at their feet.

"Must be the spark. She ain't gettin' no spark."

"No, it ain't got fuel. Look, the plug's bone-dry."

"Gotta be a stuck valve, you can feel there's no compression."

"No spark, no fuel, no compression. That 'bout covers it. What do ya figure, Bubba?"

"This is one broke lawnmower."

—Excerpted from "Mechanical Inclinations" by Tom Bodett, 1987

The author's topic is men and machines. As you read the passage, you may have smiled or laughed at the author's attitude toward the topic. He pokes fun at the notion that men have an inborn ability to repair machines. How can you tell that the article is not to be taken seriously? Write your ideas on the lines below.

_____

_____

_____

The opening sentence sets the tone for the rest of the article. The idea that a man has an agreement with machines is not to be taken seriously. Many other details tell you that the article is humorous: the author's overstatement about his inability to spit, the idea that tractors are broken if they don't sound like the air flapping through lips, and Bubba's final statement: "This is one broke lawnmower."

EXERCISE 11

Directions: Read each passage and choose the best description of tone for each.

1. I am the whistler. And I know many things, for I walk by night. I know many strange tales hidden in the hearts of men and women who have stepped in the shadows. Yes. I know the nameless terrors of which they dare not speak.

—Excerpted from the radio show *The Shadow*

(1) threatening
(2) silly
(3) joyful
(4) rude
(5) encouraging

2. Fifteen. What a weird age to be male. Most of us have forgotten about it, or have idealized it. But when you are fifteen well, things tend to be less than perfect.

   You can't drive. You are only a freshman in high school. The girls your age look older than you and go out with upperclassmen who have cars. You probably don't shave. You have nothing to do on weekends.

   —Excerpted from "Fifteen" by Bob Greene, 1982

   (1) serious
   (2) nasty
   (3) funny
   (4) grim
   (5) angry

3. About five o'clock our procession of three cars reached the cemetery and stopped in a thick drizzle beside the gate—first a motor hearse, horribly black and wet, then Mr. Gatz and the minister and I in the limousine, and, a little later, four or five servants and the postman from West Egg in Gatsby's station wagon, all wet to the skin.

   —Excerpted from *The Great Gatsby* by F. Scott Fitzgerald, 1925

   (1) somber
   (2) disrespectful
   (3) insincere
   (4) peaceful
   (5) happy

4. These devils will afflict the damned in two ways, by their presence and by their reproaches. We can have no idea how horrible these devils are. Saint Catherine of Siena once saw a devil and she has written that, rather than look again for one single instant on such a frightful monster, she would prefer to walk until the end of her life along a track of red coals.

   —Excerpted from *A Portrait of the Artist as a Young Man* by James Joyce, 1916

   (1) sarcastic
   (2) mysterious
   (3) friendly
   (4) intimidating
   (5) gentle

Answers are on pages 322–323.

Structure

Study the four designs in the following illustration. Which designs are arranged in an organized pattern?

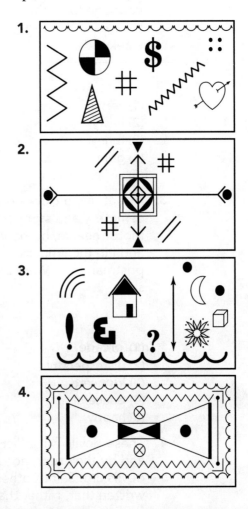

If you said design 2 and design 4, you were correct. The marks are grouped together to form an organized pattern. Therefore, you can see a particular structure in the design.

Similarly, authors structure their writing to make their ideas clear to the reader. **Structure** refers to the methods authors use to organize their message. Depending on the topic and purpose, an author devises a plan to order information.

In the following passage, a journalist discusses the problem of reporting the assassination of President John F. Kennedy:

> At first no one knew what happened, or how, or where, much less why. Gradually, bits and pieces began to fall together, and within two hours a reasonably coherent version of the story began to be possible. Even now, however, I know no reporter who was there who has a clear and orderly picture of that surrealistic afternoon; it is still a matter of bits and pieces thrown hastily into something like a whole.
>
> —Excerpted from "The Assassination" by Tom Wicker, *The New York Times*

According to this paragraph, the reporter's job was to make sense of an event that seemed disordered and confused. "Bits and pieces" had to be assembled to form a "whole"—a complete version of the story that the public would understand.

The following newspaper account by the same journalist presents a "clear and orderly picture" of that story:

> **DALLAS, Nov. 22**—President John Fitzgerald Kennedy was shot and killed by an assassin today.
>
> He died of a wound in the brain caused by a rifle bullet that was fired at him as he was riding through downtown Dallas in a motorcade.
>
> Vice President Lyndon Baines Johnson, who was riding in the third car behind Mr. Kennedy's, was sworn in as the 36th President of the United States 99 minutes after Mr. Kennedy's death.
>
> Mr. Johnson is 55 years old; Mr. Kennedy was 46.
>
> Shortly after the assassination, Lee H. Oswald, who once defected to the Soviet Union and who has been active in the Fair Play for Cuba Committee, was arrested by the Dallas police. Tonight he was accused of the killing.
>
> —Excerpted from "Kennedy Is Killed by Sniper as He Rides in Car in Dallas"
> by Tom Wicker, *The New York Times*

You probably found this article easy to understand because the reporter logically structured the information. The first sentence introduces the main idea—the assassination of President Kennedy. The remaining sentences summarize the most important facts relating to this event.

The next section of this chapter will help you analyze the structure of passages. You will learn the ways an author arranges information and how the arrangement or organization reveals the author's purpose. You will study three methods of organization:

1. time order

2. classification

3. cause and effect

Time Order

To prepare a frozen TV dinner, you follow the instructions on the package:

1. Preheat oven to 375 degrees.

2. Remove foil wrapping from tray.

3. Cook for 35–40 minutes.

These step-by-step directions illustrate a method of organization called time order. When the purpose of a piece of writing is to explain a process or an event, the author may use this structure. He or she arranges the information according to a sequence—a related series of actions.

Notice how the author uses time order in the following passage:

> Nick laid the bottle full of jumping grasshoppers against a pine trunk. Rapidly he mixed some buckwheat flour with water and stirred it smooth, one cup of flour, one cup of water. He put a handful of coffee in the pot and dipped a lump of grease out of a can and slid it sputtering across the hot skillet. On the smoking skillet he poured smoothly the buckwheat batter. It spread like lava, the grease spitting sharply. Around the edges the buckwheat cake began to firm, then brown, then crisp. The surface was bubbling slowly to porousness. Nick pushed under the browned undersurface with a fresh pine chip. He shook the skillet sideways and the cake was loose on the surface. I won't try to flop it, he thought. He slid the chip of clean wood all the way under the cake, and flopped it over onto its face. It sputtered in the pan.
>
> When it was cooked Nick regreased the skillet. He used all the batter. It made another big flapjack and one smaller one.
>
> —Excerpted from "Big Two-Hearted River" by Ernest Hemingway, 1925

In the preceding passage Hemingway shows you how Nick, a camper, cooks breakfast. Did you clearly understand the stages in this process? Did you notice that each action and movement happens in an orderly sequence? If you answered yes to these questions, you correctly analyzed the structure.

EXERCISE 12

Directions: Read the passage below, paying attention to the order of the steps the boy uses when shining shoes. Then number the steps to show the sequence in which they appeared in the passage.

When I got a customer, we both played our roles. The customer, tall and aloof, smiled, "Gimme a shine, kid," and I replied, "*Si, señor*, sir, I'll give you one that you'll have to put sunglasses on to eat the bright down."

My knees grinding against the gritty sidewalk, I adopted a serious, businesslike air. Carefully, but confidently, I snaked out my rags, polish, and brushes. I gave my cool breeze customer the treatment. I rolled his pants cuff up—"That'll keep shoe polish off"—straightened his socks, patted his shoe, assured him he was in good hands, and loosened and retied his shoes. Then I wiped my nose with a delicate finger, picked up my shoe brush, and scrunched away the first hard crust of dirt. I opened my bottle of black shoe cleaner—dab, rub in, wipe off, pat the shoe down. Then I opened my can of polish—dab on with three fingers, pat-a-pid, pat-a-pid. He's not looking—spit on the shoe, more polish, let it dry, tap the bottom of his sole, smile up at Mr. Big Tip (you hope), "Next, sir."

I repeated the process on the other shoe, then picked up my brush and rubbed the bristles very hard against the palm of my hand, scientific-like, to warm the brush hairs up so they would melt the black shoe wax and give a cool unlumpy shine. I peeked out of the corner of my eye to see if Mr. Big Tip was watching my modern shoeshine methods. The bum *was* looking. I hadn't touched his shoe, forcing him to look.

The shoe began to gleam dully—more spit, more polish, more brush, little more spit, little more polish, and a lotta rag. I repeated on the other shoe. As Mr. Big Tip started digging in his pocket, I prepared for the climax of my performance. Just as he finished saying, "Damn nice shine, kid," I said, "Oh, I ain't finished, sir. I got a special service," and I plunged my wax-covered fingers into a dark corner of my shoe box and brought out a bottle of "special shoe lanolin cream for better preservation of leather."

I applied a dab, a tiny dab, pausing long enough to say very confidently, "You can't put on too much or it'll spoil the shine. It gotta be just right." Then I grabbed the shoe rag firmly, like a maestro with a baton, and hummed a rhythm with it, slapping out a beat on the shoes. A final swish here and there, and *mira!*—finished. Sweating from the effort of my creation, I slowly rose from my knees, bent from the strain, my hand casually extended, palm flat up, and murmured, "Fifteen cents, sir," with a look that said, "But it's worth much more, don't you think?" Mr. Big Tip dropped a quarter and a nickel into the offering plate, and I said, "Thanks a mil, sir," thinking, *Take it cool*, as I cast a watchful eye at his retreating back.

—Excerpted from *Down These Mean Streets* by Piri Thomas, 1967

_____ dabs some polish on the shoe

_____ rubs in the cleaner and wipes it off

_____ brushes the shoes until they're shiny

_____ takes out the rags, polish, and brushes

_____ applies lanolin cream to preserve the shoe leather

_____ opens the bottle of black shoe cleaner

_____ opens the can of polish

_____ repeats the process on the other shoe

_____ lets the shoe dry

Answers are on page 323.

WRITING ACTIVITY 3

On a separate sheet of paper, explain a simple step-by-step process that you perform frequently. Identify the topic, then list the steps in proper sequence. Here are some topics that you might write about:

- a job responsibility, such as balancing a cash drawer or filling out a time sheet

- a household chore, such as washing clothes or waxing a floor

- a hobby, such as refinishing a piece of furniture or cooking a special dish

- a sports technique, such as throwing a curveball or dunking a basketball

Answers will vary.

Classification

When you go to a new shopping mall, you probably check the store directory. The directory lists the stores under titles describing types of merchandise, as in this example:

Men's Apparel

Women's Apparel

Men's and Women's Apparel

Children's Apparel

Shoes

Jewelry

Books and Cards

Plants and Flowers

Food Specialties and Candies

Home Furnishings and Accessories

Music, Records, and Home Entertainment

Restaurants

As you know, these categories help you plan your shopping. Sorting things, people, or ideas into categories is called **classification**. The following chart on the zodiac uses this method of organization. The information is grouped into four categories: sun sign, dates, symbol, and element.

THE ZODIAC

Sun Sign	Dates	Symbol	Element
Aries	March 21–April 20	Ram	Fire
Taurus	April 21–May 20	Bull	Earth
Gemini	May 21–June 20	Twins	Air
Cancer	June 21–July 22	Crab	Water
Leo	July 23–August 22	Lion	Fire
Virgo	August 23–September 22	Virgin	Earth
Libra	September 23–October 22	Scales	Air
Scorpio	October 23–November 22	Scorpion	Water
Sagittarius	November 23–December 21	Archer	Fire
Capricorn	December 22–January 20	Goat	Earth
Aquarius	January 21–February 19	Water-bearer	Air
Pisces	February 20–March 20	Fish	Water

Based on the chart on the preceeding page, rearrange the information on the zodiac according to these categories:

Signs Related to Fire

_____

_____

_____

Signs Related to Earth

_____

_____

_____

Signs Related to Air

_____

_____

_____

Signs Related to Water

_____

_____

_____

Did you correctly classify the sun signs? Here are the answers:

- *Fire Signs:* Aries, Leo, Sagittarius
- *Earth Signs:* Taurus, Virgo, Capricorn
- *Air Signs:* Gemini, Libra, Aquarius
- *Water Signs:* Cancer, Scorpio, Pisces

Authors use classification to structure their writing when they analyze a topic according to categories. For instance, a music critic analyzing popular music might divide the topic into blues, jazz, rock and roll, and country and western. A literary scholar classifies Shakespeare's plays as comedies, tragedies, and histories.

WRITING ACTIVITY 4

Take an informal poll of at least three friends or family members. Ask each person the following questions:

•What is your favorite kind of music?

•Do you ever attend concerts? Why or why not?

•How often do you buy a tape or CD?

Write up the results of your poll in paragraph form.

Answers will vary.

EXERCISE 13

Directions: As you read the passage below, notice the categories of information. Then complete the exercise.

The kind of vehicle you drive reveals your personality, say behavior experts.

"Surveys have shown a direct relationship between automobiles and personality," said California psychologist Dr. Stephen Brown.

Here are the personality traits revealed by different kinds of "wheels," according to Dr. Brown and New York psychiatrist Dr. Emory Breitner.

Subcompact: These drivers like to be in control, and it's easy to be in control of a tiny subcompact. They're frugal, pragmatic people who are in a hurry. Subcompact owners don't want to be bogged down by a big car—with payments to match.

Mid-size or Compact: Reserved and conservative, these drivers rarely make moves without considerable thought. They're sensitive and emotional—but never foolish. They don't gamble, they check things out, work hard, and are honest to a fault. These drivers like to blend in, not make waves.

Full-size: The drivers of these giants like to do everything in a big way. They're ambitious, desire money and material goods—and are literally driven to success. They like big homes—and if they throw a party, they want it to be an all-out affair with people singing, eating, and having a ball. They aim for important jobs and can't stand a cramped office or a tiny car that cramps their style.

Station wagon: Family comes first for these people. They're good neighbors, very friendly, enjoy children and animals, and will always try to help you out if you have a problem. Image isn't important. They just want to use their station wagon to enjoy life.

Jeep: These drivers are trailblazers who love adventure. They enjoy striking out on their own and don't mind questioning authority. They're practical, energetic survivors who like to win under tough conditions, and work best when they can make their own rules.

Convertible: The top's up one day, and down the next. These drivers are exactly like their car—changing from day to day. Convertible owners are impulsive, quick-witted and restless. But they're excellent at communicating ideas and love to shine on short-term projects—jobs where they can see instant results. They love art, music and creative activities.

Pickup truck: These people are ready to tackle any job. They have a determined, fighting spirit, and a do-it-yourself attitude that makes them self-sufficient. They're forceful, opinionated, and like to pitch right in and get a job done.

—Excerpted from "Type of Vehicle You Drive Reveals Your Personality" by Byron Lutz, *The National Enquirer,* 1986

Match the type of vehicle shown on the left with the appropriate personality trait shown on the right by writing the correct letter in the space provided.

Vehicle	Personality Trait
_____ 1. Subcompact	(a) is restless and changeable
_____ 2. Mid-size or Compact	(b) desires money and success
_____ 3. Full-size	(c) completes a job and is self-sufficient
_____ 4. Station wagon	(d) likes to control situations
_____ 5. Jeep	(e) enjoys adventure
_____ 6. Convertible	(f) is reserved and sensitive
_____ 7. Pickup truck	(g) values family

Answers are on page 323.

Cause and Effect

When you attempt to discover *how* or *why* something happened, you are analyzing through **cause** and **effect**.

When authors analyze the causes and effects of a topic, they ask two questions:

1. Why does a situation occur? (*causes*)

2. What are the results or reactions? (*effects*)

If a young family were asked, "Why did you move to this area?", the family might give the following causes for their decision:

• Housing is reasonably priced.

• The schools have an excellent reputation.

• Shopping is close to home.

• Police and fire services are very competent.

• Job opportunities are plentiful.

If a scientist were asked, "What have been the benefits of our space explorations?", the scientist might state the effects provided by the exploration of space:

• a greater understanding of the solar system

• more accurate mapping of the earth

• medical advances from studies carried out in weightlessness

• improved global satellite communications

• sharing of knowledge gained among nations

Sometimes authors focus on either causes or effects. For example, you might read an article that describes how divorce affects men and women (effects). Another article may analyze the reasons marriages end in divorce (causes). In the following dialogue from a short story, a mother explains a cause-and-effect relationship to her son.

"Oh!" said the boy. "Then what *is* luck, mother?"

"It's what causes you to have money. If you're lucky you have money. That's why it's better to be born lucky than rich. If you're rich, you may lose your money. But if you're lucky, you will always get more money."

—Excerpted from "The Rocking-Horse Winner" by D. H. Lawrence

Can you identify the cause-and-effect relationship?

The cause, _____ results in _____

If you said that *luck* (the cause) results in *money* (the effect), you were right.

EXERCISE 14

Directions: Read the following passage and notice the causes or effects. Then answer the questions that follow.

We live in a world where there is a need to be able to speak with others at any time and at any place. Our indispensable possessions are our cell phones, Palm Pilots, laptop computers, voice mail, and instant e-mail. We can't hide; we are always in reach.

In our jobs and businesses we must have instant access to our clients, our suppliers, our supervisors, and our offices. A highly competitive economy requires us to be accessible to our clients, or else we risk losing their business or our jobs. Customers also want immediate service, overnight delivery, and our constant attention. We have those tools that allow us to reach out and touch someone 24 hours a day anywhere on the earth, in the sky, or beneath the sea. No longer can we use the excuses, "I didn't get the message" or "I was away from my desk". Through the magic of wireless communication, we can even be reached while we're on vacation.

Family life has become a little more manageable as well. Schools can reach parents anywhere anytime. The children need no longer be separated from Mom and Dad during the working day: pagers and family-plan cellular phones ensure that those reassuring voices are just a few finger points away. That old excuse for lateness, "I wasn't near a phone," just doesn't work any more.

Forgot what to pick up at the grocery store or too busy to shop? No problem. Call home while pushing the cart through the aisles. Better yet, call or fax the many services that will deliver a prepared meal to the house at an appointed hour.

Technology has enabled us to keep in touch at work and at home, but where do we go when we want to get away?

The first paragraph explains the effect of new communication devices: Because of new technology, we can be reached anytime, anywhere. Below, list the causes for our need to be in contact with others.

On the job:

_____

_____

_____

For the family:

_____

_____

_____

Answers are on page 323.

Chapter Review

Directions: Read each of the following passages and answer the questions that follow.

Questions 1–2 refer to the following passage from a novel.

WHAT DOES HUCK FEAR?

Then away out in the woods I heard that kind of a sound that a ghost makes when it wants to tell about something that's on its mind and can't make itself understood, and
5 so can't rest easy in its grave, and has to go about that way every night grieving. I got so downhearted and scared I did wish I had some company. Pretty soon a spider went crawling up my shoulder, and I flipped it off
10 and it lit in the candle; and before I could budge it was all shriveled up. I didn't need anybody to tell me that that was an awful bad sign and would fetch me some bad luck, so I was scared and most shook the clothes
15 off of me. I got up and turned around in my tracks three times and crossed my breast every time; and then I tied up a little lock of my hair with a thread to keep witches away. But I hadn't no confidence. You do that
20 when you've lost a horseshoe that you've found, instead of nailing it up over the door, but I hadn't ever heard anybody say it was any way to keep off bad luck when you'd killed a spider.

—Excerpted from *Adventures of Huckleberry Finn* by
Mark Twain, 1884

1. According to Huck Finn, which of the following actions causes bad luck?

    (1) nailing a horseshoe over the door
    (2) lighting a candle
    (3) hearing ghostly sounds
    (4) killing a spider
    (5) keeping witches away

2. Which of the following words best describes Huck's immediate reaction to the sign of bad luck?

    (1) confident
    (2) calm
    (3) miserable
    (4) frightened
    (5) irritable

Questions 3–6 refer to the following excerpt from a newspaper article.

HOW SHOULD PEOPLE SEEK REVENGE ON A MACHINE?

The guy in front of me put his dime in the coffee machine. The cup dropped, the machine whirred, but nothing came out.

5 He muttered, then started to walk away looking dejected and embarrassed. That's the way many people react when a machine doesn't come through: as if they have been outwitted. They feel foolish.

"Aren't you going to do anything about 10 it?" I asked.

"What's there to do?"

What a question. If he had gone in a bar and ordered a beer, and if the bartender had taken his money but not given him a beer, 15 he'd do something. He'd yell or fight or call the police.

But he let a machine cow him. "Kick it," I said.

"What good will that do?" he said.

20 "You'll feel better," I said.

He came back and got in position to kick it, but I stopped him.

"Not like that. You are going to kick it with your toe, but you can hurt yourself that 25 way. Do it this way."

I stepped back and showed him the best way. You use the bottom of your foot, as if you're kicking in a bedroom door.

I stepped aside, and he tried it. The first 30 time he used the ball of his foot. It was a weak effort. "Use more of the heel," I suggested. That did it. He gave it two good ones and the machine bounced. He has big feet.

35 "With feet like that," I told him, "you could knock over a sandwich machine."

He stepped back looking much more self-confident.

Somebody else who had been in line 40 said: "I prefer pounding on it. I'll show you."

Leaning on it with his left hand, he put his forehead close to the machine, as if in deep despair. Then he pounded with his clenched fist.

45 "Never use the knuckles," he said, "because that hurts. Use the bottom of the fist, the way you'd pound on the table."

"Why just one fist?" someone else said. "I always use two."

50 He demonstrated, standing close to the machine, baring his teeth, and pounding with both fists, as if trying to break down a bedroom door with his hands.

Just then, another guy with a dime 55 stepped up. Seeing us pounding on the machine, he asked: "Is it out of coffee?"

We told him it had shorted on a cup.

He hesitated, then said: "Sometimes it only skips one, then it works OK."

60 "It's your money," I told him.

He put in his dime, the cup dropped, the machine whirred, and nothing came out. All he said was "Hmm," and started to walk away.

65 "Why don't you kick it?" I said.

He grimaced. "It's only a dime."

—Excerpted from "How to Kick a Machine" by Mike Royko, *Chicago Daily News*, November 15, 1971

3. Which of the following choices best describes the tone of the excerpt?

   (1) neutral
   (2) fearful
   (3) humorous
   (4) angry
   (5) sad

4. In what other situation would the writing style used in this passage be effective?

   (1) a presidential campaign speech
   (2) an advertisement for health insurance
   (3) a magazine article on city colleges
   (4) a job-application letter
   (5) a script for a TV comedy series

5. What is the author's purpose in lines 23–32?

   (1) to explain a process
   (2) to analyze causes and effects
   (3) to classify information
   (4) to contrast different events
   (5) to compare people to machines

6. Which of the following techniques does the author use to show people's reactions to the coffee machine?

   (1) summaries of complaint letters
   (2) conversations between people
   (3) newspaper reports about vending machines
   (4) interviews with bartenders
   (5) a national survey of dissatisfied customers

Questions 7–9 refer to the following excerpt from a newspaper article.

ARE THESE WORD WATCHERS "HAPPY CAMPERS"?

"Pro-active," "downsize," "happy camper" and any sentence beginning "Basically . . . " were banished from the English language Thursday in a year-end
5 cleansing by word watchers.

The annual light-hearted list of misused, overused and useless words from Lake Superior State University also exiled "team chemistry," "victimless crime," "win-win
10 situations," "open" heart surgery, "associates" (once called employees) and "pro-active" (a feeble substitute for *diligent* and *assertive*), among others.

The list is compiled from nominations
15 sent from around the country by people concerned about eroding standards of English usage. The words receiving the most nominations for banishment this time around were "basically" and "got"—as in the
20 election year cry "We've got to get the country moving again."

"Basically" is a stall word, said the verbal vigilantes. Any sentence starting out with it signals fuzzy thinking and a desire not to
25 offend.

"Got" got on the list because people are fed up with hearing "have got, has got, etc." One person who nominated it said, "If one 'gets' something, one then 'has' it. 'Got'
30 is redundant. It is the most overused word in the language."

"Downsizing" is nothing more than a $5 euphemism for layoffs and firings; "gridlock" is a needless substitute for
35 "deadlock"; "empower" was the most useless buzzword of 1992; and "victimless crime" was banished by those who doubt there could be any such thing. "'Associates'

are simply employees who haven't had a
40 raise lately," the report said.

"Happy camper" made the list after one contributor said anyone using the phrase should be made to "reside for a weekend in a campground [with] rain, hordes of children,
45 black flies, mosquitoes, raccoons, bears, drunken neighbors."

—Excerpted from "English Gets a Pro-Active Downsizing," Reuters Limited , January 1, 1993

7. According to the excerpt, to what does the word *downsizing* often refer?

(1) losing weight
(2) altering clothes
(3) firing people
(4) reducing spending
(5) cutting salaries

8. What is the purpose of the first two paragraphs?

(1) to give examples of poor word choice
(2) to introduce the main idea of the passage
(3) to invite readers to analyze their use of language
(4) to summarize the author's attitude toward the subject
(5) to help banish certain words from the English language

9. Which of the following words best describes the author's tone?

(1) assertive
(2) sincere
(3) angry
(4) lighthearted
(5) concerned

Questions 10–12 refer to the following excerpt from a short story.

WHAT IS ROSIE'S OPINION OF THE JAPANESE LANGUAGE?

The first Rosie knew that her mother had taken to writing poems was one evening when she finished one and read it aloud for her daughter's approval. It was about cats,
5   and Rosie pretended to understand it thoroughly and appreciate it no end, partly because she hesitated to disillusion her mother about the quantity and quality of Japanese she had learned in all the years
10 now that she had been going to Japanese school every Saturday (and Wednesday, too, in the summer). Even so, her mother must have been skeptical about the depth of Rosie's understanding, because she
15 explained afterwards about the kind of poem she was trying to write.

See, Rosie, she said, it was a *haiku*, a poem in which she must pack all her
20 meaning into seventeen syllables only, which were divided into three lines of five, seven, and five syllables. In the one she had just read, she had tried to capture the charm of a kitten, as well as comment on the
25 superstition that owning a cat of three colors meant good luck.

"Yes, yes, I understand. How utterly lovely," Rosie said, and her mother, either satisfied or seeing through her deception
30 and resigned, went back to her composing.

The truth was that Rosie was lazy; English lay ready on the tongue but Japanese had to be searched for and examined, and even then put forth
35 tentatively (probably to meet with laughter). It was so much easier to say yes, yes, even when one meant no, no. Besides this was what was in her mind to say: I was looking through one of your magazines from Japan

40 last night, Mother, and towards the back I found some *haiku* in English that delighted me. There was one that made me giggle off and on until I fell asleep—

It is morning, and lo!

45 *I lie awake, comme il faut,*

Sighing for some dough.

Now, how to reach her mother, how to communicate the melancholy song? Rosie knew formal Japanese by fits and starts, her
50 mother had even less English, no French. It was much more possible to say yes, yes.

—Excerpted from "Seventeen Syllables" by Hisaye Yamamoto, 1988

10. What is the purpose of paragraph two?

(1) to reveal Rosie's dislike of poetry
(2) to provide a definition for *haiku*
(3) to talk about superstitions
(4) to praise the family cat
(5) to show Rosie's willingness to learn

11. Which choice best describes Rosie's attitude in the third paragraph?

(1) helpful
(2) insulting
(3) interested
(4) critical
(5) insincere

12. What is the basis of the difference between Rosie and her mother?

(1) Rosie dislikes poetry, but her mother likes it.
(2) Rosie's mother wants her daughter to earn better grades in school.
(3) Rosie's mother has an interest in Japanese language, but Rosie does not.
(4) Rosie cannot understand her mother's ignorance of French poetry.
(5) Rosie's mother wants her daughter to be more honest.

Answers are on page 323.

Go to **www.GEDReading.com** for additional practice and instruction!

CHAPTER 4

Synthesis

In Chapter 3 you learned that some questions on the GED Language Arts, Reading Test would require you to draw inferences based upon what you observe and know from your experience. You will use your analysis skills when you draw inferences from *a part* of the passage. When you draw inferences from several parts of the passage, you will be using **synthesis** skills. Synthesis is a way of thinking—a reasoning process that draws multiple inferences from an entire passage or integrates information from outside the passage to reach a new understanding.

Solving synthesis questions is much like solving a puzzle. In a puzzle all of the pieces when linked together give you the full picture. Synthesis requires you to link the pieces you have observed and what you know from your experiences to form a new context.

Synthesis questions will ask you to

• interpret how a passage is organized

• interpret the overall tone, point of view, or purpose of a passage

• link elements of a passage

• integrate information from outside a passage with information from within the passage

This chapter will help you to practice solving synthesis questions.

Interpreting How a Passage is Organized

Writers organize their work in a way that helps the reader to follow the progression of action, the importance of ideas, examples for illustration, or points of comparison or contrast.

Authors of fictional and nonfictional texts organize their works so that the reader can better understand the author's purpose. An author can organize a passage in several different ways, including time order, classification, cause and effect, and comparison and contrast. The purpose of a passage may also be to delve into the mind of the character to show what the character is thinking or how the character is reacting to situations. In Chapter 3 you saw examples of passages organized in time order, classification, and cause and effect. In this chapter, you will look at passages that use comparison and contrast. You will need to understand all four methods of organizing passages in order to synthesize information and draw conclusions.

Comparison and Contrast

One of the seven passages you will see on the GED Language Arts, Reading Test will involve **comparison** or **contrast**. This passage may be any of the literary texts (prose fiction, poetry, drama) or a nonfiction text. You will be expected to recognize when an author is organizing a passage to analyze similarities or differences.

Comparison and contrast passages are organized by an author to balance one feature with another. For example, an author may develop one character by stating this character's traits and comparing them to the traits of another character. In this way the reader sees in what ways the characters are similar. If an author contrasts the characters' traits, readers can see how the characters differ. Writers could choose to compare or contrast

- characters
- settings
- situations
- courses of action
- points of view

You make comparisons and contrasts on a daily basis. In planning a vacation, you may want to examine the benefits of one destination over another. At work you may have to decide which course of action brings the greatest advantage to your company. You may make price comparisons or product comparisons before making a purchase.

Suppose you want to move into a new apartment. After looking at several apartments, you find two that you like. Before you choose which apartment to rent, you might evaluate certain features of each apartment:

Features	Apartment #1	Apartment #2
Monthly rent	$580.00	$610.00
Location and neighborhood	Good	Good
Amount of space	5 rooms/ 1 bedroom	4 rooms/ 1 bedroom
Condition of appliances	Fair	New
Maintenance	Good	Fair

Comparing and contrasting Apartment 1 with Apartment 2 would help you make your final decision. The comparison-and-contrast reasoning process would show you why you prefer either the first or the second apartment.

An author uses comparison and contrast to organize a passage for these purposes:

- to judge which of two similar things is better

• to show how two similar things are alike and different

For example, a sportswriter might predict the likely winner of the World Series by comparing and contrasting the strengths and weaknesses of the two baseball teams involved. A movie critic might analyze the similarities and differences between a best-selling novel and the movie version of the book.

EXERCISE 1

Directions: In the following passage, an imaginary psychologist named Dr. Applebaum discusses his opinion of television shows. Read the passage and answer the questions that follow.

"Now," said Applebaum, "have you ever said to a taxi driver, 'Follow that car and don't lose him'?"

"Not really."

"Well, if you had, the driver would have told you to blow it out your ear. No taxi driver is in a mood to follow another car because that means he's going to get involved. But on TV every cabdriver looks as if he'd like nothing better to do than to drive 90 miles an hour through a rain-swept street trying to keep up with a carful of hoods. And the worst thing is that the kids believe it."

"What else have you discovered?"

"Kids have a perverted sense of what emergency wards of hospitals are really like. On TV shows they take a kid to an emergency ward and four doctors come rushing down to bandage his leg. In a real life situation the kid would be sitting on the bench for two hours before he even saw an intern. On TV there always happens to be a hospital bed available when a kid needs it. What the kids in this country don't know is that sometimes you have to wait three days to get a hospital bed and then you have to put a cash deposit of $500 down before they give it to you."

—Excerpted from "Unreality of TV" in *The Buchwald Stops Here*
by Art Buchwald, 1978

1. The purpose of this passage is to compare and contrast

   _____ with _____

2. In paragraph 3 _____

   is compared and contrasted with _____

3. In paragraph 5 _____

   is compared and contrasted with _____

4. According to this excerpt, what can you conclude about Dr. Applebaum's opinion of television shows?

   _____

   _____

Answers are on pages 323–324.

EXERCISE 2

Directions: Read the passages and identify the nature of the comparison or contrast.

Ernest Hemingway's books are easier to know, and love, than his life. He wrote, at his early best, a prose of powerful and brilliant simplicity. But his character was not simple. In one of his stories he wrote, "The most complicated subject I know, since I am a man, is a man's life." The most complicated subject that he knew was Ernest Hemingway.

He was a violently cross-grained man. His life belonged as much to the history of publicity as to the history of literature. He was a splendid writer who became his own worst creation, a hoax and a bore. He ended by being one of the most famous men in the world, white-bearded Mr. Papa. He stopped observing and started performing. He sentimentalized and pontificated and lied and bullied.

—Excerpted from "A Quarter-Century Later, the Myth Endures"
by Lance Morrow, *Time*, August 25, 1986

1. In the first paragraph Ernest Hemingway's _____
   is contrasted with his _____

2. List two contrasts about Ernest Hemingway contained in paragraph 2.

   _____

   _____

   _____

   _____

People, black and white, say that the throngs of upstanding black men at the Million Man March showed a picture of the Black Man different from what the nation is accustomed to. Because this has always been my primary image of the Black Man—the men in my family, my father, his friends, my friends, total strangers at traffic lights, and sometimes even myself—what struck me was not the vast crowd's proud demeanor or the insult that the crowd's peacefulness was a pleasant surprise to most whites and some blacks, but that the black men deserved a message more worthy of their journey than the numerology and self-election of Louis Farrakhan.

It was not a civil rights march or even a march, though a Nation of Islam spokesman said on television that it was a march in Washington rather than a march on Washington. As more than one of the day's speechmakers insisted, they had come neither to demand nor to ask anything of government and whites. They had come for themselves and to ask something of themselves. It was billed as a day of atonement and reconciliation. It was a mass rally, a religious convocation, a camp revival meeting on a grand scale, with some competition among the speechmakers to see who could blow the emotional lid off the patient multitudes. Perhaps those black men and the women mingling among them—1.5 million, 2 million, 400,000, 870,000?—came to experience what it felt like to be in command of that place where history had been made a few times before. A lot of those present on October 16, 1995, had not been born in 1963.

—Excerpted from "Slouching Toward Washington" by Darryl Pinckney,1995

3. Identify the paragraph and the sentence(s) in that paragraph where each of these contrasts is found:

(a) The participants in the Million Man March were in the capitol demanding something of themselves rather than something of the government.

paragraph _____, sentence(s) _____

(b) The image of black men taking part in the march differed from the nation's typical perception of black men.

paragraph _____, sentence(s) _____

(c) Many observers were concerned with the crowd's behavior; the writer, however, was concerned about the message that the crowd was given.

paragraph _____ sentence(s) _____

Answers are on page 324.

WRITING ACTIVITY 1

Compare and contrast yourself with a close friend. How are your backgrounds, personalities, and physical appearances similar? How are they different? List some of these similarities and differences on a sheet of paper.

Answers will vary.

EXERCISE 3

Directions: Read the passage and answer the questions that follow.

The old lady settled herself comfortably, removing her white cotton gloves and putting them up with her purse on the shelf in front of the back window. The children's mother still had on slacks and still had her head tied up in a green kerchief, but the grandmother had on a navy blue straw sailor hat with a bunch of white violets on the brim and a navy blue dress with a small white dot in the print. Her collar and cuffs were white organdy trimmed with lace and at her neckline she had pinned a purple spray of cloth violets containing a sachet. In case of an accident, anyone seeing her dead on the highway would know at once she was a lady.

She said she thought it was going to be a good day for driving, neither too hot nor too cold, and she cautioned Bailey that the speed limit was fifty-five miles an hour and that the patrolmen hid themselves behind billboards and small clumps of trees and sped out after you before you had a chance to slow down. She pointed out interesting details of the scenery: Stone Mountain; the blue granite that in some places came up to both sides of the highway; the brilliant red clay banks slightly streaked with purple; and the various crops that made rows of green lace-work on the ground. The trees were full of silver-white sunlight and the meanest of them sparkled. The children were reading comic magazines and their mother had gone back to sleep.

"Let's go through Georgia fast so we won't have to look at it much," John Wesley said.

"If I were a little boy," said the grandmother, "I wouldn't talk about my native state that way. Tennessee has the mountains and Georgia has the hills."

"Tennessee is just a hillbilly dumping ground," John Wesley said, "and Georgia is a lousy state too."

"You said it," June Star said.

"In my time," said the grandmother, folding her thin veined fingers, "children were more respectful of their native states and their parents and everything else."

—Excerpted from "A Good Man Is Hard To Find" by Flannery O'Connor, 1953

1. The contrast in the passage is primarily between _____ and _____

2. What does the women's choice of clothing say about each woman?

   _____

   _____

   _____

3. Which choice best expresses the main differences between the two women?

(1) youth and age
(2) fear and confidence
(3) respect and indulgence
(4) north and south
(5) refinement and vulgarity

Answers are on page 324.

Interpreting the Tone, Point of View, or Purpose of a Passage

Tone

As a reader you will be expected to look at an entire passage in order to reach conclusions about the author's intent or techniques. In Chapter 3 you learned to analyze tone in short sentences and paragraphs. On the GED Language Arts, Reading Test, you will also be asked to look at the tone of an entire passage.

Read the following passage. Observe the organizational pattern used by the author, and try to determine the author's tone toward her subject.

I refuse to be upset by this. In fact, I feel good about it. Oh, yeah. Because what I did was fair, probably even an inalienable right or something.

Still, it was my first time, so naturally I'm a little shaken.

I was sitting here about to pick up the phone to call Al, the appliance repair guy. Because the washing machine broke again, just froze up in mid-rinse, leaving my delicate darks stranded in a tubful of suds. Fortunately, Al had left a little sticker on my washer with his phone number in case I ever needed him again. And according to the sticker, his shop was open only till 5, which was about five minutes away, and, really, I just wanted to get this situation handled so I could move on with my life.

So I reached for the phone and *bleep, bleep,* it rang.

"Hello?" I answered.

"Hello," said a young man. "May I speak with Miss, um Je-Anne, um Lake-us?"

Oh, brother. The only people who call my house looking for Miss Um Je-Anne Um Lake-us are telemarketers. I was not in the mood. Not that I have ever been. I have never once agreed to anything offered by any telemarketer, ever. I should, I thought, just say this. I should explain to this guy that I am a big waste of his time.

"I'm not interested in anything," was the way it came out.

"Well, Miss Je-Anne Um Lake-us, what long distance service are you using now?"

Oh, brother. He was not going to go down easy. "I don't know," I said. "That's sort of my husband's domain." Now why was I lying? Not that I think this is exactly wrong. Lying to an intruder is sort of in the same category as killing someone in self-defense, isn't it?

"You *don't know*?" he said, serving up some attitude.

"Look, this really isn't a good time," I said. "Why don't you call some other time?" And why did I say that? Now I was going to get on some list where they'd call me on, like every shift or something, until finally I'd just have to snap and use that line my friend Sara once used: "Why don't you give me *your* home number and I'll call you back to discuss this offer during *your* dinnertime, okay?"

—Excerpted from "Invasive Procedure" by Jeanne Marie Laskas,
The Washington Post Magazine, August 20, 2000

1. What is the author's problem?

_____

_____

2. The author uses two techniques to organize this passage. Identify them.

_____

_____

3. Which choice best represents the tone of the author in this passage?

(1) delighted
(2) satirical
(3) solemn
(4) embarrassed
(5) confident

1. The author addresses the nuisance of telemarketers who call at the most inopportune times. However, the author uses humor and exaggeration throughout the passage as she describes her dealing with the telemarketer.

2. The passage is organized in chronological order to show the experience to the reader. The author uses dialogue and records her own thoughts to exaggerate her humorous view of the incident.

3. Answer (2), satirical, best conveys the author's humorous portrayal of a common experience.

Point of View

As you read a passage, observe who is telling the story. In some passages writers may choose to have an individual *outside* the event tell the story. For other passages a person *who is part of the event* will tell you what happens. On pages 176–179 in Chapter 6 of this book, you will find more information on determining the point of view.

EXERCISE 4

Directions: As you read the following brief excerpts, determine the point of view chosen by the writer to tell the story. Use *O* for an outside narrator and use *I* for a narrator who is part of the story.

_____ 1. Now that she knew how many people from her past were sitting here, Maggie wished she'd have given more thought to her appearance.
—Excerpted from *Breathing Lessons* by Anne Tyler

_____ 2. Of Angela Vicaro, on the other hand, I was always receiving periodic news that inspired an idealized image in me.
—Excerpted from *Chronicle of a Death Foretold* by Gabriel García Marquéz

_____ 3. "The whole family" means the Kwongs and the Louies. The Kwongs are Auntie Helen, Uncle Henry, Mary, Frank, and Bao-bao. And these days "the Louies" really refers only to my mother and me, since my father is dead and my brother Samuel lives in New Jersey.
—Excerpted from *The Kitchen God's Wife* by Amy Tan

_____ 4. They met in Vesper County, Virginia, under a walnut tree. She had been working in the fields like everybody else, and stayed past picking time to live with a family twenty miles away from her own.
—Excerpted from *Jazz* by Toni Morrison

_____ 5. In the meantime he had sold his store; he couldn't spend time in it; he was mainly occupied now with sitting around town on rainy days smoking and 'gassin' with the boys,' or in riding to and from his farms.
—Excerpted from "Under the Lion's Paw" by Hamlin Garland

Answers are on page 324.

EXERCISE 5

Directions: Read the passage and answer the questions that follow.

WHO IS THE NARRATOR?

In my younger and more vulnerable years my father gave me some advice that I've been turning over in my mind ever since.

5   "Whenever you feel like criticizing anyone," he told me, "just remember that all the people in this world haven't had the advantages that you've had."

He didn't say any more but we've always 10 been unusually communicative in a reserved way and I understood that he meant a great deal more than that. In consequence I'm inclined to reserve all judgements, a habit that has opened up many curious natures to 15 me and also made me the victim of not a few veteran bores. The abnormal mind is quick to detect and attach itself to this quality when it appears in a normal person, and so it came about in college I was 20 unjustly accused of being a politician, because I was privy to the secret griefs of wild, unknown men. Most of the confidences were unsought—frequently I have feigned sleep, preoccupation or a hostile levity when 25 I realized by some unmistakable sign that an intimate revelation was quivering on the horizon—for the intimate revelations of young men or at least the terms in which they express them are usually plagiaristic 30 and marred by obvious suppressions. Reserving judgements is a matter of infinite hope. I am still a little afraid of missing something if I forget that, as my father snobbishly suggested and I snobbishly 35 repeat, a sense of the fundamental decencies is parcelled out unequally at birth.

—Excerpted from *The Great Gatsby*
by F. Scott Fitzgerald

1. According to the passage, which of these descriptions best matches the speaker?

   (1) a character who takes part in the action of the story
   (2) a troubled young person
   (3) an all-knowing storyteller outside the story
   (4) a teenager
   (5) a politician

2. What does the narrator state is his most important quality?

   (1) He is sought out for his wisdom.
   (2) He is not a person who makes enemies.
   (3) He finds the misery of others a delight.
   (4) He had a good relationship with his father.
   (5) He does not judge people.

3. Which of these terms best describes the tone of the passage?

   (1) light-hearted
   (2) sarcastic
   (3) thoughtful
   (4) angry
   (5) desperate

4. At the end of the novel, the narrator must pass judgement on the main character. What can you expect the narrator to do before making his announcement?

   (1) consult his father
   (2) listen to the man's enemies
   (3) consider all relevant details
   (4) follow his impulses
   (5) prejudge the man on hearsay

Answers are on page 324.

Purpose

When you are asked for the main idea or purpose of a multi-paragraph passage, you must look for the idea that ties together *all* of the details from the passage. Don't confuse the purpose of a single paragraph with the purpose of the passage as a whole. As you saw when studying the organizational pattern of a passage, paragraphs are links that lead you to the overall purpose.

As you read the following passage, think about what ideas link the paragraphs.

EXERCISE 6

Directions: Read the passage and answer the questions that follow.

When the short days of winter came dusk fell before we had well eaten our dinners. When we met in the street the houses had grown sombre. The space of sky above us was the colour of ever-changing violet and towards it the lamps of the street lifted their feeble lanterns. The cold air stung us and we played till our bodies glowed. Our shouts echoed in the silent street. The career of our play brought us through the dark muddy lanes behind the houses where we ran the gauntlet of the rough tribes from the cottages to the back doors of the dark dripping gardens where odours arose from the ash-pits, to the dark odorous stables where a coachman smoothed and combed the horse or shook music from the buckled harness. When we returned to the street, light from the kitchen windows had filled the areas. If my uncle was seen turning the corner we hid in the shadow until we had seen him safely housed. Or if Mangan's sister came out on the doorstep to call her brother in to his tea we watched her from our shadows peer up and down the street. We waited to see whether she would remain or go in and, if she remained, we left our shadow and walked up to Mangan's steps resignedly. She was waiting for us, her figure defined by the light from the half-opened door. Her brother always teased her before he obeyed and I stood by the railings looking at her. Her dress swung as she moved her body and the soft rope of her hair tossed from side to side.

Every morning I lay on the floor in the front parlour watching her door. The blind was pulled down to within an inch of the sash so that I could not be seen. When she came out on the doorstep my heart leaped. I ran to the hall, seized my books and followed her. I kept her brown figure always in my eye and, when we came near the point at which our ways diverged, I quickened my pace and passed her. This happened morning after morning. I had never spoken to her, except for a few casual words, and yet her name was like a summons to all my foolish blood.

—Excerpted from "Araby" by James Joyce

1. How old does the narrator appear to be?

   (1) 8
   (2) 21
   (3) 13
   (4) 10
   (5) 25

2. What term would best describe the entire passage?

   (1) a reminiscence
   (2) a diary entry
   (3) a love letter
   (4) a fairy tale
   (5) an adventure tale

3. What is the purpose of the passage?

   (1) to describe the poor section of town
   (2) to tell how the children used their time
   (3) to convey the speaker's friendship with Mangan
   (4) to recall the speaker's first secret love
   (5) to list the typical routine in the speaker's day

Answers are on page 324.

Linking Elements of a Passage

Paragraphs are the building blocks of writing. An author's task is to skillfully link the ideas of the paragraphs so that they logically build to the intended purpose.

Read the following passage and think about the ways the paragraphs are linked together.

EXERCISE 7

Directions: Read the passage about events after the sinking of the *Titanic* and answer the questions that follow.

Most of all they talked of getting rescued. Lightoller soon discovered Harold Bride, the junior wireless operator, at the stern of the boat, and from his position in the bow he asked what ships were on the way. Bride shouted back: the *Baltic*, the *Olympic*, the *Carpathia*. Lightoller figured the *Carpathia* should arrive at daybreak . . . passed the word around, to buck up the sagging spirits.

From then on they scanned the horizon searching for any sign. From time to time they were cheered by the green flares lit by Boxhall in Boat 2. Even Lightoller thought they must have come from another ship.

Slowly the night passed. Toward dawn a slight breeze sprang up. The air seemed even more frigid. The sea grew choppy. Bitter-cold waves splashed over the feet, the shins, the knees of the men on Boat B. The spray stabbed their bodies and blinded their eyes. One man, then another, then another rolled off the stern and disappeared from sight. The rest fell silent, completely absorbed in the battle to stay alive.

The sea was silent too. No one saw a trace of life in the waves that rippled the smooth Atlantic as the first light of dawn streaked the sky.

—Excerpted from *A Night To Remember* by Walter Lord

1. What are some of the phrases that link the paragraphs together?

   _____

   _____

   _____

   _____

   _____

2. What ideas are listed in the first paragraph?

   _____

   _____

3. What ideas are listed in the second paragraph?

   _____

   _____

4. What ideas are listed in the third paragraph?

   _____

   _____

5. What is the purpose of this passage?

      (1) to list the actions taken by the survivors
      (2) to describe the cold, icy surroundings
      (3) to reveal how the leader established order
      (4) to suggest the dangers of ocean travel
      (5) to reveal the survivors' growing fear of death at sea

Answers are on page 324.

 Go to **www.GEDReading.com** for additional practice and instruction!

Integrating Information from Outside a Passage with Information from Within the Passage

Some synthesis questions will contain additional information not found in the excerpt, and you will have to integrate that information with your understanding of the passage. There are two or three of these *expanded synthesis* questions on the test. Sometimes the new information will be something that happened before or after the selection; it may be a critical comment on the passage; or it may be information about the author.

Read the following excerpt and answer the expanded synthesis question.

> By the time Krebs returned to his home town in Oklahoma the greeting of heroes was over. He came back much too late. The men from the town who had been drafted had all been welcomed elaborately on their return. There had been a great deal of hysteria. Now the reaction had set in. People seemed to think it was rather ridiculous for Krebs to be getting back so late, years after the war was over.
>
> —Excerpted from "Soldier's Home" by Ernest Hemingway, 1925

Later in the story, we learn that Krebs is having a great deal of difficulty in readjusting to normal town life after World War I.

Based on this information and the excerpt, what was Krebs' reaction to his reception on returning home from the war?

(1) joy
(2) sadness
(3) fear
(4) resentment
(5) acceptance

The first sentence of the question provides information that unfolds as the story develops. The excerpt states that years had passed since the war's end, and all of the celebrations for the returning soldiers were long over. When you integrate those two pieces of information, you can conclude that Krebs felt (4) resentment because he did not participate in the celebrations and the honors given to other returning soldiers.

WRITING ACTIVITY 2

Read the review in your local newspaper or a magazine of a movie or play you saw, a book you read, a new TV program, a new CD or video, or a concert you attended. List the points made by the reviewer.

On a separate sheet of paper, write a reply to the reviewer in which you compare or contrast the reviewer's comments with your reactions.

Chapter Review

Directions: Read each passage below and choose the best answer to each question that follows.

Questions 1–7 refer to the following excerpt from a short story.

WHO IS CONNIE?

Her name was Connie. She was fifteen and had a quick nervous giggling habit of craning her neck to glance into mirrors, or checking other people's faces to make sure
5 her own was all right. Her mother, who noticed everything and knew everything and who hadn't much reason any longer to look at her own face, always scolded Connie about it. 'Stop gawking at yourself, who are
10 you? You think you're so pretty?" she would say. Connie would raise her eyebrows at these familiar complaints and look right through her mother, into a shadowy vision of herself as she was right at that moment: she
15 knew she was pretty and that was everything. Her mother had been pretty once too, if you could believe those old snapshots in the album, but now her looks were gone and that was why she was always
20 after Connie.

"Why don't you keep your room clean like your sister? How've you got your hair fixed—what the hell stinks? Hair spray? You don't see your sister using that junk."

25 Her sister June was twenty-four and still lived at home. She was a secretary in the high school Connie attended, and if that wasn't bad enough—with her in the same building—she was so plain and chunky and
30 steady that Connie had to hear her praised all the time by her mother and her mother's sisters. June did this, June did that, she saved money and helped clean the house and cooked and Connie couldn't do a thing,
35 her mind was filled with trashy daydreams. Their father was away at work most of the time and when he came home he wanted

supper and he read the newspaper at supper and after supper he went to bed.

—Excerpted from "Where Are You Going, Where Have You Been?" by Joyce Carol Oates, 1970

1. How does the mother feel about Connie?

(1) jealous
(2) embarrassed
(3) admiring
(4) sympathetic
(5) concerned

2. In lines 14–16 the author describes Connie as follows: "She knew she was pretty and that was everything." Why does the author include that description?

To show that Connie
(1) wants to be a fashion model
(2) needs to attract teenage boys
(3) is conceited about her looks
(4) plans to enter a beauty contest
(5) fears that her beauty will fade

3. Which of the following statements best describes the mother's opinion of June?

(1) June should get married.
(2) June should go back to school.
(3) June should be more concerned about her looks.
(4) June is a capable secretary.
(5) June has her priorities in order.

4. Why does the author use the phrase "trashy daydreams" (line 35)?

(1) to compare Connie's daydreams to her messy room
(2) to contrast Connie's mind with a garbage can
(3) to imply that the mother doesn't have those kinds of daydreams
(4) to suggest that Connie's mother thinks Connie's inner thoughts are worthless
(5) to explain why Connie doesn't enjoy housework

5. From the description of the father (lines 36–39), what can you conclude about him?

   (1) He is irritable from working long hours.
   (2) He does not spend much time with his family.
   (3) He takes pride in supporting his family.
   (4) He likes to read about current events.
   (5) He enjoys being with his wife and daughters.

6. In this passage Connie's family is described by a fiction writer. From what other person's point of view could Connie's home life also be analyzed?

   (1) housekeeper
   (2) family counselor
   (3) hairstylist
   (4) scientist
   (5) historian

7. The author commented that the mysterious man who confronts and terrorizes Connie later in the story is the Demon Lover Death who has come to claim her.

   Based on that information, which choice best represents the author's purpose for the story?

   (1) to comment on Connie's relationship with her sister
   (2) to criticize Connie's poor treatment of her mother
   (3) to suggest that an attractive appearance doesn't guarantee happiness
   (4) to reprimand Connie's parents for failing to correct her selfishness
   (5) to portray Connie as a victim of the envy of her sister and mother

Questions 8–12 refer to the excerpt from a novel.

WHAT DOES EDNA FEEL IS HER ROLE IN LIFE?

Her marriage to Leoncé Pontellier was purely an accident, in this respect resembling many other marriages which masquerade as the decrees of Fate. It was in
5 the midst of her secret great passion that she met him. He fell in love, as men are in the habit of doing, and pressed his suit with an earnestness and an ardor which left nothing to be desired. He pleased her; his
10 absolute devotion flattered her. She fancied there was a sympathy of thought and taste between them, in which fancy she was mistaken. Add to this the violent opposition of her father and her sister Margaret to her
15 marriage with a Catholic, and we need seek no further for the motives which led her to accept Mr. Pontellier for her husband.

The acme of this bliss, which would have been a marriage with the tragedian, was not
20 for her in this world. As the devoted wife of a man who worshipped her, she felt she would take her place with a certain dignity in the world of reality, closing the portals forever behind her upon the realm of
25 romance and dreams.

But it was not long before the tragedian had gone to join the cavalry officer and the engaged young man and a few others; Edna found herself face to face with the realities.
30 She grew fond of her husband, realizing with some unaccountable satisfaction that no trace of passion or excessive and fictitious warmth colored her affection, thereby threatening its dissolution.

—Excerpted from "The Awakening"
by Kate Chopin, 1899

8. According to the excerpt, what does Edna expect as the outcome of her marriage to Leoncé Pontellier ?

   (1) total happiness
   (2) peace within her father's family
   (3) lifelong sorrow in a loveless marriage
   (4) an end to youthful notions of love
   (5) children of her own

9. Which choice best describes Edna's feeling for Leoncé?

   (1) resentment
   (2) affection
   (3) love
   (4) jealousy
   (5) indifference

10. Who were the "tragedian, the cavalry officer, and the engaged young man"?

    (1) friends of Leoncé's
    (2) characters in a story
    (3) imaginary lovers
    (4) Edna's brothers
    (5) former love interests

11. What is the purpose of the third paragraph?

    (1) to convey that Edna was not in love with Leoncé
    (2) to reveal Edna's disillusionment with the marriage
    (3) to express her concern about having children
    (4) to suggest that Leoncé no longer loves Edna
    (5) to relate Edna's past fears of marriage

12. Later in the story, Edna says, "I am no longer one of Mr. Pontellier's possessions to dispose of or not."

    What change in Edna does this later comment indicate?

    (1) an awareness that she is her own person
    (2) her refusal to be a mother to Leoncé's children
    (3) her following of the role assigned to her
    (4) an acceptance of society's standards for women
    (5) her rejection of both her father and her husband

Answers are on page 325.

Go to **www.GEDReading.com** for additional practice and instruction!

PART II

Understanding Language Arts, Reading

CHAPTER 5

Nonfiction Prose

On the GED Language Arts, Reading Test, you will be asked to read and interpret two **nonfiction prose** passages with approximately ten questions. The topics of nonfiction prose include real people, places, events, and social issues. (Prose fiction deals with imaginary people and events.) The purpose of nonfiction reading selections is to present factual information or to express a viewpoint. Examples of nonfiction prose will come from three content areas:

Informational Nonfiction	Literary Nonfiction	Visual Communication
business documents	biographies	film
speeches	essays	photography
magazines	diaries	television
newspapers	memoirs	computer art
research reports	letters	painting/sculpture

Reading to Understand Nonfiction

When you study nonfiction prose, you apply all the reading skills discussed in the first four chapters of this book:

1. Understanding the literal meaning (Comprehension)
    - Identifying the main idea
    - Finding supporting details—examples, reasons, facts, descriptions

2. Applying information and ideas from a passage (Application)
    - Transferring concepts from a passage to a new context

3. Analyzing content, style, and structure (Analysis)
    - Making inferences based on details from a single passage
    - Drawing conclusions from supporting details
    - Interpreting figurative language
    - Examining the effects of the language used in a passage
    - Determining how an author organizes information

4. Making connections between separate sources of information (Synthesis)
    - Applying information to a specific context

- Making multiple inferences

- Integrating information from outside the passage with information within

The exercises in this chapter will provide you with extensive practice in applying these reading skills. Many of the exercises contain a purpose question like those you'll find on the actual GED Test. Use the purpose question to focus your reading.

The reading selections are grouped according to the content areas they explore—informational nonfiction, literary nonfiction, and visual communication. In each category there are different kinds of essays. An essay is a type of writing in which the author combines facts and personal opinions. An author's purpose and intended readers determine what he or she includes in the essay and how he or she presents the facts and opinions. In this chapter you will find examples of informative essays, critical essays, and reviews.

Informative Essays

In an informative essay the author's intention is to educate the readers about the selected subject. He or she may provide historical background, descriptive summaries, or biographical sketches. In purely informative essays the author withholds personal judgments, because the purpose is to instruct readers rather than to persuade them to agree with his or her opinions. Newspapers and magazines often contain informative essays.

Critical Essays

Critical essays present in-depth analysis of a subject. The word *criticism* is often associated with a negative view. However, a critical essay attempts to interpret or explain as fully as possible both positive and negative elements of a subject. Critical essays are usually directed to readers who already have a solid base of knowledge about the particular subject. Critical essays may analyze events; documents; or works of literature, music, dance, and art. The author of a critical essay often interprets artistic techniques, such as style and structure or shape and form. The critic may also discuss the meaning or significance of the subject and judge its merits. For example, a critical essay about a world leader might analyze that leader's decisions about world events and might also interpret their impact.

Reviews

Reviews of movies, plays, books, and other art forms frequently appear in newspapers and magazines. Intended for the general reading public, reviews briefly describe the content of a work of art and evaluate its strengths and weaknesses. Reviewers assume that most readers are unfamiliar with their subject. Their purpose is to present their opinions and help readers decide whether they would enjoy the work being reviewed. After reading a movie review, you might ask yourself, "According to the reviewer, should I see the movie?"

To prepare you for the GED Language Arts, Reading Test, this chapter will present a wide range of nonfiction prose from the three content areas— informational nonfiction, literary nonfiction, and visual communication. You will apply the reading skills discussed throughout this book. In addition, you will focus on some of the elements that reviewers, critics, and authors use in developing their topics and commentaries:

- Facts and opinions

- Descriptive language

Recognizing these elements will help you determine the author's viewpoint as well as the style and the structure of nonfiction prose.

Facts and Opinions

In Chapter 1 you were told that the fiction writer Ralph Ellison attended Tuskegee Institute in Alabama, where he studied music and composition. Through research you could prove that this statement is true. A statement that can be proved is a **fact**.

Suppose a literary critic comments, "Ralph Ellison's musical training strongly influenced his prose style. His rhythmical sentences, his attention to the sound of words, and the balanced structure of his stories all reveal how his craft as a musician was transferred to his writing." The critic's statement is an **opinion**—a judgment about Ralph Ellison's prose style.

You can verify the truth of factual information. By contrast, you cannot prove or disprove a critic's interpretation of an event or work. When you read commentaries, you need to distinguish between facts and opinions. You cannot dispute the accuracy of facts. However, you have the option of agreeing or disagreeing with an author's opinion. Recognizing the difference between facts and opinions will enhance your understanding of commentaries in the following ways:

- Your literal understanding of the passage will improve if you grasp the factual information.

- You will be able to pinpoint sentences in the passage that express the author's beliefs.

- You will be able to identify facts that are used to support the critic's opinions or main idea.

EXERCISE 1

Part I **Directions:** Carefully read the four short commentaries about Ntozake Shange's play *For Colored Girls Who Have Considered Suicide/When the Rainbow Is Enuf*. Then read the statements after each commentary. Write *F* if the statement is a fact or *O* if it is an opinion.

1. *For Colored Girls Who Have Considered Suicide/When the Rainbow Is Enuf* is a "choreopoem"—a theatrical production combining music, dance, and poetry. Seven black women, each wearing a dress in one of the rainbow colors, relate their personal experiences onstage. Written by Ntozake Shange, the show was first produced in November 1975. Soon after, the show was staged on Broadway for two years. The show's continued popularity reflects Shange's insightful portrayal of black women.

      _____ 1. A "choreopoem" combines music, dance, and poetry.

      _____ 2. The show was staged on Broadway for two years.

      _____ 3. Shange insightfully portrays the experiences of black women.

2. [This play is a] stirringly acted, intimate production of Ntozake Shange's Tony Award-winning drama that explores the lives of seven black women, presented by Pegasus Players.

          —Excerpted from a drama review in the Chicago Tribune, *July 25, 1986*

      _____ 1. The show was a Tony Award-winning drama.

      _____ 2. The show explores the lives of seven black women.

      _____ 3. The production is stirringly acted and intimate.

3. When Ntozake Shange wrote this "choreopoem" ten years ago, it seemed like an outspoken affirmation of black women. Today, it sounds like the seven black women in this plotless play think only about black men. The adolescent poetry is flaccid and self-indulgent, and the production, despite some high-energy performances, can't pump much strength into it.

          —Excerpted from a drama review in Chicago *magazine, August 1986*

      _____ 1. Despite some good performances, the play no longer has the strong impact it originally had.

      _____ 2. Shange's poetry is adolescent.

      _____ 3. The production of the play is weak.

4. *Colored Girls,* as directed by Sydney Daniels, suffers from a slow start, but as Ntozake Shange's lovely poetry gets rolling, the pace picks up. And it isn't long before the Pegasus Players cast begins to make a strong connection. The tale-telling session becomes comfortable and irresistible in this cleanly delivered and forcefully presented production.

          —Excerpted from a drama review in the Chicago Sun-Times, *July 27, 1986*

      _____ 1. Sydney Daniels is the director.

      _____ 2. The acting is performed by the Pegasus Players cast.

      _____ 3. Shange's poetry is lovely.

      _____ 4. The production is cleanly delivered and forcefully presented.

Part II   **Directions:**   Reread the preceding commentaries. Then write the number of the commentary that correctly answers each of the following questions.

1. Which commentary expresses the most negative opinion of the production?

    _____

2. Which commentary praises Shange's poetry?

    _____

3. Which commentary does not judge a specific production of the show?

    _____

4. Which commentary implies that the show is out of date?

    _____

Answers are on page 325.

WRITING ACTIVITY 1

Watch your favorite television show and write a short commentary in which you include both factual information and your opinion. In the first paragraph, record facts about the show. Include the title of the show, the names of the leading actors and the characters they portray, and a brief summary of the plot.

In the second paragraph, state your opinion of the show. Answer the following questions: Why is the show your favorite? How would you rate the actors' performances? Would you recommend the show to a friend? Use a separate sheet of paper for your commentary.

Answers will vary.

Descriptive Language

Descriptive language often characterizes the writing style of commentaries on the arts. As you have already observed, reviewers rely on colorful adjectives in phrasing their opinions. An **adjective** is a part of speech that describes a person, a place, a thing, or an idea. The following are examples of adjectives used in movie and play reviews:

• wild, witty, and wonderful

• delightful, funny, and sophisticated

You probably noticed that all of these adjectives are flattering. The reviewers have chosen words praising the movie or play described.

On the other hand, you can also infer a reviewer's disapproval of a play or a movie from the descriptive language. The following adjectives from play and movie reviews are uncomplimentary:

- unimaginative and predictable

- strained and clumsy

Recognizing descriptive language enables you to determine the reviewer's opinion—positive or negative—about an artistic work. The following statement is excerpted from a review of *The Toxic Avenger*, a horror film. Underline the descriptive words that reveal the reviewer's impression of the movie.

> *The Toxic Avenger* is a monstrously crude, blatantly tasteless film reminiscent of the now by-gone drive-in movies.
>
> —Excerpted from a movie review by Sid Smith

Did you underline "monstrously crude" and "blatantly tasteless"? These phrases express Sid Smith's viewpoint. He obviously disliked the film.

EXERCISE 2

Directions: The following are reviewers' statements about a theater company, a singer, a novel, and a movie. Read the statements and answer the questions that follow.

Part I: Comments about Steppenwolf Theatre Company

"Nervy, electric, physically charged style"

—Michael Billington, *The Guardian*

"Steppenwolf Theatre Company is not merely good. It's simply great!"

—Glenna Syse, *Chicago Sun-Times*

"Steppenwolf, as always, is spectacular."

—Linda Winer, *USA Today*

"The strongest, most energetic theatre company in America today"

—*Vogue* magazine

From the preceding statements, write four adjectives that praise the Steppenwolf Theatre Company.

_____   _____

_____   _____

Part II: Comments about Singer Pia Zadora

"A big, brash, pop singing voice. . . "

—*New York Times*

"Her voice is . . . strong, mature, and it envelops the lyrics with a caress."

—*Variety*

"She has a tremendous voice . . . big, clear and good . . . the audience went crazy."

—*Detroit Free Press*

Write four adjectives from the preceding comments that describe Pia Zadora's singing voice.

_____   _____

_____   _____

Part III: Comments about Ernest Hemingway's Novel *The Garden of Eden*

"A highly readable story"

—E. L. Doctorow, *The New York Times Book Review*

"Wonderful writing. Hemingway at the top of his form"

—Charles P. Corn, *San Francisco Chronicle*

"Hemingway dialogue at its best . . . a novel worth having"

—Peter S. Prescott, *Newsweek*

Write two adjectives from the preceding comments that describe the quality of Hemingway's writing.

_____

_____

Part IV: Comments about the Movie *The Children*

A nuclear power plant releases a radioactive mist that turns some schoolchildren into monsters. The nasty tykes commit such despicable acts as killing their parents with deadly hugs. It's a cheaply made, lackluster horror film with a predictable script, dreadful acting, and the usual amount of gore.

—Excerpted from a review of *The Children* in *Rating the Movies* by Jay Brown and the editors of *Consumer Guide*

1. Copy the sentences that summarize the plot.

   _____

   _____

   _____

   _____

2. Write the adjective that describes the script.

   _____

3. Write the adjective that describes the acting.

   _____

Answers are on page 326.

WRITING ACTIVITY 2

Directions: On the following lines, write adjectives describing each topic:

1. The voice of your favorite singer

Singer's name:_____

Adjectives:

_____

_____

2. A movie that you disliked

Movie title: _____

Adjectives:

_____

_____

3. A TV series that you would recommend to a friend

Series title: _____

Adjectives:

_____

_____

Answers will vary.

Suggestions for Reading Commentaries

As you read the examples of nonfiction text in the rest of this chapter, use the following list of suggestions to develop your skills in reading commentaries:

- Find the main idea to focus your reading.

- If the author expresses an opinion, look for facts, examples, or other evidence that he or she uses to support it.

- To understand the context of an author's comments, pay close attention to brief summaries or descriptions of the artistic work.

- Notice characteristics of style and structure—that is, the author's choice of language and arrangement of information. Evaluate the overall effects of these techniques.

- Draw your own conclusions from the ideas and supporting details presented in the commentary.

Apply these suggestions when you read the commentaries in this chapter.

Informational Nonfiction

The following exercises will help you apply your analysis skills to essays and articles from magazines, newspapers, and speeches.

EXERCISE 3

Directions: Read the passage below and answer the questions that follow.

WHAT MAKES A MANAGER GOOD?

Every few years business leaders celebrate the birth of "new" management techniques and new gimmicks that promise to solve employee, customer and product quality problems. It's as if new were synonymous with better. Well, it isn't.

Management By Walking Around (MBWA), one of the newer techniques, is nothing more than caring enough about what's going on in the organization to talk to the people who know. Nothing new there. And, Total Quality Management (TQM), still another "new" technique, is a matter of instilling old-fashioned pride.

While new management techniques may look different from those they are supposed to replace, they don't qualify as a better means of accomplishing the results corporate executives are paid to produce. New techniques do not improve morale, productivity, quality or profits. At best, they offer short-lived hope and excitement, which any changes, even superficial ones, usually engender. They also generate a new vocabulary, buzzwords—which seem to give techniques legitimacy—and structured programs designed to implement the techniques.

Experience shows that technique-oriented programs eventually die, but not because the techniques themselves are bad. The problem is that many users are not true believers of the emotional and intellectual assumptions the techniques reflect.

Suppose, for example, a manager learns how to use the techniques of Management By Objectives, but really believes that the only objectives that count are the manager's. MBO is doomed to fail.

Many managers employ techniques that do not represent their basic values or true feelings. Yet, they go through the motions because they would like to think that the techniques they've learned have powers—independent of anything else—to accomplish results. The fact is, techniques for managing people that do not come from the soul—from emotions—from a genuine caring attitude, come across as phony and artificial. Unless managers' people-managing techniques are extensions of their values and beliefs, they will, almost invariably, revert to their natural ways.

—Excerpted from "Techniques Do Not a Manager Make" by Jack H. Grossman

1. Name two "new" management techniques that, according to the excerpt, are popular. Then briefly explain what each consists of.

   _____

   _____

   _____

   _____

   _____

2. What does the writer feel is most important in helping to solve employee problems?

   _____

   _____

   _____

Answers are on page 326.

EXERCISE 4

Directions: Read the passage and answer the questions that follow.

HOW SHOULD NEWS REPORTERS WRITE STORIES?

Unlike the novelist and the poet, the journalist cannot spend hours searching for the truth, much less the right word. No other writer is asked to commit words to paper with such speed, under such pressure. All the more reason, then, for the journalist to borrow from those whose struggles have cleared paths toward good writing. There are writing rules that apply to a three-paragraph item about a service station holdup and to a detailed investigative story on the state's deposits in non-interest-bearing bank accounts.

We might start with Tolstoy who, in describing the strength of his masterwork *War and Peace*, said, "I don't tell; I don't explain. I show; I let my characters talk for me."

In short, one of the reporter's first writing rules might be: Show, don't tell. Telling makes the reader or listener passive. Showing engages him. Good writers let the words and actions of the participants do the work. John Ciardi elaborates on Tolstoy's advice: "One of the skills of the good poet is to enact his experiences rather than to talk about having had them. 'Show it, don't tell it,' he says. 'Make it happen, don't talk about its happening.'"

When the reporter makes it happen, the reader moves into the story. The reporter disappears as middleman between the event and the reader.

Covering the funeral of a child killed by a sniper, a reporter wrote, "The grief-stricken parents wept during the service." Another reporter wrote, "The parents wept quietly. Mrs. Franklin leaned against her husband for support." The first reporter tells us the parents are "grief-stricken." The other reporter shows us with the picture of the mother leaning against her husband.

—Excerpted from *News Reporting and Writing* by Melvin Mencher

1. How does a journalist's writing process differ from a novelist's or a poet's?

   A journalist
   (1) spends more time researching stories
   (2) is pressured to meet strict deadlines
   (3) pays more attention to elements of style
   (4) is unconcerned with his choice of words
   (5) borrows techniques from other creative writers

2. Why does the author quote the novelist Leo Tolstoy and the poet John Ciardi?

   (1) to impress the reader with his literary background
   (2) to show that fiction and poetry are more interesting than news stories
   (3) to support the validity of the writing rule "show, don't tell"
   (4) to explain why novelists and poets admire news reporters
   (5) to suggest that novelists and poets teach journalism classes

3. Put a check mark next to the sentence in each pair that creates the more specific picture of the action described.

1. _____(a) The baseball coach was angry about the umpire's decision.

_____(b) After the "strike three" call, the baseball coach rushed from the dugout and shook his fist in the umpire's face.

2. _____(a) Two police officers at City Hall arrested the mayor for possessing an unregistered handgun.

_____(b) The police officers took the man into custody because he had an illegal weapon.

3. _____(a) Because she took the initiative to develop her skills, the office worker was moved into a position with more responsibilities.

_____(b) After completing evening management courses at XYZ Community College, the secretary was promoted to office supervisor.

Answers are on page 326.

WRITING ACTIVITY 3

On a separate sheet of paper, write a paragraph in which you report an event. It could be an event that you witnessed in person or something that you saw on TV or in a movie. Use words and details that create a vivid picture of the action in the reader's mind.

Answers will vary.

GED PRACTICE

EXERCISE 5

Directions: Read the passage below and choose the best answer to each question that follows.

WHY IS FELIPE BEING FOLLOWED?

White men in suits follow Felipe Lopez everywhere he goes. Felipe lives in Mott Haven, in the South Bronx. He is a junior at Rice High School, which is on the corner of 124th Street

5 and Lenox Avenue, in Harlem, and he plays guard for the school basketball team, the Rice Raiders. The white men are ubiquitous. They rarely miss one of Felipe's games or tournaments. They have absolute recall of his

10 best minutes of play. They are authorities on his physical condition. They admire his feet, which are big and pontoon-shaped, and his wrists, which have a loose, silky motion. Not long ago, I sat with the white men at a game between Rice

15 and All Hallows High School. My halftime entertainment was listening to a debate between two of them—a college scout and a Westchester contractor who is a high-school basketball fan—about whether Felipe had

20 grown a half inch over Christmas break. "I know this kid," the scout said as the second half started. "A half inch is not something I would miss." The white men believe that Felipe is the best high-school basketball player in the country.

25 They often compare him to Michael Jordan, and are betting he will become one of the greatest basketball players to emerge from New York City since Kareem Abdul-Jabbar. This conjecture provides them with suspended, savory

30 excitement and a happy premonition. Following Felipe is like hanging around with someone you think is going to win the lottery someday.

—Excerpted from "Shoot the Moon" by Susan Orlean,
The New Yorker, March 22, 1993

1. Which statement best summarizes what this excerpt is mainly about?

   (1) Government agents follow Felipe because they think he may be involved in illegal betting.
   (2) Boys who grow up and go to school in Harlem can become great basketball players.
   (3) The white men who follow Felipe know the scores for all his tournaments.
   (4) Many fans and scouts pay attention to Felipe because they believe he'll be a star player.
   (5) White men in suits are scouting around to find the best basketball player in the country.

2. In the sentence "The white men are ubiquitous" (line 7), what does the word *ubiquitous* mean?

   (1) suspicious
   (2) everywhere
   (3) wealthy
   (4) hidden
   (5) talented

3. Why does the writer say, "Following Felipe is like hanging around with someone you think is going to win the lottery someday" (lines 30–32)?

   (1) People are eager to associate with someone who they believe will become a winner.
   (2) People expect Felipe to be very generous when he gets rich.
   (3) The fans think Michael Jordan may show up at one of Felipe's basketball games.
   (4) The scouts need to make sure they don't miss a single game.
   (5) People are buying lottery tickets as gifts for Felipe.

Answers are on page 326.

EXERCISE 6

Directions: Read the passage and choose the best answer to each question.

WHAT IS THE REVIEWER'S OPINION OF THE FILM?

One of the movies' great strengths is the way they can cross cultures, connecting us with other countries and peoples. A prime example is "Chunhyang," a spectacular, engrossing, big-hearted film based on one of Korea's great national epics and made by that country's top filmmaker, Im Kwon Taek. It's a movie charmingly traditional and richly cinematic, and I'm not damning with faint praise when I say it's the best Korean film I've seen—that country's equivalent to "Gone With the Wind" or the 1966–67 Russian "War and Peace."

In a way, "Chunhyang" is also a great gateway movie for South Korea, just as Akira Kurosawa's "Rashomon" was for Japan and Zhang Yimou's "Red Sorghum" for China: a movie that opens up a whole national cinema. There's a special excitement in watching it, not the least part of which is the way director Im revives an old Korean art form, the pansori, to tell his story.

The film begins on a nearly bare stage where a seated drummer is accompanying a standing actor screaming out the verses of the pansori, a traditional Korean long narrative song performance. His voice hoarse with passion, drumbeats thundering behind him, the singer holds spellbound his theater audience (whom we glimpse in darkness). The song is "Chunhyang" itself, written by Cho Sang Hyun: a robust and stirring tale of star-crossed lovers, evil governors and comical servants in the 18th century.

After that spare prelude, Im opens up the story with all the tools of epic filmmaking: wide-screen color cinematography, gorgeous sets and locations, exquisite costumes, thousands of extras. Weaving the song through the entire movie, he fashions a grandly entertaining spectacle, full of tenderness and violence, beauty and humor. Evoked by the pansori singer's fierce narration, lovely maidens soar beneath trees on silken swings, lovers stage magical trysts and tyrants wage heartless persecutions, all in a world green and fresh as a fairytale forest.

It's one of those primal tales that resonate through many cultures. Mongryong (Cho Seung Woo), son of Namwon province's governor, falls in love with a girl of lower station, Chunhyang (Lee Hyo Jung), the proud, lovely but illegitimate daughter of courtesan Wolmae (Kim Sung Nyu). But, after the pair are secretly married, Mongryong is forced by his class-conscious parents to leave her for Seoul and his studies.

—Excerpted from "Epic Tale Provides Insight into Korean Culture, Tradition" by Michael Wilmington, *Chicago Tribune* Internet Edition, February 2, 2001

1. Which statement conveys the author's purpose?

   (1) American audiences will identify with the film's message.
   (2) The film shares Korean culture with other countries' audiences.
   (3) The director used foreign films to help him make "Chunhyang."
   (4) "Chunhyang" is a remake of American and Russian classics.
   (5) Audiences view elements of their own cultures in the film.

2. Which of the following groups of readers would be interested in this passage?

   Readers of the
   (1) sports pages
   (2) local news
   (3) arts
   (4) editorials
   (5) want ads

3. According to the writer, what is the function of the *pansori*?

   (1) to give the audience information that is not in the film
   (2) to provide a framework for the story by means of song
   (3) to introduce the element of music to epic filmmaking
   (4) to follow strict Korean guidelines for the epic tale
   (5) to prepare the audience for the film's magical scenes

4. Which of the following words best describes the writer's opinion of the film?

   (1) complimentary
   (2) disapproving
   (3) neutral
   (4) tolerant
   (5) confused

Answers are on page 326.

WRITING ACTIVITY 4

What games do you remember playing as a child? Choose one game that you played often. On a separate sheet of paper, describe the game. Explain why you enjoyed it. Then describe the skills or knowledge you gained from playing the game.

Answers will vary.

EXERCISE 7

Directions: Read the passage and choose the best answer to each question that follows.

HAVE WE GONE TOO FAR?

Roger Pearson, a Detroit area teacher, was walking his dog when he saw a small boy fall off his bike. Pearson stopped to help him up, but the boy became terrified and ran away and hid.

5 "He was so scared of me," Pearson said, "he didn't even take his bike with him."

Nancy Zimmerman of Washington, D.C. drives three miles out of her way to shop at a store that puts her groceries in plain bags. She

10 also buys milk in plastic, gallon containers because the paper half gallons she used to buy all bear the pictures of missing children. "Every morning when they eat breakfast, my kids don't need to see pictures of children who have been

15 separated from their parents," she says. "Children feel powerless enough as it is."

America suddenly seems full of missing children. Their faces are everywhere, on grocery store bags, on TV specials, on huge corporate-

20 sponsored banners in children's clothing stores. Book and toy store shelves are flooded with books and games that warn children against the "stranger danger." Companies selling personal alarms, insurance policies and dental identity

25 disks have sprung up overnight. Safety programs have proliferated in schools promoting the "yell and tell" message. Shopping centers host fingerprinting campaigns.

Surely one missing child is too many, but

30 experts who work in the field of missing, sexually abused and runaway children say the avalanche of publicity has grossly distorted the situation. Indeed, many feel that by overstating the problem we are poisoning relations between

35 children and adults and creating a national paranoia that may permanently damage the psyches of our children.

—Excerpted from "Are We Filling Our Children with Fear?" by Gini Hartzmark, *Chicago Tribune*, April 6, 1986

1. Who is Roger Pearson?

   (1) the parent of a missing child
   (2) a teacher who lives in the Detroit area
   (3) a detective who searches for missing children
   (4) an activist for children's rights
   (5) a person who has been convicted of kidnapping

2. Why did the small boy run away from Pearson?

   Because the boy
   (1) was riding a stolen bicycle
   (2) didn't want to go to the emergency room
   (3) was afraid Pearson wanted to harm him
   (4) feared Pearson would tell his parents he fell
   (5) had hit Pearson's dog with his bicycle

3. Why does Nancy Zimmerman buy milk in plastic containers instead of paper cartons?

   (1) Plastic is a stronger material.
   (2) Milk in plastic containers is cheaper.
   (3) Milk spoils more quickly in paper cartons.
   (4) Her grocery store doesn't sell milk in paper cartons.
   (5) Pictures of missing children don't appear on plastic cartons.

4. What conclusion does the author reach about the topic?

   (1) Because the issue of missing children is not a serious problem, publicity is unnecessary.
   (2) Too much publicity about the problem of missing children is damaging to children and their relationships with adults.
   (3) Many missing children are runaways, not kidnap victims.
   (4) Fingerprinting children makes them feel like criminals.
   (5) School safety programs effectively teach children how to avoid strangers.

Answers are on pages 326–327.

WRITING ACTIVITY 5

In the preceding passage, you read about some tactics being used to address the problem of missing children. Do you believe that these tactics help to resolve the problem, or do they worsen the situation? Choose two of the following tactics. Then, on a separate sheet of paper, state and support your opinion on the effectiveness of each.

- fingerprinting children

- school safety programs

- children's pictures on milk cartons and grocery store bags

- television specials

- banners in children's stores

- books and games about "stranger danger"

Answers will vary.

GED PRACTICE

EXERCISE 8

Directions: Read the passages and choose the best answer to each question that follows.

Questions 1–5 refer to the following essay from a newspaper.

ARE PEOPLE INADVERTENTLY RUDE TO THE DISABLED?

One of my friends runs etiquette programs for business people. The last time I went out with her, she was pushing my wheelchair when she saw another friend. She introduced us
5 graciously—and then they proceeded to carry on a conversation above me.

There was no evil intent, but since I was in my manual chair, I was not able to either turn and join in the conversation or rejoin the rest of
10 our party. I sat and waited, staring down the hall.

Ironically, I had helped write my friend's business brochure two years ago, before becoming disabled. Her programs address
15 different social situations, cultural clashes, ages and sexes—but nothing in her sessions relates to etiquette in dealing with the disabled.

Unfortunately, many people—even the most polite—need lessons on living, working and
20 generally interacting with the disabled. In most cases, all that is required is some thought or sensitivity.

When I was still getting out and about in the business world, I used to enjoy meeting up with
25 a certain Philadelphia councilman at various functions. Even though he is more than a foot taller than I, he never loomed over us shorter people. He always seemed to find a way to bring the conversation to a comfortable level,
30 by leaning on a wall or finding a seat.

When I later met his wife, in her wheelchair, I discovered one secret to his sensitivity.

For those of you who aren't accustomed to being around someone with disabilities, here are
35 a few pointers.

• Don't park a wheelchair facing a wall.

• Be aware of where you leave a wheelchair-bound person.

• Can they see and reach what they need,
40 such as a drink or reading material? Those of us who can't stand get tired of talking to belt buckles. Try to park us near chairs or a low wall so people speaking with us can be at our level. Cocktail parties are the worst—extra effort must
45 be made to find a congenial spot for conversation.

• Don't block curb cuts—ever.

That means even if you are a street vendor just trying to make a buck or a delivery man
50 who will "just be a minute."

A high curb can be an insurmountable obstacle for some people (I sat at one intersection in downtown Philadelphia for 15 minutes one noon hour and counted five people
55 with wheelchairs, walkers or canes that needed the low curb to cross the street—one every three minutes). A simple inconvenience for you might keep someone else from a critical business or doctor's appointment.

60 • Putting a ramp at the entrance isn't enough if the bathroom door is too small.

The Americans with Disabilities Act (ADA) is one year old now, so more restaurants have ramps. A friend of mine who is a quadriplegic
65 and enjoys going out for a few drinks with the boys has found lots of bars that make it possible for him to come in and spend his money.

However, getting to their bathrooms in a wheelchair is impossible. Corners are too sharp
70 for turns, doorways and stalls are too narrow. Those of us with primary caregivers of the opposite sex need to be able to use a simple, roomy, unisex facility.

• We are not all deaf, mute or mentally
75 incapacitated—so don't treat us as if we were. Address us directly, in a normal voice, if you have a question—don't assume someone else speaks for us. If necessary, most of us have developed some form of compensatory
80 communication—lip reading, note writing, or in my case slow, deliberate speech.

I still think in complex compound sentences, but my disease affects my tongue movement, making it difficult to get words out quickly.
85 Patience and attention are required.

The unifying theme of all the suggestions above is inclusiveness. We, the disabled, are part of the everyday world and wish to be treated accordingly—not as "special" or
90 "different."

—Excerpted from "Lessons in Living with the Disabled"
by Dale O'Reilley, *Chicago Tribune*, March 15, 1993

1. Which of the following statements summarizes the author's main message?

   (1) Getting into an ordinary bathroom in a wheelchair is impossible.
   (2) Always include a person who is in a wheelchair in your conversation.
   (3) More federal funding is needed for the disabled.
   (4) The Americans with Disabilities Act ensures equal access for people in wheelchairs.
   (5) People with disabilities want to be treated as part of the everyday world.

2. What does the writer mean when he says "I still think in complex compound sentences" (line 82)?

   (1) He has normal, healthy intelligence.
   (2) He is smarter than most people.
   (3) People shout when speaking to a disabled person.
   (4) People should speak slowly to make sure the disabled person understands them.
   (5) His thought process is difficult to figure out.

3. In the first paragraph, why does the writer makes a point of telling us that his friend specializes in etiquette programs for businesspeople?

To show that
(1) he has intelligent friends who know how to get along with people
(2) he knows how to get out and make friends with interesting people
(3) even experts in good manners may not know how to relate to the disabled
(4) his friend always knows how to behave properly for all types of occasions
(5) disabled people like her are able to run their own businesses

4. Which word best describes the writer's focus?

(1) disability
(2) friends
(3) inclusiveness
(4) obstacle
(5) etiquette

5. Imagine that you are throwing a party. According to the excerpt, which of the following actions would be the most helpful to your wheelchair-bound guests?

(1) politely requesting that your other guests give them preferential treatment
(2) seating your other guests so that everyone is at the same eye level
(3) making sure the disabled sit together at their own special table
(4) directing questions and comments to disabled persons' caregivers
(5) speaking more loudly, slowly, and distinctly than you normally do

Questions 6–10 refer to the following speech.

WHAT DID A NEW PRESIDENT EXPECT FROM US?

In your hands, my fellow citizens, more than mine, will rest the final success or failure of our course. Since this country was founded, each generation of Americans has been summoned
5 to give testimony to its national loyalty. . . .

Now the trumpet summons us again—not as a call to bear arms, though arms we need—not as a call to battle, though embattled we are—but a call to bear the burden of a long twilight
10 struggle, year in and year out, "rejoicing in hope, patient in tribulation"—a struggle against the common enemies of man: Tyranny, poverty, disease and war itself.

Can we forge against these enemies a grand
15 and global alliance, North and South, East and West, that can assure a more fruitful life for all mankind? Will you join in that historic effort?

In the long history of the world, only a few generations have been granted the role of
20 defending freedom in its hour of maximum danger.

I do not shrink from this responsibility—I welcome it. I do not believe that any of us would exchange places with any other people or
25 any other generation. The energy, the faith, the devotion which we bring to this endeavor will light our country and all who serve it—and the glow from that fire can truly light the world.

And so, my fellow Americans: Ask not what
30 your country can do for you—ask what you can do for your country.

My fellow citizens of the world: Ask not what America will do for you, but what together we can do for the freedom of man.

35 Finally, whether you are citizens of America or citizens of the world, ask of us here the same high standards of strength and sacrifice which we ask of you. With a good conscience our only sure reward, with history the final judge of our
40 deeds, let us go forth to lead the land we love, asking His blessing and His help, but knowing that here on earth God's work must truly be our own.

—Excerpted from "Inaugural Address" by
John F. Kennedy, 1960

6. What is the main idea of the passage?

   (1) War and poverty are our worst enemies.
   (2) The American people are responsible for the fate of the nation.
   (3) Americans are selfishly preoccupied with their individual problems.
   (4) Military strength is necessary in the struggle for freedom.
   (5) Only the president of the United States can solve the country's problems.

7. According to the speaker, what has each generation of Americans demonstrated?

   (1) freedom of speech
   (2) fear of illness
   (3) financial success
   (4) national loyalty
   (5) hatred toward foreign countries

8. Which adjective best describes the tone of the speech?

   (1) frightening
   (2) overemotional
   (3) inspiring
   (4) tragic
   (5) argumentative

9. According to this passage, what is John F. Kennedy's attitude toward the presidency?

   (1) He is overwhelmed by the enormous responsibilities.
   (2) He enthusiastically accepts the challenges of leadership.
   (3) He is greedy with power and wants total control of the government.
   (4) He welcomes the opportunity to build the military.
   (5) He looks forward to shaping economic policies.

10. Which of the following does the writing style of the concluding sentence most clearly resemble?

   (1) a newscaster's report
   (2) a lawyer's appeal
   (3) a preacher's sermon
   (4) a historian's analysis
   (5) a magazine advertisement

Answers are on page 327.

Business-related Documents

Society seeks high school graduates who are prepared for the world of college and work. In our information-based economy, students need greater education and training to obtain entry-level jobs and to qualify for advancement on the job. Employers expect their prospective employees to demonstrate a level of competency in understanding and following written guidelines for their jobs. On the GED Language Arts, Reading Test, you may find that one of your nonfiction passages will be a business-related document. These business documents may include the following:

* mission and goals statements

* excerpts from employee handbooks

* information from training manuals

* legal documents regarding the workplace

Companies use *mission statements* to clarify their purpose for existing in the marketplace and to spell out their unique benefits for clients and customers. Employees need to understand the focus of these statements and goals in order to contribute to the success of the company.

Employees use *employee handbooks* to learn essential elements regarding conditions of their employment. Handbooks provide guidance in employee expectations and behavior, salary and benefits, grievance procedures, and training opportunities.

Training manuals guide employees with practical step-by-step assistance in performing their jobs according to company policy and procedure.

Legal documents advise employees of federal and local laws governing behavior in the workplace, such as avoidance of sexual harassment, prohibitions against hiring discrimination, and safety requirements.

EXERCISE 9

Directions: Read the mission statement below and answer the questions that follow.

CORPORATE MISSION

Education

- Educate the general public, small businesses, and organizations about the internet and World Wide Web. That way, clients can make informed and intelligent decisions regarding the use of media in their businesses or organizations. By educating clients about the World Wide Web and other new forms of media, they will have a competitive advantage.

Design

- Design informative and eye-catching homepages for clients to make their product or service information available throughout the world. The internet publishing of World Wide Web homepages will be done by experienced web page designers and computer professionals. We will provide internet publishing services such as HTML programming and developing, homepage design, installation, and maintenance. Our expertise and experience in developing, creating and maintaining homepages will provide you with a strong internet presence. Our staff is constantly monitoring the newest developments in internet, and will make sure your company can take advantage of all the latest developments.

Service

- Provide a reliable server to host homepages for small businesses, individuals, and organizations for a competitive price, and respond quickly and courteously to inquires or problems regarding your homepage.

—Adapted from SuN sTuDIoS, Inc. web site

1. According to its mission statement, what unique services does this company believe that it offers its clients?

   _____

   _____

   _____

2. What advantages does this company believe that it has over its competitors?

   _____

   _____

   _____

3. Who would benefit from the services offered by this company?

   _____

   _____

4. What are some of this employer's expectations of its staff members?

   _____

   _____

   _____

   _____

Answers are on page 327.

WRITING ACTIVITY 6

Part I. Write a letter of introduction to the company in Exercise 9 telling them how your work and training experience would benefit them in achieving the company's mission.

Part II. Write a brief letter to the company as a prospective client describing how the company can help you meet your goals.

Answers will vary.

EXERCISE 10

Directions: Review the personnel action form below and answer the questions on the following page.

Personnel Action Form

Employee Name: _____

Instructions

Check the appropriate personnel action and fill in the information in the blanks below. Employee signs only if he or she initiates action or payroll deduction is required. Supervisor signs in all cases.

_____ Increase	_____ Separation
_____ Decrease	_____ Payroll deduction
_____ Classification change	_____ Change of address
_____ Transfer	_____ Change in dependents
_____ Promotion	_____ Other
_____ Leave of Absence	

Change in Pay or Classification

From	To
Pay: per	Pay: per
Classification:	Classification:

To Be Effective _____

Separation

_____ Laid off for lack of work	_____ Discharged for felonious conduct
_____ Left work voluntarily	_____ Other reason
_____ Discharged for repeated willful misconduct	_____
	_____

Remarks (final paycheck, date, amount, etc.) _____

Eligible for rehire?

_____ Yes	_____ No

Other (changes, deductions etc.)? _____

Employee signature _____

Date _____

Supervisor _____

Date _____

—Based on a form from *HRnext.com* web site

1. What is the purpose of the Personnel Action Form?

   (1) to explain why an employee was dismissed
   (2) to evaluate an employee's performance on the job
   (3) to explain an employee's grievance with an employer
   (4) to record changes in status, pay, or job termination
   (5) to request a job interview

2. What information does this form *not* provide an employee dismissed from a job?

   (1) information about final pay
   (2) additional training required
   (3) qualification for re-employment
   (4) reason for dismissal
   (5) supervisor's acknowledgment

3. When would an employee be required to sign the form?

   When the employee
   (1) was separated for lack of work
   (2) was released for criminal conduct
   (3) was promoted to a new position
   (4) was dismissed for willful misconduct
   (5) resigned by his or her own choice

Answers are on page 327.

EXERCISE 11

Directions: Read the passage from a hospital's employee handbook and answer the questions that follow.

EXPECTATIONS FROM A TO Z

ATTIRE

Proper attire in a hospital setting is very important. A professional appearance generates confidence and respect for the Institution. Employees should dress in a fashion that fosters this positive, reassuring image. Attire also should be appropriate to duties performed and for maintaining the health and safety of patients, visitors and other employees in a health care environment.

In addition, dress code standards are required of all departments within Johns Hopkins. Certain departments may determine that a specific business or health care need justifies more defined appearance standards, career apparel and/or uniforms.

ATTENDANCE

Regular and reliable attendance and punctuality are essential responsibilities of each employee in delivering quality patient care and services. The Hospital is committed to establishing and maintaining work schedules on a fair and consistent basis and to providing opportunities for employees and managers to jointly manage attendance. For more information, refer to Attendance Management Policy in the *HR Policy & Procedure Manual.*

CHANGE OF STATUS

Changes of name, address, telephone number, emergency contact and phone number, and dependent or marital status must be reported to supervisors and the Human Resources Department so that the Hospital can keep up-to-date employment records.

CONFIDENTIAL INFORMATION

All information about a patient, employee or Hospital business is considered confidential and is to be released only to authorized personnel. A confidentiality statement is provided to every employee to advise of Hospital expectations regarding confidentiality. See also, Employment Verification in the *HR Policy & Procedure Manual.*

CONFLICT OF INTEREST

Hospital employees should refrain from engaging in any outside activities of financial interest that are incompatible with the performance of work duties. Employees should not realize personal gain in any form that would influence improperly the conduct of their Hospital duties. Employees shall not knowingly use Hospital property, Funds, position or power for personal or political gain.

ELECTRONIC MAIL REGULATIONS

The Hospital provides electronic mail (e-mail) to employees at the Institution's expense for their use in performing their work duties. All electronic communication systems and all communication and information transmitted by, received from or stored in these systems are the property of Johns Hopkins and as such are to be used for job-related communications only. Equipment used by employees may be monitored from time to time, and employees should not expect privacy when using this equipment.

EMPLOYMENT VERIFICATION

Persons or institutions from outside Johns Hopkins that request information on an employee will be referred to Employment Records. This office will release only information in compliance with Hospital policy.

—Excerpted from the Johns Hopkins Hospital Employee Handbook

1. What is the primary purpose of this document?

(1) to detail the specific duties of a health care provider
(2) to list all possible conflicts of interest with policy
(3) to define expected behaviors and their rationale
(4) to state the hospital's position on dealing with patients
(5) to review hospital policies regarding employee training

2. Who maintains the job records for an employee?

(1) hospital director
(2) attendance manager
(3) employment records
(4) human resources department
(5) department supervisor

3. Identify three reasons, or factors, why employees must dress appropriately.

_____

_____

_____

_____

4. Read the statements below. If a statement defines permissible behavior according to the document, circle *P*. If a behavior is not permissible, circle *N*.

P   **N**   (1) Use e-mail to invite coworkers to a party in your home.

P   **N**   (2) Promptly provide quality patient care and services.

P   **N**   (3) Discuss patient and employee information only with authorized personnel.

P   **N**   (4) Inform supervisor and Human Resources when you change your address.

P   **N**   (5) Wear attire on the job that is comfortable and reflects personal standards.

P   **N**   (6) Read the Attendance Management Policy.

P   **N**   (7) Refrain from activities that conflict with work duties and lead to personal financial gain.

P   **N**   (8) Excuse yourself often from work to attend to personal matters.

Answers are on pages 327–328.

WRITING ACTIVITY 7

Look over the behaviors and expectations listed in Exercise 11. On a separate sheet of paper, write a brief paragraph justifying an employer's setting standards for employee behavior and listing expectations for all its employees.

Answers will vary.

EXERCISE 12

Directions: Read the following description of employment law and answer the questions that follow.

The federal Occupational Safety and Health Act (OSH Act) governs safety and health in the private employment sector (but not the public sector, either state or federal). It applies to every private employer that is involved in interstate commerce, regardless of company size. The term *interstate commerce* is given a very liberal interpretation, making the OSH Act applicable to all but the smallest enterprises. The following are not covered by the OSH Act:

- Self-employed persons

- Farms at which only immediate members of the farmer's family are employed

- Working conditions regulated by other federal agencies under other federal statues, including mining, nuclear energy, and nuclear-weapons manufacture, and many segments of the transportation industry

- Employees of state and local governments (unless located in a state with an approved safety and health program)

The law is enforced by the Occupational Safety and Health Administration (OSHA). The OSH Act, however, encourages states to develop their own job safety and health plans with OSHA guidance.

State laws. Some states have an occupational safety and health plan approved by federal OSHA. States with approved plans are called state-plan states, and their laws must be equivalent to or more protective than the federal law. Because the OSH Act was written to provide a minimal and generally uniform national standard, states that do not have an approved work safety plan are not permitted to enforce their own occupational safety and health laws in private sector workplaces.

—from *HRnext.com* web site

1. Why are miners, nuclear engineers and manufacturers, and transportation workers not covered under the OSH Act?

   _____

2. What is meant by *interstate commerce?*

   _____

   _____

3. Why would an employee want to work for a company covered by the OSH Act?

   In order to be
   (1) assured that the federal government would control unlawful competition
   (2) confident that he or she would be entitled to Social Security benefits
   (3) convinced that his or her employer was supported by federal money
   (4) secure in knowing that an approved job-safety plan was in force
   (5) satisfied that he or she could not be dismissed from a job unfairly

4. What type of employer would be exempt from the provisions of the OSH act?

   (1) a contractor who lives in one state but works in another
   (2) a cable TV shopping network that sells throughout the country
   (3) a major hotel chain with hotels in every big city
   (4) a manufacturer that distributes products across the country
   (5) a home consulting business operated by a single individual

5. Under what condition may a state *not* have its own OSH plan?

   (1) when it offers more protection than the federal plan
   (2) when it provides fewer protections than the government act
   (3) when it has been approved by the Occupational Safety and Health Administration
   (4) when it uses OSHA guidance in development of its state plan
   (5) when its protection is the same as that offered by the federal act

Answers are on page 328.

Literary Nonfiction

The literary essays that appear on the GED Language Arts, Reading Test can include excerpts from biographies, memoirs or selected events, diaries, letters, essays, commentaries, or reviews of works of literature. Read the selections below for some practice in working with literary nonfiction.

EXERCISE 13

Directions: Read the following passage from a memoir and answer the questions that follow.

WHAT DOES A PLAIN LOOK LIKE?

A single knoll rises out of the plain in Oklahoma, north and west of the Wichita range. For my people, the Kiowas, it is an old landmark, and they gave it the name Rainy Mountain. The hardest weather in the world
5 is there. Winter brings blizzards, hot tornadic winds arise in the spring, and in the summer the prairie is an anvil's edge. The grass turns brittle and brown, and it cracks beneath your feet. There are green belts along the rivers and creeks, linear groves of hickory and pecan, willow and witch hazel. At a distance in July or August the steaming foliage seems
10 almost to writhe in fire. Great green and yellow grasshoppers are everywhere in the tall grass, popping up like corn to sting the flesh, and tortoises crawl about on the red earth, going nowhere in the plenty of time. Loneliness is an aspect of the land. All things in the plain are isolate; there is no confusion of objects in the eye, but *one* hill or *one*
15 tree or *one* man. To look upon that landscape in the early morning, with the sun at your back, is to lose the sense of proportion. Your imagination comes to life, and this, you think, is where Creation was begun.

—Excerpted from *The Way to Rainy Mountain* by N. Scott Momaday, 1969

1. What is the name of the author's Indian tribe?

   _____

2. Write a phrase from the passage that appeals to each of the following senses:

   Sight: _____

   Hearing: _____

   Touch: _____

3. Why does the author state that "the steaming foliage seems almost to writhe in fire" in lines 9–10?

   (1) to emphasize the intense summer heat
   (2) to suggest that forest fires are commonplace
   (3) to describe the fiery sunset
   (4) to explain the effects of daylight on plant growth
   (5) to show that Native Americans worship the sun

4. With which of the following can the author's description of the plain be compared?

(1) a weather report
(2) a map of Oklahoma
(3) a passage from the Bible
(4) a landscape painting
(5) a real estate brochure

5. What can you infer that the word *knoll* in line 1 means?

(1) hill
(2) landmark
(3) blizzard
(4) tornado
(5) prairie

Answers are on page 328.

EXERCISE 14

Directions: Read the following passage and answer the questions about the Harlem Unit's production of Shakespeare's *Macbeth*. (The Harlem Unit was part of the Federal Theatre Project, a theatrical program organized in 1935.)

When Rose McClendon died in 1936 at the age of fifty-one, John Houseman carried on the directorial duties of the Harlem Unit alone. One of its first major productions was a black version of *Macbeth*. The black actors and actresses of the Harlem Unit wanted to prove
5 that they could perform the classics as well as portray servants, but this would be no ordinary version of Shakespeare's play.

Macbeth is about a power-mad Scottish nobleman who murders the king of Scotland with the help of his wife. He is urged to commit the crime by a group of witches who prepare mysterious potions
10 and chant, "Double, double, toil and trouble, fire burn and cauldron bubble!" Because Houseman wanted an experienced director with a flair for the dramatic to stage this exciting play, he hired a young white man named Orson Welles, who had just wound up a tour of Shakespeare's *Romeo and Juliet*.

15 It was unanimously decided to change the locale of the play from Scotland to Haiti. Haiti, famous for its "voodoo" and witchcraft, made a much more exciting setting than Scotland and allowed the black-magic theme of the drama to be played to the hilt.

20   When Welles discovered a touring African dance group stranded in New York for lack of return passage, he immediately signed them up. He also hired a practicing African witch doctor whom he had somehow found in New York. The musical score for the show was full of voodoo drums and witches' cries, and the jungle sets were
25 exotic and eerie. All the roles were played by blacks: Jack Carter and Edna Thomas were Lord and Lady Macbeth, Canada Lee played Banquo, and Eric Burroughs played the evil Hecate.

     The show was a tremendous success. Drama critic Brooks Atkinson praised the Haitian setting as follows in his review of the
30 production: "The witches have always worried the life out of the polite tragic stage. . . . But ship the witches down to the rank and fever-stricken jungle of Haiti, dress them in fantastic costumes, crowd the stage with mad and gabbing throngs of evil worshippers, beat the jungle drums, raise the voices until the jungle echoes, stuff
35 a gleaming, naked witch doctor into the cauldron, hold up Negro masks in baleful light—and there you have a witches' scene that is logical and stunning and a triumph of theatre art."

—Excerpted from "The Harlem Unit" by James Haskins, *Black Theater in America*, 1982

1. What is the main idea of the passage?

   (1) Classic dramas continue to attract large audiences.
   (2) The cast of *Macbeth* consisted of black actors and actresses.
   (3) Shakespeare was fascinated by witches and the supernatural.
   (4) The Harlem Unit staged an unusual production of *Macbeth*.
   (5) Macbeth, the main character, was a cold-blooded murderer.

2. In your own words, briefly summarize the plot of Shakespeare's play *Macbeth*.

_____

_____

_____

3. What is the setting for Shakespeare's version of *Macbeth*?

_____

4. Where does the play take place in the Harlem Unit's production?

_____

5. How does the author describe the musical score for the show?

_____

6. Write *F* if a statement is a fact or *O* if it is an opinion.

_____ (1) Shakespeare wrote *Macbeth* and *Romeo and Juliet*.

_____ (2) Orson Welles directed the Harlem Unit's production of *Macbeth*.

_____ (3) Orson Welles was a remarkably gifted and creative individual.

_____ (4) Haiti is a more exciting country than Scotland.

_____ (5) An African dance group and a practicing African witch doctor were cast for the show.

_____ (6) Edna Thomas played the role of Lady Macbeth.

7. Which of the following statements best expresses drama critic Brooks Atkinson's impression of the show?

(1) The show was a popular success.
(2) The jungle sets were exotic and eerie.
(3) The witches' scene was a theatrical masterpiece.
(4) The hiring of a practicing African witch doctor made the show authentic.
(5) Shakespeare's *Macbeth* is an exciting play.

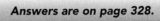

Answers are on page 328.

Go to **www.GEDReading.com** for additional practice and instruction!

EXERCISE 15

Directions: Read the passage and choose the best answer to each question that follows.

WHAT DO YOU LEARN ABOUT DETECTIVE FICTION?

The novel rode out of Spain on the horse and donkey of Don Quixote and Sancho Panza, and the modern short story had its early masters in Russia, France and England. But the
5 hard-boiled detective was born in America. His popularity has remained in force for half a century. He can be seen on countless shelves of paperbacks and hardcovers, and he has appeared on prime time since the first vacuum
10 tube was plugged in. . . . As he was in the films of the '40s, so he is today, in Raymond Chandler's memorable phrase, a man "who is neither tarnished nor afraid" as he walks down America's mean streets.

15 Good cases have been made for locating his origins in the boot steps of the lonesome pioneer. Robert B. Parker, creator of Spenser, a private investigator so sure of himself that he needs only one name, even wrote a Ph.D. thesis
20 on the subject. According to the traditional ideal, to survive with dignity on the American frontier required a touch of ruthlessness and a personal code of honor. "When the wilderness disappeared at the end of the 19th century,"
25 says Parker, the hero "became a man, alone, facing an urban wilderness." A more precise definition of the breed came naturally enough from Chandler, the American-born, British-educated creator of Philip Marlowe, the
30 detective who got more similes to the mile than anybody before or since ("as inconspicuous as a tarantula on a slice of angel food"). Laid down in his essay *The Simple Art of Murder*, Chandler's description of the fictional American detective
35 has the power of an ecclesiastical oath: "He is a relatively poor man, or he would not be a detective at all. He is a common man or he could not go among common people. He has a sense of character, or he would not know his
40 job. He will take no man's money dishonestly

and no man's insolence without a due and dispassionate revenge. He is a lonely man and his pride is that you will treat him as a proud man or be very sorry you ever saw him. He talks
45 as the man of his age talks—that is, with rude wit, a lively sense of the grotesque, a disgust for sham, and a contempt for pettiness."

—Excerpted from "Neither Tarnished nor Afraid" by A. Z. Shepherd, *Time*, June 16, 1986

1. On which of the following fictional elements does the passage focus?

(1) plot
(2) setting
(3) point of view
(4) theme
(5) characterization

2. Where did the hard-boiled detective originate?

(1) in Spain
(2) in the United States
(3) in Russia
(4) in France
(5) in England

3. According to Robert B. Parker, what influenced the portrayal of fictional detectives?

(1) detectives in TV series
(2) nineteenth-century pioneers
(3) heroes of modern short stories
(4) characters in Spanish novels
(5) private investigators in movies

4. According to Raymond Chandler, what characteristic is not typical of a fictional American detective?

(1) loneliness
(2) pride
(3) wealth
(4) wit
(5) honesty

5. What kind of language does Philip Marlowe often use in his speech (lines 29–32)?

(1) literal
(2) formal
(3) ungrammatical
(4) figurative
(5) technical

Answers are on page 328.

EXERCISE 16

The following excerpt from a book review is longer than the reading selections on the GED Language Arts, Reading Test. However, by reading a longer excerpt, you will acquire a better understanding of this type of commentary.

Directions: Read the passage and answer the questions that follow.

Once upon a time, 86 years ago in the city of Chicago, a man named Lyman Frank Baum sat down at the insistence of his mother-in-law to write out a bedtime story that he liked to tell to his children. The yarn was about a little girl named Dorothy, her feisty
5 dog Toto, cyclones, Kansas and an enchanted kingdom of silver slippers, flying monkeys, fighting trees, and good and bad witches. Baum and his illustrator, W. W. Denslow, had to agree to share the publishing costs, but when "The Wonderful Wizard of Oz" appeared, it quickly became the best selling children's book of 1900,
10 and Dorothy was established as America's most famous and endearing astral explorer.

By the time Baum died in Hollywood in 1919, he had written 14 Oz books, each of which had its magical and enduring moments. But "The Wonderful Wizard" has remained his most famous. The gray of
15 Kansas—the word is used 10 times in five paragraphs—gives way to the colorful rainbow of potential available in Oz, and we enter a compensatory, utopian landscape in which the power of Good is greater than the power of Evil, and where the pastoral, wilderness and technological aspects of our culture exist in beneficent
20 harmony. Cast ashore in this forbidding territory with one fresh dress, some worn-out shoes and a picnic basket, the bedraggled Dorothy becomes a Miss Liberty, liberating the Munchkins and Winkies from the oppressive rule of the Wicked Witches and leading the Scarecrow, Tin Woodman, and Cowardly Lion to kingship, glory
25 and self-confidence. Her struggles to get back home mirror her life and flights of fancy as a prairie child, from the bran and pins of the

Scarecrow's brain to the way the Wicked Witch imprisons her with housework, and she revenges herself by "liquidating" the villainess with a bucket of cleaning water.

30   Although a continuing favorite with children, Oz has never received the admiration, or critical attention, of Lewis Carroll's famous Alice adventures. It is a less astonishing book—more traditional in concept, more commonplace in detail, less playfully daring, and more truly devoted to seeing the world with a child's
35 eye. And, as befits the pleasant adventure, W. W. Denslow's original illustrations are charming and silly rather than striking in their own right. [Dover offers a fine paperback reprint of the original edition.] But whether you remember "Oz" through Denslow's amusing, squat little figures or as immortalized in the radiant technicolor of the
40 1939 film, color has always been an essential part of the story's spell: a way to distinguish character and demonstrate how reality changes depending on the distorting lenses you're looking through.

     All this has changed. Barry Moser and his Pennyroyal Press have been coming up with startling new visions of old classics for some
45 time, many of which have been reissued in trade editions by the University of California—"Alice's Adventures in Wonderland" and "Through the Looking-Glass," "Frankenstein," "Adventures of Huckleberry Finn." Now Moser has turned his eye and mind to "Oz." The result is a visually stunning, if suspiciously adult, reading
50 of Baum's homely tale.

—Excerpted from "New Illustrations Make 'Oz' a Sadder, More Adult World"
by Paul Skenazy, *Chicago Tribune*, August 3, 1986

1. Write *F* if a statement is a fact or *O* if it is an opinion.

_____ (1) *The Wonderful Wizard of Oz* became a best-selling children's book in 1900.

_____ (2) W. W. Denslow was the first artist to illustrate *The Wonderful Wizard of Oz*.

_____ (3) Denslow's illustrations are silly and charming.

_____ (4) *Alice's Adventures in Wonderland* is a better written and more imaginative book than *The Wonderful Wizard of Oz*.

_____ (5) Dorothy is America's most famous explorer of new worlds.

_____ (6) *The Wonderful Wizard of Oz* is told from a child's point of view.

_____ (7) The film *The Wizard of Oz* was released in 1939.

_____ (8) Barry Moser's illustrations reveal an adult interpretation of the book.

2. How does Dorothy kill the Wicked Witch of the West?

   _____

   _____

3. Why does the author begin the book review with the phrase "Once upon a time"?

   (1) He is telling a bedtime story.
   (2) His description of L. Frank Baum is imaginary.
   (3) He is writing the review for children.
   (4) He is poking fun at children's literature.
   (5) His topic is a children's fairy tale.

4. What is the major theme of *The Wonderful Wizard of Oz*?

   (1) Cyclones endanger people's lives.
   (2) Animals behave like humans.
   (3) Good overpowers evil.
   (4) Adults deceive children.
   (5) Life is a dream.

Answers are on pages 328–329.

 Go to **www.GEDReading.com** for additional practice and instruction!

EXERCISE 17

Directions: Read each passage and answer the questions that follow.

Questions 1–6 refer to the following excerpt from a critical essay.

WHAT IS EMILY DICKINSON'S POETRY LIKE?

Emily Dickinson, born in 1830 in Amherst, Massachusetts, lived a very secluded life. She was alone most of the time; she didn't know other writers. Almost no one knew she wrote
5 poetry. She wrote her poems in the midst of doing other things. She wrote them on the backs of envelopes and on other scraps of paper. These poems were discovered, and published, only after her death. These
10 circumstances probably have something to do with the peculiar way her poetry is written, the way it's unlike anyone else's— with its odd use of capitals, dashes, and strange rhymes—and with its peculiar point of view. She seems to
15 have been, more than other poets, writing just for herself.

Her way of looking at things seems, at first, innocent, like the innocence of children. But Emily Dickinson knows and feels things that
20 children don't. Her view is not so much innocent, really, as it is gentle and resigned to the way things are. It's as if she felt that simply watching were the only thing left to do. She watches nature—trees, brooks, bees, flies,
25 flowers, snakes, wind. She watches people. She seems even to watch herself in the same way she watches everything else—with impartial curiosity and from a distance.

In Emily Dickinson's poetry, the whole
30 universe becomes very private and domestic. It is as if all of nature, all its gentle and violent forces, were noticed and wondered about with the kind of simple familiarity with which you might wonder about your neighbors. And
35 everything that happens seems almost equally important. The arrival of winter, a storm, or the coming of death gets no more space than a bird's song or a fly's buzz. This makes her poems about death seem particularly strange and
40 chilling.

—Excerpted from *Sleeping on the Wing* by Kenneth Koch and Kate Farrell, 1981

1. Which of the following statements expresses an opinion about Emily Dickinson?
   (1) She was born in 1830 in Amherst, Massachusetts.
   (2) She wrote some poems about death.
   (3) Her poems were published after she died.
   (4) She punctuates her poetry with dashes.
   (5) Her poems show her gentle, resigned view of the world.

2. According to the excerpt, who was probably Emily Dickinson's intended audience for her poems?
   (1) other poets
   (2) herself
   (3) children
   (4) neighbors
   (5) women

3. What is the main purpose of the second paragraph?
   To discuss Emily Dickinson's
   (1) childlike innocence
   (2) style of observation
   (3) interest in people
   (4) subjects of poetry
   (5) curiosity about herself

4. Which of the following is *not* reflected in Emily Dickinson's poetry?
   (1) a private view of the universe
   (2) a unique way of writing
   (3) an impression of everyday events
   (4) a morbid fear of death
   (5) a familiarity with nature

5. From the passage, what can you infer about Emily Dickinson?
   She was
   (1) sociable
   (2) ambitious
   (3) solitary
   (4) immature
   (5) depressed

6. One of Dickinson's poems begins with these lines:

Because I could not stop for Death—
He kindly stopped for me—
The carriage held but just Ourselves—
And Immortality.

What aspect of her poetry discussed in the article is illustrated in this excerpt?

(1) her habit of writing poems on scraps of paper
(2) the use of the seasons of nature in her poetry
(3) a surrender to the joys and trials of life
(4) an observation of herself as if from a distance
(5) an attitude of simple familiarity toward all of nature and experience

Questions 7–14 refer to the following excerpt from an autobiography.

HOW DID MALCOLM X IMPROVE HIMSELF DURING HIS PRISON TERM?

The Norfolk Prison Colony's library was in the school building. A variety of classes was taught there by instructors who came from such places as Harvard and Boston universities. The
5 weekly debates between inmate teams were also held in the school building. You would be astonished to know how worked up convict debaters and audiences would get over subjects like "Should Babies Be Fed Milk?"

10 Available on the prison library's shelves were books on just about every general subject. Much of the big private collection that Parkhurst had willed to the prison was still in crates and boxes in the back of the library—thousands of
15 old books. Some of them looked ancient: covers faded, old-time parchment-looking binding. Parkhurst, I've mentioned, seemed to have been principally interested in history and religion. He had the money and the special interest to have
20 a lot of books that you wouldn't have in general circulation. Any college library would have been lucky to get that collection.

As you can imagine, especially in a prison where there was heavy emphasis on
25 rehabilitation, an inmate was smiled upon if he demonstrated an unusually intense interest in books. There was a sizable number of well-read inmates, especially the popular debaters. Some were said by many to be practically walking
30 encyclopedias. They were almost celebrities. No university would ask any student to devour literature as I did when this new world opened to me, of being able to read and *understand*.

I read more in my room than in the library
35 itself. An inmate who was known to read a lot could check out more than the permitted maximum number of books. I preferred reading in the total isolation of my own room.

When I had progressed to really serious
40 reading, every night at about ten P.M. I would be outraged with the "lights out." It always

seemed to catch me right in the middle of something engrossing.

Fortunately, right outside my door was a
45 corridor light that cast a glow into my room. The glow was enough to read by, once my eyes adjusted to it. So when "lights out" came, I would sit on the floor where I could continue reading in that glow.

—Excerpted from *The Autobiography of Malcolm X* by
Malcolm X with Alex Haley, 1965

7. Who taught the academic classes at the prison?

(1) prison guards
(2) librarians
(3) college-educated convicts
(4) professional debaters
(5) university instructors

8. Based on information in the excerpt, what can you infer about the weekly debates between teams of inmates?

The debates were
(1) popular with the inmate debaters and their audiences
(2) dangerous to guards because the debates often became heated
(3) fun for Mr. Parkhurst and other influential people who came to watch
(4) frustrating to inmate debaters, who did not have access to books
(5) discouraged by the prison system, which viewed them as a waste of time

9. What was the prison officials' reaction to inmates who were interested in books?

(1) suspicion
(2) criticism
(3) indifference
(4) approval
(5) surprise

10. Why does Malcolm X refer to certain inmates as "walking encyclopedias" (lines 29–30)?

(1) They were responsible for carrying books.
(2) They used to sell encyclopedias door to door.
(3) They were well informed on a variety of topics.
(4) They paced around the library while they read.
(5) They liked to exercise their minds.

11. Why was Malcolm X annoyed with the "lights out" rule at 10:00 P.M.?

(1) He was afraid of the dark.
(2) He had difficulty falling asleep.
(3) His reading was interrupted.
(4) He was outraged with unfair prison regulations.
(5) He disliked childish treatment.

12. What is the major impression that Malcolm X conveys in the passage?

(1) his respect for his fellow inmates
(2) his enthusiasm for reading and learning
(3) his support of rehabilitating convicts
(4) his attitude toward the prison system
(5) his interest in books about history and religion

13. If Malcolm X were alive today, which of the following statements would he be most likely to support?

(1) Classroom instruction is not effective.
(2) Debates often result in arguments.
(3) People have the ability to educate themselves.
(4) Prison libraries are poorly stocked.
(5) University students know less than self-taught convicts.

14. Traditionally, debate has been an important element in many literary circles. It provides for a free and lively discussion of literature and a clarification of ideas.

Why did Malcolm X believe that the weekly inmates' debates "worked up debaters and audiences"?

(1) The inmates gained greater insight from their readings.
(2) Debaters could win influence and favors from prison officials.
(3) The interest in the debates demonstrated that prisoners were rehabilitated.
(4) The debates provided an escape from prison jobs and routine.
(5) Inmates who debated could keep their lights on later.

Answers are on page 329.

Visual Communication

Visual Arts

Sculpture, painting, and photography are all examples of the *visual arts*. In commentaries about the visual arts, the authors often re-create the physical appearance of the art in words. Therefore, when you read descriptions, try to imagine how the work of art looks. Authors may also interpret the emotions or the message that the art seems to convey.

EXERCISE 18

Directions: The picture below is described in the passage that accompanies it. Read the passage and answer the questions.

WHAT DOES EDMONIA LEWIS PORTRAY IN
"OLD ARROW MAKER"?

Edmonia Lewis, the daughter of a black father and a Chippewa mother, was drawn to subjects from both her racial backgrounds. In this sculpture, she examines her Indian heritage by showing a moment of quiet reflection being enjoyed by father and daughter—
5 a universal theme that transcends ethnic boundaries. The work is small, so that the viewer feels the intimacy of the moment as well as

the gentleness of a race often characterized elsewhere as brutal and savage. The
10 arrowmaker wears an animal-skin loincloth, moccasins, and a bear-tooth necklace; his daughter is clothed in a fur bodice, long skirt, moccasins,
15 and a necklace of stones. An arrow, perhaps just freshly made, rests near the father's left foot, and a dead deer lies at his feet, a symbol of the
20 traditional hunt. The marble shows an impressive variety of textures that display Lewis's skill gained in her studies in Rome, where she
25 spent most of her career.

One of several women sculptors working in Rome, Lewis settled there in 1865 to learn marble-carving techniques (although late in her career she, like other sculptors, directed assistants in the actual carving), to pursue her career with greater artistic freedom, and to
30 avoid much of the racial discrimination that she had faced in America. She was successful on every count.

1. Which part of Lewis's racial background is reflected in the sculpture "Old Arrow Maker"?

_____

2. List three reasons why Edmonia Lewis decided to live in Rome.

_____

_____

_____

3. According to the reviewer, how are American Indians often characterized?

    (1) gentle
    (2) savage
    (3) intimate
    (4) quiet
    (5) impressive

4. Why does this reviewer think that the small size of the statue is effective?

Because it
(1) was easier for the sculptor to work on
(2) is easier to reproduce than a large work
(3) captures the intimacy of the father-daughter relationship
(4) shows texture better than a larger statue would
(5) made it easier to transport it from Rome to the Smithsonian

Answers are on pages 329–330.

EXERCISE 19

Directions: Read the passage and answer the questions that follow.

IS TATTOOING AN ART?

Tattoo artists have always felt that their work deserved more acceptance as an art and that it was discredited because of the nature of the medium. But if the medium is put aside, it is easy to see the craft, the fancy, the individuality, and the art of the
5 practitioner. Whatever one may think of tattooing itself, one must acknowledge that it is a true folk art.

Tattooing as the art of marking the human skin is quite ancient. One of the earliest known examples was discovered recently on the body of a Scythian chieftain found, frozen and perfectly preserved,
10 in a tomb in Russia dating back to 2500 B.C. The earliest records of the use of the tattoo are Egyptian ones dating to 2000 B.C., and tattoo markings have been revealed on mummies. Libyan figures from the tomb of Set I, built in 1330 B.C., are tattooed symbols of the Egyptian goddess Neith which, in a simplified form, are still
15 employed as tattoo designs in North Africa today. Tattooing existed in southwest China in 1100 B.C. In Japan it thrived in the middle of the first century A.D., but has also been traced to its origin in the sixth century B.C. It is now thought that from Japan it was taken to the South Sea Islands, where today one still sees the most intricate
20 and delicate patterns in the raised skin of the natives.

—Excerpted from *America's Forgotten Folk Arts* by Frederick and Mary Fried, 1978

1. According to the passage, what would tattoo artists probably believe?

   (1) that more tattoo parlors should open in the suburbs
   (2) that all women should wear tattoos to express their individuality
   (3) that replicas of their work should be exhibited in art museums
   (4) that marking human skin is an uncivilized practice
   (5) that the designs of Chinese tattoos are outdated

2. What evidence do the authors present to support their view that tattooing is an ancient art?

   (1) They conducted research in African and Asian museums.
   (2) They traveled around the world looking for evidence.
   (3) They specified dates and countries where tattooing was practiced.
   (4) They interviewed South Seas natives whose ancestors wore tattoos.
   (5) They described historical photographs belonging to tattoo artists.

3. From the passage, what can you conclude about the authors' attitude toward tattoos?

   (1) They dislike highly decorated tattoo designs.
   (2) They practice tattooing as a hobby.
   (3) They prefer African tattoos to Russian tattoos.
   (4) They discredit the craftsmanship of modern tattoo artists.
   (5) They appreciate the artistic qualities of tattooing.

4. The following statements draw conclusions based on the passage. Write *V* if a statement is valid or *I* if it is invalid.

   _____ (1) Tattooing is primarily a North American art.

   _____ (2) Many people do not think of tattooing as an art form.

   _____ (3) Although attractive, tattoos are dangerous.

   _____ (4) The earliest examples of tattoos date back to the sixth century B.C.

Answers are on page 330.

WRITING ACTIVITY 8

Look in a book, magazine, or newspaper to find a reproduction of a photograph, sculpture, painting, or sketch that you like. On a separate sheet of paper, write a description of the visual you selected. Your description should help readers picture what the item looks like as well as what your opinion of the item is.

Answers will vary.

GED PRACTICE

EXERCISE 20

Directions: Read the passage and answer the questions that follow.

HOW DOES A POLICE ARTIST PERFORM HIS JOB?

Initially, Mr. Hagenlocher tries to put witnesses at ease so they trust him, rather than barging up and identifying himself as a police officer. When questioning someone, the artist
5 tries to exact as much detail as possible about the suspect, though he can get by on remarkably few facts. As a rule, he looks for five features: shape of face, hair, eyes, ears, and mouth. Distinguishing scars, birthmarks, beards,
10 and mustaches are an artist's dream for producing a useful sketch, but they don't often crop up.

Mr. Hagenlocher always carts along 150 to 200 of the 900,000 mug shots the police
15 force keeps. Witnesses are asked to leaf through these to try to find a similar face, and then subtle changes can be made in the sketch. "You could use just one photo and work from that," Mr. Hagenlocher says.

20 "Using that as a base, you have the witness compare the hair—is it longer or shorter?—the mouth—is it thinner or wider?—and so forth. But that's harder and takes more time. It's usually much quicker to show him a lot of
25 photos and have them pick the one that's close."

"But I remember one time," the artist goes on, "when a girl flipped through a mess of photos and finally picked one. 'That looks
30 exactly like him,' she said, 'except the hair was longer, the mouth was wider, the eyes were further apart, the nose was smaller, and the face was rounder.' She was a big help."

Besides the five basic features, Mr.
35 Hagenlocher also questions witnesses about a suspect's apparent nationality and the nature of the language he used. This can be of subtle assistance in sketching the suspect, but it can also sometimes link several sketches together.
40 For instance, if over a short period of time three suspects are described as soft-spoken, in addition to having other similar traits, then chances are they are the same person. It is also a good idea to ask a witness if a suspect
45 resembled a famous person. Suspects have been compared to Marlon Brando, Rod Steiger, Winston Churchill, Nelson Eddy, Jack Palance, Jackie Gleason, Mick Jagger and a Greek god.

After Mr. Hagenlocher completes a sketch,
50 he shows it to the witness or witnesses for their

reaction. Usually, there will be lots of minor, and sometimes not too minor, changes to be made. When it's finished, the sketch isn't intended to approach the polished form of a portrait.

55 "We're just trying to narrow down the possibilities," Mr. Hagenlocher says. "If you've just got a big nose and a thin mouth to go with, then at least you've ruled out all the people with small noses and thick mouths. There are still
60 millions of people still in the running, but millions have also been eliminated."

—Excerpted from "Portraits of a Cop" by N. R. Kleinfield, *The Best of the Wall Street Journal,* 1973

1. What is the major purpose of the entire passage?

    (1) to analyze witnesses' observations
    (2) to explain the process of sketching a suspect
    (3) to classify different types of suspects
    (4) to compare drawing to photography
    (5) to describe how witnesses remember faces

2. What does Mr. Hagenlocher do when he first meets witnesses?

    (1) He badgers them with questions.
    (2) He emphasizes that he is a police officer.
    (3) He mistrusts their descriptions.
    (4) He makes them feel comfortable.
    (5) He evaluates their intelligence.

3. Why do witnesses examine mug shots?

    (1) to determine whether the suspect is a former convicted criminal
    (2) to find faces similar to the suspect's
    (3) to test their photographic memories
    (4) to study criminal-looking faces
    (5) to observe how criminals pose for photographs

4. Which of the following questions would Mr. Hagenlocher *not* ask a witness?

    (1) Does the suspect resemble a famous person?
    (2) What is the suspect's apparent nationality?
    (3) How does the suspect use language?
    (4) Was the suspect armed?
    (5) Does the suspect have a distinguishing birthmark?

5. Which of the following techniques does the author use to develop the topic?

    (1) the court testimony of witnesses
    (2) interviews with arrested suspects
    (3) a description of a notorious suspect
    (4) excerpts from an official police report
    (5) quotations from Mr. Hagenlocher

6. Which of the following people could most closely identify with Mr. Hagenlocher's work?

    (1) a photographer
    (2) a plastic surgeon
    (3) a portrait painter
    (4) a film director
    (5) a sculptor

Answers are on page 330.

Performing Arts

As opposed to the visual arts, where the piece of art is created from an inanimate material such as paint or stone, in the *performing arts*, the people themselves are the art, creating their work from their movements, voices, and actions. Music, dance, theater, film, and TV are all examples of performing arts. Just as with the visual arts, reviewers of the performing arts often write essays describing and expressing their opinions about an artist or a performance. In this section you will read a variety of commentaries about the performing arts.

EXERCISE 21

Directions: Read the descriptive passage below and answer the questions that follow.

One of the all-time classics, this thrilling espionage adventure was the first film to establish Hitchcock as the Master of Suspense. What are the "39 Steps," and where do they lead? Which vital secrets are in the mind of a performer named Mr. Memory? Can the
5 British Empire be saved from imminent destruction? These are only some of the baffling questions faced by Richard Hannay, a happy-go-lucky Canadian tourist who innocently visits a London music hall and ends up in a terrifying chase across the country. After the music hall show is abruptly interrupted by a gunshot, a strange woman
10 asks Hannay for his protection from deadly secret agents. Later, she appears in his room—with a knife in her back! Pursued by the police for the murder, Hannay sets out to find the spy organization's sinister leader, who can be identified only by the fact that part of his finger is missing. Like many later Hitchcock heroes, Hannay is an
15 ordinary man suddenly caught up in a chaotic world where nothing is certain and all appearances are deceptive.

—Excerpted from a description of *The 39 Steps* in *Video Yesteryear* catalog, 1985

1. In lines 3–5, why does the author pose questions?

   (1) to test the reader's knowledge
   (2) to arouse the reader's curiosity
   (3) to plant misleading clues in the reader's mind
   (4) to imitate a lawyer's speaking style
   (5) to baffle the main character

2. According to the excerpt, what choice best describes the heroes in Alfred Hitchcock's films?

   (1) notorious murderers
   (2) happy-go-lucky tourists
   (3) sinister spies
   (4) tough police officers
   (5) ordinary people

3. Moments from the movie's plot are listed here in jumbled order. Rearrange the plot details according to the sequence described in the passage. Number the statements 1–6 to show the correct order.

_____ Suspected of murder, Richard Hannay is pursued by the police.

_____ A strange woman asks Richard Hannay to protect her from deadly secret agents.

_____ Richard Hannay tries to track down the spy organization's sinister leader.

_____ Richard Hannay visits a London music hall.

_____ The strange woman appears in Richard Hannay's room with a knife in her back.

_____ A gunshot interrupts the music show.

4. Which of the following newspaper headlines would most likely appeal to Hitchcock?

(1) FBI Agents Screened for Drug Use
(2) Detectives Undergo Rigorous Training
(3) Police Officers Demand Higher Wages
(4) Suburban Man Finds Body in Car Trunk
(5) Local Politician Ticketed for Speeding

5. Which of the following statements best summarizes the author's opinion of *The 39 Steps*?

(1) The film represents Hitchcock's best work.
(2) The stereotyped characters are unbelievable.
(3) The thrilling spy adventure is masterfully directed.
(4) The plot is overly complicated.
(5) The film is excessively violent.

Answers are on page 330.

WRITING ACTIVITY 9

Part I. In a paragraph, summarize the highlights from a movie that impressed you. Write your summary on a separate sheet of paper.

Part II. On a separate sheet of paper, write a letter to your favorite performing artist, such as a singer, a comedian, a musician, or an actor. Tell the person why you admire him or her. Use specific details to support your opinion.

Answers will vary.

EXERCISE 22

Directions: The following passage is about Harold and Fayard Nicholas, a famous tap-dancing team. Read the passage and answer the questions that follow.

HOW DID THE NICHOLAS BROTHERS SUCCEED IN SHOW BUSINESS?

"We never had teachers," Nicholas says. "Fayard could watch and pick up things. . . . He was a natural."

After mastering the basics, the brothers began choreographing their own routines.

5   "When they found out that we had something going," Nicholas says, "our folks stopped doing their jobs to take care of us. They decided to manage us."

By the late-'30s, the Nicholas family moved back to New York and the brothers entered the world of vaudeville at Harlem's famed
10 Cotton Club.

"That was the main job we had when we were kids," Nicholas says.

At the Cotton Club they performed on the same bill with some of the most acclaimed black performers of the era, including Cab
15 Calloway and Duke Ellington. Unlike most of the black stars, the young Nicholas Brothers were allowed to mingle with the all-white audience. But Nicholas says that their privileges didn't hold much significance for him at the time.

"It didn't matter to me. We were so young," he says. "Nothing
20 mattered. I just enjoyed the work."

The enthusiastic response the Nicholas Brothers received at the Cotton Club led one of its managers to take charge of the budding tap-dancing act. In 1940, the brothers, then 10 and 16 respectively, were contracted to Hollywood's 20th Century-Fox studio for their
25 dance routines. They debuted in "Down Argentine Way."

Choreographer Nick Castle designed many of the Nicholas Brothers' routines, including their famed Staircase Dance in "Stormy Weather" in which the hoofers leapt over each others' backs all the way down a giant staircase, landing in full splits. Castle worked with
30 the duo throughout their movie career and also helped Harold develop some of his signature stunts, such as backflipping into a split, and sliding through a tunnel of open legs.

"He thought of all the crazy, impossible things for us to do," Nicholas says. "My brother and I started something different in tap
35 dancing when we did the movies. People always asked us if we studied ballet because we used our hands so much."

—Excerpted from "Star of 'Tap Dance Kid' Started Living Title Role
More Than Half a Century Ago" by Robert Blau

1. How did the Nicholas Brothers learn to dance?

_____

_____

2. Where was the Cotton Club located?

_____

3. What can you infer that a choreographer does?

(1) manages entertainers
(2) recruits new talent
(3) reviews dance performances
(4) designs dances
(5) supervises a nightclub

4. Whose point of view does the author rely on to trace the Nicholas Brothers' career?

(1) Cab Calloway's
(2) Harold Nicholas's
(3) Nick Castle's
(4) Duke Ellington's
(5) one of the dancing team's fans

Answers are on page 330.

EXERCISE 23

Directions: Read the passage and answer the questions that follow.

WHAT KINDS OF SHOWS DOES THE ZAPATO PUPPET THEATER PERFORM?

The Zapato Puppet Theater, a two-person company run by Michael and Laura Montenegro, utilizes several types of puppets as well as 2-foot masks. Much of its current production, "The Rickety Wheel Makes the Most Noise," is comic, yet its dreamlike and
5 serious approach appeals to both adults and children.

Among its pieces, the show includes Chilean folktales told by Saldania, a cantankerous old man; a dance performed by La Llorona, a tragic character from New Mexican folklore; and a mask scene between a man and woman. For this the Montenegros have created
10 2-foot masks that entirely cover their heads.

As Laura Montenegro explains, "The reason the puppets really appeal to us is they sort of live in the world between the conscious and the unconscious. When you go into a museum you see little characters—wooden figures, masks and puppets—and they have a
15 certain life.

"But when they're used and they're moved and they come alive, they reveal something mythic about our humanness. It's kind of an ancient thing. It's almost ritualistic, something that people don't have a chance to experience very much anymore. What we'd like to
20 accomplish is to make people get a little more insight into our humanness."

To get that insight, the Montenegros dip frequently into folktales for the source of their vignettes and treat them in a dreamlike manner.

25 Chilean folktales in particular have been a source of material for the Montenegros, reflecting Michael Montenegro's roots. "My father was born in Chile," he says, "and his father was a writer, a foreign correspondent for the *New York Times*, and among other writing endeavors he put together two volumes of Chilean folktales.
30 And this tradition of storytelling and folklore, especially Hispanic folklore, was a very strong influence on myself and my brothers."

—Excerpted from "Puppet Theater Can Make All Our Dreams Come True" by Robert Wolf, *Chicago Tribune*, July 25, 1986

1. What is the title of the Zapato Puppet Theater production described in the passage?

    _____

2. Write three adjectives that the author uses to describe this production.

    _____

3. Where was Michael Montenegro's father born?

    _____

4. According to Laura Montenegro, what is the major goal of the Zapato Puppet Theater?

    (1) to represent an ancient form of entertainment
    (2) to depict ridiculous characters
    (3) to imitate art exhibits at museums
    (4) to display lifelike wooden masks
    (5) to provide insights into human nature

5. What is the author's attitude toward the Montenegros?

    (1) cynical
    (2) joking
    (3) boastful
    (4) respectful
    (5) ridiculing

6. The following statements draw conclusions based on the passage. Write *V* if a statement is valid or *I* if it is invalid.

    _____ (1) Puppet shows appeal only to children.

    _____ (2) Hispanic folklore influences the subjects of Michael Montenegro's art.

    _____ (3) Folktales and myths express stories about a particular culture.

    _____ (4) Puppet shows are more creative than plays performed by human actors.

    _____ (5) All artists intentionally portray their cultural heritage in their art.

Answers are on pages 330–331.

Chapter Review

Directions: Read each passage and choose the best answer to the questions that follow.

Questions 1–5 refer to the following excerpt from an informative essay.

WHAT IS THE ARCHITECTURE OF THE NATIVE AMERICAN INDIAN CENTER?

The building that houses the Native American Indian Center in Niagara Falls is, by any standards, an unconventional one. Built for noncommercial purposes—to house an Indian
5   Cultural Center and to serve as a symbol of the Iroquois nation—the structure was designed in the shape of a turtle. There were several motives for choosing the design. Graphically, it was a strong image and would surely make a
10 vivid impression on the observer. In addition, the turtle was a universal symbol of good luck, long life, and toughness. The turtle had a special meaning to the Iroquois, who call North America "the great turtle island" and whose
15 myths hold that the earth was created on the back of a turtle. The building was designed by Dennis Sun Rhodes, an Arapaho architect, who believed that it was important that modern architecture be adapted to traditional Indian
20 values.

The turtle is 63,000 square feet and three stories high. Inside its multipurpose body is a 250-seat amphitheatre and exhibit hall; the surrounding concrete walls support a geodesic
25 dome, 160 feet in diameter. The hall is illuminated by a huge skylight in the shape of a thunderbird. All the turtle's appendages are functional spaces: the four legs contain a Contemporary Crafts Hall, a National Indian Art
30 Gallery, a museum workshop, and the building's mechanical systems. The head and neck area contain a restaurant and a dining galley (in the turtle's mouth), administration offices, and, at the top of the head, an apartment for the
35 center's artist in residence. The forehead holds an observation deck, from which the visitor can view "the smoking waters"—Niagara Falls.

Throughout the building are traditional Indian symbols, including a large circle, set into the
40 central wooden floor, representing the continuity of life, and a compass design representing the four winds.

—Excerpted from *The Well-Built Elephant* by J. C. C. Andrews, 1984

1. Why is the Native American Indian Center considered unique?

   It is
   (1) located in Niagara Falls
   (2) three stories high
   (3) designed in the shape of a turtle
   (4) used for cultural purposes
   (5) an example of modern architecture

2. Which of the following statements best represents Dennis Sun Rhodes's opinion about architecture?

   (1) Buildings should make a vivid impression on the observer.
   (2) Modern architecture should be adapted to traditional values.
   (3) Architectural design should imitate forms found in nature.
   (4) Buildings should be used for noncommercial purposes.
   (5) Modern architecture should reflect contemporary American culture.

3. What is the main purpose of the second paragraph?

   (1) to discuss the architect's creativity
   (2) to describe the anatomy of a turtle
   (3) to interpret the symbols of Native American culture
   (4) to describe the building's physical structure
   (5) to convince readers to visit the center

4. Which of the following words best describes the tone of the passage?

(1) informative
(2) persuasive
(3) critical
(4) entertaining
(5) personal

5. Which of the following buildings also strongly shows how meaningful cultural symbols influence architectural design?

(1) churches
(2) skyscrapers
(3) apartment complexes
(4) factories
(5) department stores

Questions 6–10 refer to the following excerpt from a review.

HOW HAS THE MEANING OF ART CHANGED?

It used to be that viewing works of art was an experience marked by a certain decorum. A hushed setting encouraged the serenity and detachment necessary to absorb truths revealed
5 in works of timeless beauty. Whether or not you could rely on your fellow cultural pilgrims to behave in a civilized manner, one thing was certain: the art, at least, would mind its own business.

10 Imagine instead a world where artworks talk back, where they sense your presence and are, perhaps, not at all pleased to see you. Peace of mind disappears as once passive objects turn the tables, responding to you in unpredictable
15 ways. This is no longer merely a theoretical notion; interactivity is the buzzword in art as well as in the electronic media. As increasing numbers of artists avail themselves of the latest technologies, artworks—like the latest toys—
20 are becoming responsive, causing turbulence in the previously one-way flow of information. Sensors pick up our every gesture, provoking changes in the works themselves—sounds, movements or more disturbing effects.
25 Embedded microchips allow participants to "play" sculptures like musical instruments.

Nowhere are these radical transformations more apparent than in the realm of virtual reality, a new frontier for artists who believe that
30 the encounter between viewer and art object should be anything but passive. One of the most ambitious art projects involving this new technology is "Spirited Ruins," an imaginary world created by HiPArt (High Performance
35 Computing in the Arts), a team of computer-savvy artists and software developers from Boston University's Scientific Computing and Visualization group who have joined forces to explore the outer reaches of the virtual realm.

40   For the moment, to view "Spirited Ruins" one must go to the university's Computer Graphics Laboratory, pick up a navigating wand and don a pair of 3-D goggles; one drawback of such advanced technology is that it won't yet
45 run on your home computer. Standing in front of an ImmersaDesk—the wide screen onto which a computer projects the interactive, three-dimensional scene—viewers (called pilots) can travel through an imaginary landscape where
50 sculptures spring to life and the laws of physics are routinely violated.

—Excerpted from "In a Virtual Sculpture Park, the Art Talks Back" by Miles Unger, *New York Times*, January 2001

6. According to the first paragraph, what is the meaning of the word *decorum*?

    (1) education
    (2) rudeness
    (3) mystery
    (4) respectability
    (5) conversation

7. What is the author's purpose in this passage?

    (1) to criticize a modern interpretation of art
    (2) to explain how technology has changed art
    (3) to suggest a more traditional meaning for art
    (4) to expose faults in virtual art theory
    (5) to praise an effort to bring culture to people

8. Which choice best explains what the author means in paragraph two when he says, ". . . microchips allow participants to 'play' sculptures like musical instruments"?

The participants
    (1) learn to play many musical instruments
    (2) listen to music from the sculptures
    (3) direct the sculpture's responses
    (4) create their own imaginary worlds
    (5) free themselves from their troubles

9. Which choice best describes the author's attitude toward virtual sculpture?

It is
    (1) too unrealistic for modern audiences
    (2) promising but limited in its availability
    (3) lacking three-dimensional capability
    (4) expensive for developers and viewers
    (5) impractical to interact with art

10. Later in the review, the author quotes an artist who says she loves the technology but is not willing to give up control.

What does this information say about the experience of the viewers?

Their experience is
    (1) limited by their background
    (2) exciting and self-directed
    (3) similar to a museum visit
    (4) directed by the designing artist
    (5) spoiled by a sponsor's advertising

Questions 11–15 refer to the following business-related document.

WHEN ARE AN EMPLOYER'S ACTIONS UNFAIR JOB DISCRIMINATION?

Federal fair employment laws prohibit employment practices that discriminate on the basis of age, race, color, gender, national origin, religion, and disability. The laws also prohibit employers from retaliating against employees who file discrimination complaints. Nearly all public and private employers are subject to some of these provisions. The following chart lists the major federal civil rights statutes, who they cover, and what the basic requirements are.

Statute	Coverage	Basic Requirements
Age Discrimination in Employment Act (ADEA)	Employers with 20 or more employees	Prohibits discrimination in employment against individuals aged 40 or over
Americans with Disabilities Act (ADA)	Employers with 15 or more employees	Prohibits discrimination in employment against individuals with a disability
Civil Rights Act, Title VII	Employers with 15 or more employees	Prohibits discrimination in employment based on race, color, sex, religion, national origin
Equal Pay Act (EPA)	Employers engaged in interstate commerce	Requires equal pay between employees of different sexes for equal work
Executive Order 11246	Government contractors	Requires nondiscriminatory employment practices of all contractors; requires contractors with 50 or more employees and contracts of $50,000 or more to implement a written affirmative action plan for women and minorities
Vocational Rehabilitation Act	Government contractors and employers who receive federal financial assistance	Prohibits discrimination in employment against individuals with disabilities

—From *HRnext.com* web site

11. What is a major consideration in determining if a federal discrimination law can be applied to a case?

    (1) the number of discrimination cases against an employer
    (2) the number of employees or federal contracts
    (3) the intent of the company charged with discrimination
    (4) the employment history of the person bringing the charge
    (5) the financial loss suffered by the discriminated employee

12. If an employer has 60 employees and a government contract for $150,000, what must that employer have done to be in compliance with federal law?

    (1) submit to government inspections of hiring practices
    (2) hire only those employees who are physically capable
    (3) employ only members of certain religions, nationalities, and color
    (4) fill positions with individuals who have physical disabilities
    (5) carry out an affirmative action plan for women and minorities

13. If a federal contractor dismissed an individual who is legally blind unfairly, the individual could then seek remedy through which act?

    (1) Executive Order 11246
    (2) Age Discrimination in Employment Act
    (3) Vocational Rehabilitation Act
    (4) Equal Pay Act
    (5) Civil Rights Act

14. What is the primary purpose for the federal civil rights statutes on the chart?

    (1) to ensure that all capable individuals are protected from inequity
    (2) to protect employers from hiring physically unable workers
    (3) to permit employees to criticize harmful work conditions by their employers
    (4) to provide safe working conditions for all employees on government contracts
    (5) to define job discrimination by all private employers not under government contracts

15. What practice is *not* covered by federal statutes listed on the chart?

    (1) safeguards from retaliation by employers charged with discrimination
    (2) protection for individuals of different races, sexes, religions
    (3) equal health and life insurance benefits for all workers
    (4) guarantee of equal pay for equal work
    (5) assurance that workers over age 40 may continue working

Answers are on page 331.

Prose Fiction

The content of the GED Language Arts, Reading Test is divided into two parts: *nonfiction text*, which includes articles about visual communication, editorials, essays, biographies, and business-related documents, and *literary text*, which includes excerpts from novels, short stories, poems, and plays.

You may recall from looking at some of the sample test passages that they appear different in print. The excerpts from novels, short stories, and nonfiction articles appear in paragraphs. Writing in paragraph form is called **prose**. Poems are written in lines and groups of lines called **stanzas**. Excerpts from plays provide the reader with the names of the characters who speak and those characters' words, or **dialogue**.

This chapter focuses on selections from *fiction*. Fiction writers invent a self-contained world where imaginary events unfold. The writers also create characters who play roles in these events.

Three of the seven passages you will see on the test will be *prose fiction*. One passage will be selected from each of the following time periods:

- before 1920

- 1920–1960

- after 1960

In addition, the passages will include two types of fiction—the novel and the short story. The **novel** is a book-length story, a fully developed portrayal of people, situations, and places. Because it is more concise, the **short story** usually focuses on one major event or a series of closely related incidents. In this chapter you will study the following elements of fiction:

- setting

- plot

- point of view

- characterization

- figurative language

- theme

Understanding these elements will help you analyze and interpret fiction.

When you study prose fiction, you will be applying the same reading skills discussed in the first four chapters of this book.

Setting

Fiction writers stage the action of their stories by establishing **setting**—the place, the time, and the atmosphere in which dramatic situations occur.

The **place** confines the action to a specific location or geographical area. For example, the following are some of the places described in short stories and novels:

- a bingo parlor
- a jungle island off the Brazilian coast
- a supermarket
- a small town in Ohio
- a roadside diner
- a southern plantation

The **time** frames the action of the story by explaining when the events happened—the time of day, the season, or the historical period. Ralph Ellison's short story "King of the Bingo Game" takes place in the evening. John Updike's short story "A & P" occurs during the summer. F. Scott Fitzgerald's novel *The Great Gatsby* is set in the 1920s.

The **atmosphere** conveys the emotions associated with the story's physical environment. Descriptions of specific places often create the atmosphere. An intimate, candlelit restaurant may evoke romantic feelings. The emotions associated with funeral parlors are grief and loss.

Apply your understanding of the terms *place*, *time*, and *atmosphere* as you read the following paragraph:

> It was raining that morning, and still very dark. When the boy reached the streetcar café he had almost finished his route and he went in for a cup of coffee. The place was an all-night café owned by a bitter and stingy man called Leo. After the raw, empty street the café seemed friendly and bright: along the counter there were a couple of soldiers, three spinners from the cotton mill, and in a corner a man who sat hunched over with his nose and half his face down in a beer mug.
>
> —Excerpted from "A Tree. A Rock. A Cloud." by Carson McCullers

In the following spaces, identify the three elements of setting:

Place:_____

Time of day:_____

Atmosphere of the place:_____

If you wrote that the scene occurs in the morning at a streetcar café, you correctly named the time and the place. The phrase *friendly and bright* describes the atmosphere of the café.

In the preceding excerpt you see a young boy and some customers. The fictional setting provides the background in which characters act out the events of the story.

How Authors Establish Setting

As you noticed in the excerpt from "A Tree. A Rock. A Cloud.," the author establishes the place, the time, and the atmosphere. Sometimes authors directly state these elements of setting. Here are some examples.

DIRECT STATEMENTS OF PLACE

We went to the only nightclub on a short, dark street, downtown. The village of Loma is built, as its name implies, on a low round hill that rises like an island out of the flat mouth of the Salinas Valley in central California.

—Excerpted from "Sonny's Blues" by James Baldwin

Murphy slams the phone down and bounds back upstairs to his room in the YMCA to sit alone . . .

—Excerpted from "Murphy's Xmas" by Mark Costello

The military school of St. Severin. The gymnasium. The class in their white cotton shirts stand in two rows under the big gas lights.

—Excerpted from "Gym Period" by Rainer Maria Rilke

DIRECT STATEMENTS OF TIME

I sit in the sun drinking gin. It is ten in the morning.

—Excerpted from "The Fourth Alarm" by John Cheever

It was the second day of Easter week.

—Excerpted from "The Peasant Marey" by Fyodor Dostoyevsky

The morning of June 27th was clear and sunny, with the fresh warmth of a full-summer day.

—Excerpted from "The Lottery" by Shirley Jackson

It was December—a bright frozen day in the early morning.

—Excerpted from "A Worn Path" by Eudora Welty

DIRECT STATEMENTS OF ATMOSPHERE

The oiler swung the boat then and, seated in the stern, the cook and the correspondent were obliged to look over their shoulders to contemplate the lonely and indifferent shore.

—Excerpted from "The Open Boat" by Stephen Crane

The room in which I found myself was very large and lofty. . . . I felt that I breathed an atmosphere of sorrow. An air of stern, deep, and irredeemable gloom hung over and pervaded all.

—Excerpted from "The Fall of the House of Usher" by Edgar Allan Poe

Inferring Place and Time

When authors do not name the place or time, you can infer this information from descriptive details. Infer where the action in the following paragraph occurs.

The pass was high and wide and he jumped for it, feeling it slap flatly against his hands, as he shook his hips to throw off the halfback who was driving at him. The center floated by, his hands desperately brushing Darling's knee as Darling picked his feet up high and delicately ran over a blocker and an opposing linesman in a jumble on the ground near the scrimmage line.

—Excerpted from "The Eighty Yard Run" by Irwin Shaw

If you said the action occurs on a football field, you were correct. What are some of the clues that support this inference? Write the words or phrases on the following lines:

_____

_____

_____

_____

When taken together, the terms *pass, halfback, blocker,* and *scrimmage line* all refer to football. You can conclude that the men are playing this sport on a football field.

In the next example the author does not tell the reader the era in which the story is set. However, you can infer the historical period from the description of the main character, a man who is hanged for treason.

Peyton Farquhar was a well-to-do planter, of an old and highly respectable Alabama family. Being a slave owner and like other slave owners a politician he was naturally an original secessionist and ardently devoted to the Southern cause.

—Excerpted from "An Occurrence at Owl Creek Bridge" by Ambrose Bierce

What clues from the character description suggest that the story happens during the Civil War years? On the following lines, write two phrases that support this inference about setting:

_____

_____

As you probably noted, Peyton Farquhar is a "slave owner" who is "devoted to the Southern cause," which included preserving the institution of slavery.

Inferring Atmosphere

Recall that *atmosphere* refers to the emotional qualities associated with a place. An author usually suggests an atmosphere by describing the physical appearance of a place or by showing how characters react to their environment.

The following paragraph describes an abandoned house. Notice the feelings conveyed by the descriptive language.

> On a night the wind loosened a shingle and flipped it to the ground. The next wind pried into the hole where the shingle had been, lifted off three, and the next, a dozen. The midday sun burned through the hole and threw a glaring spot on the floor. The wild cats crept in from the fields at night, but they did not mew at the doorstep any more. They moved like shadows of a cloud across the moon, into the rooms to hunt the mice. And on windy nights the doors banged, and the ragged curtains fluttered in the broken windows.

—Excerpted from *The Grapes of Wrath* by John Steinbeck

This excerpt illustrates how the sun and the wind are gradually destroying an empty house. What is your impression of the atmosphere? desolate? bleak? dreary? These are some of the words that capture the overall feeling of this place. John Steinbeck, the author, conveys the atmosphere through images relating to sights and sounds. Reread his concluding sentence. Try to imagine hearing doors banging on a windy night and seeing ragged curtains fluttering in broken windows.

WRITING ACTIVITY 1

Where would you like to be at this moment? at the beach? in the mountains? at a party with friends and family? On a separate sheet of paper, write a paragraph describing the setting and atmosphere of the scene you envision. Use plenty of descriptive details to make your paragraph vivid.

Answers will vary.

EXERCISE 1

Directions: Read the passage below and choose the best answer to each question that follows.

WHAT DO THE CHILDREN HEAR?

And so the house came to be haunted by the unspoken phrase: There must be more money! There must be more money! The children could hear it all the time, though
5 nobody said it aloud. They heard it at Christmas, when the expensive and splendid toys filled the nursery. Behind the shining modern rocking-horse, behind the smart doll's house, a voice would start whispering: "There must be more
10 money! There must be more money!" And the children would stop playing, to listen for a moment. They would look into each other's eyes, to see if they had all heard. And each one saw in the eyes of the other two that they too
15 had heard. "There must be more money! There must be more money!"

It came whispering from the springs of the still-swaying rocking-horse, and even the horse, bending his wooden, champing head, heard it.
20 The big doll, sitting so pink and smirking in her new pram, could hear it quite plainly, and seemed to be smirking all the more self-consciously because of it. The foolish puppy, too, that took the place of the teddy-bear, he
25 was looking so extraordinarily foolish for no other reason but that he heard the secret whisper all over the house: "There must be more money!"

Yet nobody ever said it aloud. The whisper
30 was everywhere, and therefore no one spoke it. Just as no one ever says: "We are breathing!" in spite of the fact that breath is coming and going all the time.

—Excerpted from "The Rocking-Horse Winner" by
D. H. Lawrence, 1926

1. Which of the following statements about the children is true?

   (1) They wish they had more toys.
   (2) They fear running short of money.
   (3) Their house is haunted by ghosts.
   (4) They don't take care of their possessions.
   (5) Their whispering annoys their parents.

2. Where does the action described in the excerpt take place?

   (1) in a school
   (2) on a playground
   (3) at a toy store
   (4) in a daycare center
   (5) in a nursery

3. Which word best describes the atmosphere of the house?

   (1) peaceful
   (2) cheerful
   (3) tense
   (4) joyous
   (5) angry

Answers are on page 331.

EXERCISE 2

Directions: Read the passage and answer the questions that follow.

It was freezing cold, with a fog that caught your breath. Two large searchlights were crisscrossing over the compound from the watchtowers at the far corners. The lights on the perimeter and the lights inside the camp were on full force. There were so many of them that they blotted out the stars.

With their felt boots crunching on the snow, prisoners were rushing past on their business—to the latrines, to the supply rooms, to the package room, or to the kitchen to get their groats cooked. Their shoulders were hunched and their coats buttoned up, and they all felt cold, not so much because of the freezing weather as because they knew they'd have to be out in it all day. But the Tartar in his old overcoat with shabby blue tabs walked steadily on and the cold didn't seem to bother him at all.

They went past the high wooden fence around the punishment block (the stone prison inside the camp), past the barbed-wire fence that guarded the bakery from the prisoners, past the corner of the HQ where a length of frost-covered rail was fastened to a post with heavy wire, and past another post where—in a sheltered spot to keep the readings from being too low—the thermometer hung, caked over with ice. Shukhov gave a hopeful sidelong glance at the milk-white tube. If it went down to forty-two below zero they weren't supposed to be marched out to work. But today the thermometer wasn't pushing forty or anything like it.

—Excerpted from *One Day in the Life of Ivan Denisovich* by Alexander Solzhenitsyn

1. Where does the story most likely take place?

    (1) a military academy
    (2) an army post
    (3) a prison camp
    (4) a combat zone
    (5) a reform school

2. What is the atmosphere depicted in this passage?

    (1) violent
    (2) suspenseful
    (3) dull
    (4) hopeful
    (5) oppressive

3. List four phrases in the passage that refer to the weather.

_____

_____

_____

_____

Answers are on pages 331-332.

Plot

The **plot** of a story refers to the action—the sequence of events. A writer structures and organizes events to suit the purpose of the story he or she wants to tell. As author John Steinbeck once explained, "Of course, a writer rearranges life, shortens the intervals, sharpens events, and devises beginnings, middles, and ends." In other words, writers present an organized version of experiences that may occur in real life.

In fiction the action progresses toward a believable conclusion. Individual incidents or episodes are connected logically. For example, the events may unfold in a series of cause-and-effect relationships. When you are reading a fictional passage, ask yourself why an event happened, what the outcome was, and what will happen next.

Summarizing the action of a scene can also help you see how plot details are related. Identify the main incident described in the following excerpt.

The dogs were cast, still on leash. They struck immediately. The trail was good, easily followed because of the dew. The fugitive had apparently made no effort whatever to hide it. They could even see the prints of his knees and hands where he had knelt to drink from a spring. "I never yet knew a murderer that had more sense than that about the folks that would chase him," the deputy said. "But this durn fool don't even suspect that we might use dogs."

"We been putting dogs on him once a day ever since Sunday," the sheriff said. "And we ain't caught him yet."

"Them were cold trails. We ain't had a good hot trail until today. But he's made his mistake at last. We'll get him today. Before noon, maybe."

"I'll wait and see, I reckon," the sheriff said.

"You'll see," the deputy said. "This trail is running straight as a railroad. I could follow it, myself almost. Look here. You can even see his footprints. The durn fool ain't even got enough sense to get into the road, in the dust, where other folks have walked and where the dogs can't scent him. Them dogs will find the end of them footprints before ten o'clock."

Which the dogs did. Presently the trail bent sharply at right angles. They followed it and came onto a road, which they followed behind the lowheaded and eager dogs who, after a short distance, swung to the roadside where a path came down from a cotton house in a nearby field. They began to bay, milling, tugging, their voices loud, mellow, ringing; whining and surging with excitement. "Why, the durn fool!" the deputy said. "He set down here and rested: here's his footmarks: them same rubber heels. He aint a mile ahead right now! Come on, boys!" They went on, the leashes taut, the dogs baying, the men moving now at a trot.

—Excerpted from *Light in August* by William Faulkner, 1932

Which statement best summarizes the action of this passage?

(1) A murderer runs away from the law.

(2) A fugitive outsmarts the sheriff and his deputy.

(3) A sheriff, a deputy, and his dogs try to track down a murderer.

(4) A sheriff and his deputy disagree on plans for a manhunt.

(5) The dogs are useless in capturing the fugitive.

Answer (3) is the right response. The entire scene traces the pursuit of the murderer by the sheriff, the deputy, and their dogs. Answer (1) describes the reason for the manhunt but does not summarize the action. Answers (2) and (5) are possible outcomes, but they do not convey the main action in the passage. Answer (4) describes a specific moment from the scene.

As you read the passage, did you also notice that the setting changes? The author reveals this shift in location by showing where the sheriff and his deputy have found the fugitive's handprints and footmarks. Study the passage again. On the following lines, describe the locations where the passage begins and ends:

_____

_____

_____

_____

The two locations are an area near a spring and a path coming down from a cotton house in a nearby field.

Conflict in Plot

Headlines often report **conflicts**—clashes between opposing forces:

Hurricane off Florida Coastline Forces Residents to Evacuate

Professional Athlete Struggles to Overcome Drug Problems

Citizens Stage Protest Against Nuclear Weapons and the Arms Race

Two Men Arrested in Barroom Brawl

Movie Star Tells About Battle to Recover from Stroke

As these newspaper headlines illustrate, conflict is a part of everyday life. People find themselves at odds with their environment, society, or other individuals. They also confront personal problems that result in inner conflicts. These kinds of real-life conflicts also occur in fictional plots.

The events of a story often arise when characters defy society or other individuals, cope with dangerous surroundings, or struggle with their own emotions. These conflicts create moments of tension in the plot.

The following excerpt from Ralph Ellison's novel *Invisible Man* shows the main character in conflict.

How had I come to this? I kept unswervingly to the path placed before me, had tried to be exactly what I was expected to be, had done exactly what I was expected to do—yet, instead of winning the expected reward, here I was stumbling along, holding on desperately to one of my eyes in order to keep from bursting out my brain against some familiar object swerved into my path by my disordered vision. And now to drive me wild I felt suddenly that my grandfather was hovering over me, grinning triumphantly out of the dark. I simply could not endure it. For, despite my anguish and anger, I knew of no other way of living, nor other forms of success available to such as me. I was so completely a part of that existence that in the end I had to make my peace. It was either that or admit that my grandfather had made sense. Which was impossible, for though I still believed myself innocent, I saw that the only alternative to permanently facing the world of Trueblood and the Golden Day was to accept the responsibility for what had happened. Somehow, I had convinced myself, I had violated the code and thus would have to submit to punishment. Dr. Bledsoe is right, I told myself, he's right; the school and what it stands for have to be protected. There was no other way, and no matter how much I suffered I would pay my debt as quickly as possible and return to building my career . . .

Back in my room I counted my savings, some fifty dollars, and decided to get to New York as quickly as possible. If Dr. Bledsoe didn't change his mind about helping me get a job, it would be enough to pay my room and board at Men's House, about which I had learned from fellows who lived there during their summer vacations. I would leave in the morning.

—Excerpted from *Invisible Man* by Ralph Ellison, 1947

On the lines, state the conflict and explain how it was resolved.

The conflict is between _____ and

_____

The conflict is resolved when _____

_____

    The conflict is one between the narrator and *himself.* Dr. Bledsoe accused the narrator of a school code violation and subjected him to punishment; however, the narrator was innocent of the charge. By choosing to leave voluntarily, the narrator resolved the conflict between his innocence and the punishment. The narrator made a sacrifice for the good of his school.

GED PRACTICE

EXERCISE 3

The following excerpt is from a short story set in South Africa, where apartheid, the official policy of racial segregation, was strictly enforced for many years. The laws under apartheid denied blacks certain human rights.

Directions: As you read the excerpt, be aware of how the setting influences Karlie and his actions. Then choose the best answer to each question that follows.

WHAT DOES THE BENCH MEAN?

    Here was his challenge! *The bench.* The railway bench with "Europeans Only" neatly painted on it in white. For one moment it symbolized all the misery of the plural South
5 African society.

    Here was his challenge to the rights of a man. Here it stood. A perfectly ordinary wooden railway bench, like thousands of others in South Africa. His challenge. That bench now had
10 concentrated in it all the evils of a system he could not understand and he felt a victim of. It was the obstacle between himself and humanity. If he sat on it, he was a man. If he was afraid he denied himself membership as a human being in
15 a human society. He almost had visions of righting this pernicious system, if he only sat down on that bench. Here was his chance. He, Karlie, would challenge.

    He seemed perfectly calm when he sat
20 down on the bench, but inside his heart was thumping wildly. Two conflicting ideas now throbbed through him. The one said, "I have no right to sit on this bench." The other was the voice of a new religion and said, "Why have I no
25 right to sit on this bench?" The one voice spoke of the past, of the servile position he had occupied on the farm, of his father, and his father's father who were born black, lived like blacks, and died like mules. The other voice
30 spoke of new horizons and said, "Karlie, you are a man. You have dared what your father and your father's father would not have dared. You will die like a man."

—Excerpted from "The Bench" by Richard Rive, 1960

1. In Karlie's eyes, what does the bench represent?

   (1) a peaceful place to rest
   (2) the European railway system
   (3) an unreasonable fear of whites
   (4) the importance of obeying the law
   (5) the pain of racial segregation

2. What outside conflict triggers Karlie's inner conflict in paragraph 3?

A conflict with
(1) his father
(2) his grandfather
(3) South African society
(4) the bench
(5) European police

3. Which of the following words best describes Karlie's behavior?

(1) calm
(2) courageous
(3) reckless
(4) silly
(5) cowardly

4. If Karlie were living in the United States today, which of the following would he probably support?

(1) people opposed to school busing
(2) stronger law enforcement
(3) financial aid to foreign countries
(4) discrimination against protesters
(5) the human rights movement

Answers are on page 332.

WRITING ACTIVITY 2

On a separate sheet of paper, write about a conflict from your own experience. Some suggested topics include a conflict with another person—a relative, a friend, a boss, or an enemy; and an inner conflict about making a decision—getting married, returning to school, or breaking a rule. Organize your paragraphs by answering each of these questions:

Paragraph 1: What were the two opposing sides of the conflict?

Paragraph 2: What caused the conflict?

Paragraph 3: What tense moments did the conflict create?

Answers will vary.

Point of View

When you read stories, through whose eyes do you see the setting, the plot, and the characters? Sometimes, an author chooses to tell a story through the eyes of someone completely outside the action of the story. Other times, an author chooses to tell a story through the eyes of a character who takes part in the story. The person telling the story is the **narrator**. The kind of narrator determines the way that you see people, actions, and situations. This is called the narrator's **point of view**.

"Outside" Narrator

The "outside" narrator does not participate in the conflict of a story. In fact, usually the outside narrator is not a character at all. This kind of narrator is, instead, a voice relating a story from a distance. The narrator recounts the characters' experiences and may tell you about their thoughts and feelings, as if able to read their minds.

The outside narrator is used in many types of fiction. As you read the following excerpt from a fairy tale, notice whose voice is conveying information about the characters, their circumstances, and their environment.

> Close to a large forest there lived a woodcutter with his wife and his two children. The boy was called Hansel and the girl Gretel. They were always very poor and had very little to live on. And at one time when there was famine in the land, the woodcutter could no longer procure daily bread.
>
> One night when he lay in bed worrying over his troubles, he sighed and said to his wife, "What is to become of us? How are we to feed our poor children when we have nothing for ourselves?"
>
> "I'll tell you what, husband," answered the woman. "Tomorrow morning we will take the children out quite early into the thickest part of the forest. We will light a fire and give each of them a piece of bread. Then we will go to our work and leave them alone. They won't be able to find their way back, and so we shall be rid of them."
>
> "Nay, wife," said the man, "we won't do that. I could never find it in my heart to leave my children alone in the forest. Wild animals would soon tear them to pieces."
>
> "What a fool you are!" she said. "Then we must all four die of hunger. You may as well plane the boards for our coffins at once."
>
> She gave him no peace till he consented. "But I grieve over the poor children all the same," said the man.
>
> —Excerpted from "Hansel and Gretel" by The Brothers Grimm

In the preceding passage, who tells you about a poverty-stricken family living in a forest?

(1) the woodcutter

(2) the woodcutter's wife

(3) Hansel

(4) Gretel

(5) an unnamed narrator

Answer (5) is the correct response. The narrator is not identified. You do not sense the narrator's actual presence in the story. Instead, you are aware of a voice describing the situation. The authors, the Brothers Grimm, act as a single storyteller who tells you about the family's financial problems and the parents' plan to abandon the children.

This method of narration, or storytelling, is also used in this passage from a science fiction novel.

> Montag had done nothing. His hand had done it all, his hand, with a brain of its own, with a conscience and a curiosity in each trembling finger, had turned thief. Now it plunged the book back under his arm, pressed it tight to sweating armpit, rushed out empty, with a magician's flourish! Look here! Innocent! Look!
>
> —Excerpted from *Fahrenheit 451* by Ray Bradbury

As you read the paragraph, did you discover from an unidentified narrator Montag's state of mind when he took the book?

Character as Narrator

An author may also invent a character to tell the story. The character participates in the action, and you witness the events through his or her eyes. In this method of narration, the story sounds like a firsthand report.

For example, in Mark Twain's novel *The Adventures of Huckleberry Finn*, Huck Finn, the central character, is the narrator. The novel begins with Huck introducing himself to the reader:

> You don't know about me without you have read a book by the name of *The Adventures of Tom Sawyer*; but that ain't no matter. That book was made by Mr. Mark Twain, and he told the truth, mainly. There was things which he stretched, but mainly he told the truth.
>
> —Excerpted from *The Adventures of Huckleberry Finn* by Mark Twain

In his own language, Huck relates the experiences that follow. You personally observe the way in which Huck, a teenage boy, views his surroundings and other characters.

WRITING ACTIVITY 3

Reread the excerpt from *Fahrenheit 451* on the previous page. As you already know, an outside narrator reports the event. Imagine that you are Montag, a fireman in the novel. Using the pronoun *I*, tell your supervisor why you took the book. You should know that the story takes place in the future, in a time when books were banned. Firemen did not put out fires but burned books as dangerous. You can invent plot details not included in the original excerpt. Write your version on a separate sheet of paper.

Answers will vary.

Characterization

You get to know fictional characters, like real people, by their actions, relationships, conversations, and environment. How do you form impressions about the people you meet? In the list that follows, check the numbered items that show how you judge others:

_____ **1.** physical appearance

_____ **2.** age

_____ **3.** clothing

_____ **4.** possessions

_____ **5.** action

_____ **6.** conversations

_____ **7.** other people's opinions

_____ **8.** past experiences

_____ **9.** family life

_____ **10.** neighborhood

Add your own:

11. _____

12. _____

13. _____

14. _____

15. _____

You can get to know fictional characters in all of these ways as well. The methods an author uses in presenting characters to the reader are called **characterization**. The author uses various techniques to portray the human characteristics—physical appearance, personality traits, and actions—of imaginary individuals.

When you are reading a short story or a novel, pay close attention to the following means of revealing character:

- outside narrator's comments
- other characters' comments
- dialogue
- scenes depicting characters in action

Outside Narrator's Comments

One way of learning about a character is from an outside narrator's point of view. The narrator may describe how a character looks, give you background information, summarize moments from the character's past, or tell you what a character is thinking.

What does the outside narrator tell you about the Mooneys? Read the passage and answer the questions that follow.

> Mrs. Mooney was a butcher's daughter. She was a woman who was quite able to keep things to herself: a determined woman. She had married her father's foreman and opened a butcher's shop near Spring Gardens. But as soon as his father-in-law was dead Mr. Mooney began to go to the devil. He drank, plundered the till, ran headlong into debt. It was no use making him take the pledge: he was sure to break out again a few days after. By fighting his wife in the presence of customers and by buying bad meat he ruined his business. One night he went for his wife with the cleaver and she had to sleep in a neighbour's house.
>
> After that they lived apart. She went to the priest and got a separation from him with care of the children.
>
> —Excerpted from "The Boarding House" by James Joyce, 1916

1. What two personality traits of Mrs. Mooney are described in the passage?

_____

_____

2. How does Mr. Mooney's behavior change after his father-in-law's death?

_____

3. How does Mr. Mooney ruin his business?

_____

_____

4. Why does Mrs. Mooney seek a separation from her husband?

_____

Here are the correct responses: (1) private and determined; (2) he drank and went into debt; (3) he fought his wife in front of customers and bought bad meat; and (4) Mr. Mooney went after her with a meat cleaver.

You derived information about the characters, their behavior, and their relationship from the narrator's statements. From these direct statements, you can make additional inferences about Mr. and Mrs. Mooney. For instance, because Mr. Mooney went after his wife with a meat cleaver, you can infer that he is capable of physical violence. Since Mrs. Mooney asked her priest for a separation from her husband, you can assume that she is Catholic. Once you understand what the narrator directly tells you, you will be better prepared to draw your own conclusions about the characters.

EXERCISE 4

Directions: Read the passage and answer the questions that follow.

He had been as Tony a kid of many dreams and schemes, especially getting out of this tenement-crowded, kid-squawking neighborhood, with its lousy poverty, but everything had fouled up against him before he could. When he was sixteen he quit the vocational school where they were making him into a shoemaker, and began to hang out with the gray-hatted, thick-soled-shoe boys, who had the spare time and the mazuma and showed it in fat wonderful rolls down in the cellar clubs to all who would look, and everybody did, popeyed. They were the ones who had bought the silver caffe espresso urn and later the television, and they arranged the pizza parties and had the girls down; but it was getting in with them and their cars, leading to the holdup of a liquor store, that had started all the present trouble. Lucky for him the coal-and-ice man who was their landlord knew the leader in the district, and they arranged something so nobody bothered him after that. Then before he knew what was going on—he had been frightened sick by the whole mess—there was his father cooking up a deal with Rosa Agnello's old man that Tony would marry her and the father-in-law would, out of his savings, open a candy store for him to make an honest living. He wouldn't spit on a candy store, and Rosa was too plain and lank a chick for his personal taste, so he beat it off to Texas and bummed around in too much space, and when he came back everybody said it was for Rosa and the candy store, and it was all arranged again and he, without saying no, was in it.

—Excerpted from "The Prison" by Bernard Malamud, 1950

Part I: Factual Statements About Characterization

1. Where did Tony grow up?

_____

2. How old was Tony when he quit vocational school?

_____

3. Who were his friends?

_____

4. How did Tony break the law?

_____

5. What arrangement did Tony's father make with Rosa Agnello's father?

_____

Part II: Making Inferences About Characterization

6. What was Tony's life like before his marriage?

_____

7. Why did Tony marry Rosa?

_____

Answers are on page 332.

Other Characters' Comments

Frequently, a character narrating a story comments on the other characters. This type of narrator may have direct contact with these characters, and you see them from the narrator's point of view. Through the narrator's descriptions of and relationship with the other characters, you learn about both the narrator's personality and the characters that he or she knows.

This method of characterization is used in the following passage. A mother, the narrator of the story, recalls the hardships of raising her daughter alone during the 1930s and 1940s. Like most single parents, she is torn between two conflicting responsibilities—holding down a job and taking care of her child. In the following excerpt, notice what the mother says about herself, her daughter, and their relationship:

I will never total it all. I will never come in to say: She was a child seldom smiled at. Her father left me before she was a year old. I had to work her first six years when there was work, or I sent her home and to his relatives. There were years she had care she hated. She was dark and thin and foreign-looking in a world where the prestige went to blondeness and curly hair and dimples, she was slow where glibness was prized. She was a child of anxious, not proud, love. We were poor and could not afford for her the soil of easy growth. I was a young mother, I was a distracted mother.

—Excerpted from "I Stand Here Ironing" by Tillie Olsen, 1956

From the mother's point of view, you catch a glimpse of the daughter's physical appearance—"dark and thin and foreign-looking." The mother also tells you about the conditions affecting her daughter's upbringing. Summarize these circumstances.

_____

_____

_____

You should have included the following information about the daughter:

(1) Her father abandoned her before she was a year old.

(2) She was frequently separated from her mother.

(3) She had a deprived childhood.

In the last sentence of the excerpt, the mother admits some of her own shortcomings as a parent: "I was a young mother, I was a distracted mother."

WRITING ACTIVITY 4

From what the mother says about herself and her daughter, what is your impression of these two characters? On a separate sheet of paper, write a brief paragraph describing your feelings about the mother and the daughter.

Answers will vary.

EXERCISE 5

Directions: As you read the following passage, notice how Nick Carraway describes Tom Buchanan's physical appearance. Then answer the questions.

The front was broken by a line of French windows, glowing now with reflected gold, and wide open to the warm windy afternoon, and Tom Buchanan in riding clothes was standing with his legs apart on the front porch.

He had changed since his New Haven years. Now he was a sturdy, straw haired man of thirty with a rather hard mouth and a supercilious manner. Two shining, arrogant eyes had established dominance over his face and gave him the appearance of always leaning aggressively forward. Not even the effeminate swank of his riding clothes could hide the enormous power of that body—he seemed to fill those glistening boots until he strained the top lacing and you could see a great pack of muscle shifting when his shoulder moved under his thin coat. It was a body capable of enormous leverage—a cruel body.

—Excerpted from *The Great Gatsby* by F. Scott Fitzgerald

1. What is Tom wearing?

   _____

2. Identify these facts about Tom:

   Age: _____

   Hair color: _____

3. Nick uses emotionally charged words to describe Tom's facial features and build. Write the word next to the physical trait it describes.

   "_____ mouth"

   "_____ eyes"

   "_____ body"

4. List some words or phrases from the passage that suggest Tom's strength and force.

   _____

   _____

   _____

   _____

5. Based on details in the excerpt, what can you can infer is Nick's attitude toward Tom?

(1) cautious
(2) critical
(3) sympathetic
(4) unbiased
(5) respectful

Answers are on page 332.

Dialogue

Another way you can learn about characters is through what they say. Characters reveal their personalities when they communicate aloud. **Dialogue** is a conversation between characters. As you read, you "hear" the characters' speech—the actual words they use to express their thoughts, feelings, and attitudes.

An author encloses a character's exact spoken words in quotation marks. This punctuation signals to you, the reader, that a character is talking. When the conversation switches to another speaker, the author begins a new paragraph. Words not enclosed in quotation marks identify the speaker, comment on the character, or present additional plot details.

This format indicating dialogue is used in the following passage, an excerpt from a 1920s gangster novel.

EXERCISE 6

Directions: Read the passage and identify the character who says each of the following lines of dialogue.

The men looked uneasily at Arnie. Little by little they were losing their nerve.

"Speak up," said Pepi, "where you guys from?"

"We're from Detroit," said one of the men.

"Where the hell's that?" Joe Sansone inquired. "I never heard of it."

"Say," said Pepi, "don't you know that tough guys like you oughtn't to be running around loose. No sir. You're liable to get arrested for firing a rod in the city limits."

"Listen," said one of the men from Detroit, "what you guys got against us? We ain't done nothing. We just got in."

They were thoroughly intimidated.

—Excerpted from *Little Caesar* by W. R. Burnett

1. "Speak up, where you guys from?" _____

2. "We're from Detroit." _____

3. "Where the hell's that? I never heard of it." _____

4. "Say, don't you know that tough guys like you oughtn't to be running around loose. No sir. You're liable to get arrested for firing a rod in the city limits." _____

5. "Listen, what you guys got against us? We ain't done nothing. We just got in." _____

Answers are on page XXX.

Hints for Reading Dialogue

When you read dialogue, ask yourself the following questions:

- What is the topic of conversation?

- What is the literal meaning of the speaker's statements? Does the speaker's tone emphasize or change the literal meaning?

- What does the dialogue reveal about the character's personality and background? about his or her relationship with others?

In the next example, a woman seeks the advice of a fictional detective. What do you learn about him from the dialogue?

"Good-morning, madam," said Holmes, cheerily. "My name is Sherlock Holmes. This is my intimate friend and associate, Dr. Watson, before whom you can speak as freely as before myself. Ha! I am glad to see that Mrs. Hudson has had the good sense to light the fire. Pray draw up to it, and I shall order you a cup of hot coffee, for I observe that you are shivering."

"It is not cold which makes me shiver," said the woman, in a low voice, changing her seat as requested.

"What, then?"

"It is fear, Mr. Holmes. It is terror." She raised her veil as she spoke, and we could see that she was indeed in a pitiable state of agitation, her face all drawn and gray, with restless, frightened eyes, like those of some hunted animal. Her features and figure were those of a woman of thirty, but her hair was shot with premature gray, and her expression was weary and haggard. Sherlock Holmes ran her over with one of his quick, all-comprehensive glances.

"You must not fear," said he, soothingly, bending forward and patting her forearm. "We shall soon set matters right, I have no doubt."

—Excerpted from "The Speckled Band" by Sir Arthur Conan Doyle

Holmes's Dialogue	Holmes's Personality Traits
"I shall order you a cup of hot coffee, for I observe that you are shivering."	considerate and observant
"We shall soon set matters right, I have no doubt."	helpful and self-confident

The sentences not enclosed in quotation marks are the comments of Dr. Watson, Sherlock Holmes's associate, who is telling the story. From Watson's point of view, you see the woman's physical appearance and both the woman's and Holmes's facial expressions and gestures.

EXERCISE 7

Directions: In the following passage two brothers are talking to each other. Read the passage and answer the questions that follow. To guide your reading, be aware of the following format for indicating dialogue:

- The words *I asked* or *I said* signal that the older brother is speaking.

- The words *he said* signal that Sonny, the younger brother, is speaking.

- When the conversation switches to another speaker, a new paragraph begins.

- Sentences not enclosed in quotation marks are the comments of the older brother, from whose point of view the story is told.

"What do you want to do?" I asked him.

"I'm going to be a musician," he said.

For he had graduated, in the time I had been away, from dancing to the juke box to finding out who was playing what, and what they
5 were doing with it, and he had bought himself a set of drums.

"You mean, you want to be a drummer?" I somehow had the feeling that being a drummer might be all right for other people but not for my brother Sonny.

"I don't think," he said, looking at me very gravely, "that I'll ever
10 be a good drummer. But I think I can play a piano."

I frowned. I'd never played the role of the older brother quite so seriously before, had scarcely ever, in fact, *asked* Sonny a damn thing. I sensed myself in the presence of something I didn't really know how to handle, didn't understand. So I made my frown a little
15 deeper as I asked: "What kind of musician do you want to be?"

He grinned. "How many kinds do you think there are?"

"Be *serious*," I said.

He laughed, throwing his head back, and then looked at me. "I *am* serious."

20 "Well, then, for Christ's sake, stop kidding around and answer a serious question. I mean, do you want to be a concert pianist, you want to play classical music and all that, or—or what?" Long before I finished he was laughing again. "For Christ's *sake*, Sonny!"

He sobered, but with difficulty. "I'm sorry. But you sound so—
25 *scared*!" and he was off again.

"Well, you may think it's funny now, baby, but it's not going to be so funny when you have to make your living at it, let me tell you *that*." I was furious because I knew he was laughing at me and I didn't know why.

30 "No," he said, very sober now, and afraid, perhaps, that he'd hurt me, "I don't want to be a classical pianist. That isn't what interests me. I mean"—he paused, looking hard at me, as though his eyes would help me to understand, and then gestured helplessly, as though perhaps his hand would help—"I mean, I'll have a lot of
35 studying to do, and I'll have to study *everything*, but, I mean, I want to play with—jazz musicians." He stopped. "I want to play jazz," he said.

Well, the word had never before sounded as heavy, as real, as it
sounded that afternoon in Sonny's mouth. I just looked at him and I
40 was probably frowning a real frown by this time. I simply couldn't
see why on earth he'd want to spend his time hanging around
nightclubs, clowning around on bandstands, while people pushed
each other around a dance floor. It seemed—beneath him,
somehow. I had never thought about it before, had never been
45 forced to, but I suppose I had always put jazz musicians in a class
with what Daddy called "good-time people."

—Excerpted from "Sonny's Blues" by James Baldwin

1. What is the overall topic of conversation in this passage?

   (1) famous jazz musicians
   (2) the brothers' relationship
   (3) Sonny's choice of career
   (4) appreciation of classical pianists
   (5) high-paying jobs

2. In lines 26–29, what is the older brother's tone of voice?

   (1) angry
   (2) understanding
   (3) polite
   (4) depressed
   (5) suspicious

3. In lines 30–36, what is Sonny's tone of voice?

   (1) childish
   (2) sarcastic
   (3) rude
   (4) sincere
   (5) bitter

4. Write *V* on the line if an inference is *valid*. If the passage does not support an inference, write *I* for *invalid*.

_____ (1) There is tension between the two brothers.

_____ (2) Sonny's brother doesn't respect jazz musicians.

_____ (3) Sonny's brother doesn't believe that Sonny is musically talented.

_____ (4) Sonny wants to study music at a fine arts college.

_____ (5) Sonny and his brother understand each other.

_____ (6) Sonny doesn't take life seriously.

_____ (7) The older brother is protective of Sonny.

_____ (8) Sonny wants to make his own decisions.

Answers are on page 332.

Scenes Depicting Characters in Action

Showing a character in action is another method of characterization. You judge characters by what they do. Is a character drawn to threatening or safe situations? In a crisis, does the character behave responsibly or irresponsibly? What are the character's motives for his involvement in the story's events? Selfishness? Adventure? Concern for others? You discover the answers to these questions by observing the character's behavior.

In the following excerpt from a short story, the central character finds himself in a predicament. Johnny Hake, a 36-year-old businessman living in a wealthy suburb, doesn't tell his wife, Christina, that they're broke. What steps does Johnny take to get money? In the next exercise you'll find out how Johnny solves his financial problems.

EXERCISE 8

Directions: Read the passage below and complete the exercises that follow.

I tossed my cigarette into the toilet (ping) and straightened my back, but the pain in my chest was only sharper, and I was convinced that the corruption had begun. I had friends who would think of me kindly, I knew, and Christina and the children would surely keep alive an affectionate memory. But then I thought about money again, and the Warburtons, and my rubber checks approaching the clearinghouse, and it seemed to me that money had it all over love. I had yearned for some women—turned green, in fact—but it seemed to me that I had never yearned for anyone the way I yearned that night for money. I went to the closet in our bedroom and put on some old blue sneakers and a pair of pants and a dark pullover. Then I went downstairs and out of the house. The moon had set, and there were not many stars, but the air above the trees and hedges was full of dim light. I went around the Trenholmes' garden then, gumshoeing over the grass, and down the lawn to the Warburtons' house. I listened for sounds from the open windows, and all I heard was the ticking of a clock. I went up the front steps and opened the screen door and started across the floor from the old Ritz. In the dim night light that came in at the windows, the house looked like a shell, a nautilus, shaped to contain itself.

I heard the noise of a dog's license tag, and Sheila's old cocker came trotting down the hall. I rubbed him behind the ears, and then he went back to wherever his bed was, grunted, and fell asleep. I knew the plan of the Warburtons' house as well as I knew the plan of my own. The staircase was carpeted, but I first put my foot on one of the treads to see if it creaked. Then I started up the stairs. All the bedroom doors stood open, and from Carl and Sheila's bedroom, where I had often left my coat at big cocktail parties, I could hear the sound of deep breathing. I stood in the doorway for a second to take my bearings. In the dimness I could see the bed, and a pair of pants and a jacket hung over the back of a chair. Moving swiftly, I stepped into the room and took a big billfold from the inside pocket of the coat and started back to the hall. The violence of my emotions may have made me clumsy, because Sheila woke. I heard her say, "Did you hear that noise, darling?" "S'wind," he mumbled, and then they were quiet again. I was safe in the hall—safe from everything but myself. I seemed to be having a nervous breakdown out there. All my saliva was gone, the lubricants seemed to drain out of my heart, and whatever the juices were that kept my legs upright were going. It was only by holding on to the wall that I could make any progress at all. I clung to the banister on my way down the stairs, and staggered out of the house.

Back in my own dark kitchen, I drank three or four glasses of water. I must have stood by the kitchen sink for a half hour or longer before I thought of looking in Carl's wallet. I went into the cellarway and shut the cellar door before I turned the light on. There was a little over nine hundred dollars. I turned the light off and went back into the dark kitchen. Oh, I never knew that a man could be so miserable and that the mind could open up so many chambers and fill them with self-reproach.

—Excerpted from "The Housebreaker of Shady Hill" by John Cheever, 1978

Part I: A Character's Role in the Plot

Actions from the passage are listed in jumbled order below. Number the statements 1–7 according to the sequence reported by Johnny.

_____ stepped swiftly into the bedroom

_____ took a big billfold from inside the pocket of the coat

_____ found a little more than $900 in Carl's wallet

_____ went down the lawn to the Warburtons' house

_____ went into the cellarway and shut the cellar door

_____ left his own house

_____ returned to his own dark kitchen

Part II: Characterization

Read each of the following statements about Johnny Hake. Circle *T* if the statement is true or *F* if it is false.

T F 1. Johnny believes that love is more important than money.

T F 2. He is a loner who doesn't have any friends.

T F 3. He feels that what he has done is corrupt and disgraceful.

T F 4. He is concerned about how his wife and children will remember him.

T F 5. He thinks that robbing his neighbor is a thrilling experience.

T F 6. He is greedy and can't wait to count the stolen money.

T F 7. He is an inexperienced thief.

T F 8. Financial pressures cause him to behave like a criminal.

Answers are on pages 332-333.

WRITING ACTIVITY 5

In this exercise, you will apply the techniques that professional authors use in portraying a character. On a separate sheet of paper, write about a person you know as though he or she were a character in a story. You want your reader to "see" this person. The following topics will help you organize your information:

- character
- physical appearance
- background
- personality strengths
- personality weaknesses

Then write a short dialogue involving your character and another person. The words enclosed in quotation marks should imitate the way these people really talk.

Answers will vary.

Figurative Language

In the chapters on analysis and synthesis you learned that figurative language suggests a meaning beyond the literal definition of the words. Through figurative language, authors invent original ways of describing a subject or expressing feelings. In fictional prose, descriptions using figurative language are often vivid and emotionally powerful.

Review the differences between literal and figurative language. Then read the following sentences from Toni Morrison's novel *The Bluest Eye*. Write *L* if a statement uses literal language or *F* if it uses figurative language.

_____ **1.** "The air seemed to strangle him, hold him back."

_____ **2.** "Soon, like bright bits of glass, the events of that afternoon cut into him."

_____ **3.** "Rosemary Villanucci, our next-door friend who lives above her father's café, sits in a 1939 Buick eating bread and butter."

_____ **4.** "The rags have fallen from the window crack, and the air is cold."

_____ **5.** "The big, the special, the loving gift was always a big, blue-eyed Baby Doll."

_____ **6.** "And the years folded up like pocket handkerchiefs."

_____ **7.** "Meridian. The sound of it opens the windows of a room like the first four notes of a hymn."

_____ **8.** "And these houses loomed like hothouse sunflowers among the rows of weeds that were the rented houses."

_____ **9.** "In Kentucky they lived in a real town, ten to fifteen houses on a single street, with water piped right into the kitchen."

_____ **10.** "Each pale yellow wrapper has a picture on it."

Sentences 3, 4, 5, 9, and 10 use literal language. Sentences 1, 2, 6, 7, and 8 use figurative language.

In sentences 2, 6, 7, and 8, the phrase that states the comparison is introduced by the word *like*. A comparison using the word *like* or *as* is a figure of speech called a **simile**. Toni Morrison uses a simile to compare the passing of years with folded handkerchiefs: "And the years folded up *like* pocket handkerchiefs."

A **metaphor** is an implied comparison in which the writer states that something *is* something else. The words *like* and *as* are not used in a metaphor. If Toni Morrison had stated, "The passing years have become folded handkerchiefs," she would have made the comparison in a metaphor.

Chapter 7, on poetry, will describe types of figurative language in more detail. On the GED Language Arts, Reading Test, you will be asked to read figures of speech and interpret their meaning. You will not have to define what kind of language is used.

Interpreting Figurative Language

After you recognize that a fiction writer is using figurative language, how do you infer the meaning? Here are some suggestions:

1. Identify the comparison between two different things.

2. Picture the two images being compared.

3. Determine the author's purpose in drawing the comparison. What is he or she trying to show?

Apply these steps as you read the following sentence:

> Now he faced the raging crowd with defiance, its screams penetrating his eardrums like trumpets shrieking from a juke-box.

—Excerpted from "King of the Bingo Game" by Ralph Ellison

What two things is the author comparing?

_____ are compared to _____

What does the comparison show?

_____

You correctly identified the comparison if you said that the crowd's screams are compared to trumpets shrieking from a jukebox. This figure of speech emphasizes the shrill, ear-piercing sound coming from the crowd.

EXERCISE 9

Directions: Carefully read the following sentences from Flannery O'Connor's short novel *Wise Blood*. In each sentence, identify the two things the author is comparing. Then interpret the author's comparison.

1. "Nearer, the plowed fields curved and faded and the few hogs nosing in the furrows looked like large spotted stones."

   _____ are compared to _____

   Interpretation: _____

   _____

2. "He moved like a crow, darting from table to table."

   _____ is compared to _____

   Interpretation: _____

   _____

3. "Her mouth was open and her eyes glittered on him like two chips of green bottle glass."

   _____ are compared to _____

   Interpretation: _____

   _____

4. "Mrs. Watts's grin was as curved and sharp as the blade of a sickle."

   _____ is compared to _____

   Interpretation: _____

   _____

5. "It began to drizzle rain and he turned on the windshield wipers; they made a great clatter like two idiots clapping in church."

   _____ are compared to _____

   Interpretation: _____

   _____

Answers are on page 333.

EXERCISE 10

Directions: Read the passage and choose the best answer to each question that follows.

WHAT DOES COKETOWN LOOK LIKE?

It was a town of red brick, or of brick that would have been red if the smoke and ashes had allowed it; but as matters stood it was a town of unnatural red and black like the painted
5 face of a savage.

It was a town of machinery and tall chimneys, out of which interminable serpents of smoke trailed themselves for ever and ever, and never got uncoiled.

10 It had a black canal in it, and a river that ran purple with ill-smelling dye, and vast piles of building full of windows where there was a rattling and a trembling all day long, and where the piston of the steam-engine worked
15 monotonously up and down like the head of an elephant in a state of melancholy madness.

—Excerpted from *Hard Times* by Charles Dickens, 1854

1. In lines 4–5, what does the author's comparison of the town's red-and-black brick to a savage's painted face suggest?

(1) Savages live in the city.
(2) The town is overrun with violence.
(3) The buildings need repainting.
(4) The town appears wild and uncivilized.
(5) Painting faces is socially unacceptable.

2. What impression is the phrase *serpents of smoke* (lines 7–8) used to create?

An impression of
(1) evil
(2) prosperity
(3) slyness
(4) selfishness
(5) deceit

3. Why does the author compare the motions of a piston (an engine part) to an elephant's head?

(1) to analyze how machines affect animal behavior
(2) to suggest that elephants should replace machines
(3) to give the reader an image of the steam engine's motion
(4) to show that machines are more durable than animals
(5) to explain what a steam engine does

4. From the descriptive details in this passage, what can you conclude about Coketown?

That it is
(1) a fast-paced modern city
(2) an ugly industrial city
(3) a smog-free, unpolluted city
(4) a thriving, wealthy city
(5) a quiet, peaceful city

5. Charles Dickens was a writer who used many of his stories to criticize the dehumanizing effect of the Industrial Revolution in the mid 1800s in England.

What line from the excerpt dehumanizes the inhabitants of Coketown?

(1) "It had a black canal in it, and a river that ran purple. . . . "
(2) " . . . it was a town of unnatural red and black like the painted face of a savage."
(3) "It was a town of machinery and tall chimneys . . . "
(4) " . . . the piston of a steam-engine worked monotonously up and down. . . "
(5) "It was a town of red brick or of brick that would have been red . . . "

Answers are on page 333.

Theme

The **theme** is the underlying meaning of a story. In fables the significance of the plot is usually stated directly at the end of the tale. Read the following fable.

The Shepherd Boy and the Wolf

A shepherd boy who tended his sheep grew lonely. Thinking to have some fun and pass the time he cried out, "Wolf! Wolf!"

His neighbors rushed over to help him, but of course there was no wolf. He merely laughed at them for coming. Three times he raised a false cry of *Wolf*. Three times the neighbors came running.

At last the wolf really did come. The shepherd boy cried out in terror, "Wolf, Wolf! The wolf is killing the sheep."

No one came or paid any attention to his cries. The wolf, having nothing to fear, proceeded to destroy the entire flock.

The point—No one believes a liar—even when he speaks the truth.

—Excerpted from *Myths and Folklore* by Henry I. Christ

The point, or theme, of the fable is stated as follows: "No one believes a liar—even when he speaks the truth." This theme has also been revealed by the characters and their actions. Three times the shepherd boy jokingly cries "Wolf!" to fool his neighbors. His neighbors ignore the real plea for help because they assume that the boy is lying. The theme of "The Shepherd Boy and the Wolf" is a moral judgment about human behavior. Did you notice that you can apply this moral to situations outside the story? You may have heard parents telling their children, "Don't be like the boy who cried 'Wolf!'"

Themes in short stories and novels express beliefs and opinions about life. The central message reflects the author's attitudes toward political or social issues and his or her perceptions about human nature and relationships. Unlike the statement at the end of a fable, the theme of a short story or novel is usually implied rather than stated directly. In addition, the theme may be more complex and sophisticated than the "lesson in life" stated at the end of a fable.

The following passage by Ernest Hemingway is an account of an actual event.

. . . [A]n old man fishing alone in a skiff out of Cabanas hooked a great marlin that, on the heavy sashcord line, pulled the skiff far out to sea. Two days later the old man was picked up by fishermen sixty miles to the eastward, the head and forward part of the marlin lashed alongside. What was left of the fish, less than half, weighed eight hundred pounds. The old man had stayed with him a day, a night, a day, and another night while the fish swam deep and pulled the boat. When he had come up, the old man had pulled the boat up on him and harpooned him. Lashed alongside, the sharks had hit him and the old man had fought them out alone in the Gulf Stream in a skiff, clubbing them, stabbing at them, lunging at them with an oar until he was exhausted and the sharks had eaten all that they could hold. He was crying in the boat when the fishermen picked him up, half crazy from his loss, and the sharks were still circling the boat.

—Excerpted from "On the Blue Water: A Gulf Stream Letter" by Ernest Hemingway

Hemingway based a novel on the old man described above. Study the following excerpt from the novel. Then underline the two sentences that state an important theme—the old man's insight about his situation.

"He took about forty pounds," the old man said aloud. He took my harpoon too and all the rope, he thought, and now my fish bleeds again and there will be others.

He did not like to look at the fish anymore since he had been mutilated. When the fish had been hit it was as though he himself were hit.

But I killed the shark that hit my fish, he thought. And he was the biggest *dentuso* that I have ever seen. And God knows that I have seen big ones.

It was too good to last, he thought. I wish it had been a dream now and that I had never hooked the fish and was alone in bed on the newspapers.

"But man is not made for defeat," he said. "A man can be destroyed but not defeated." I am sorry that I killed the fish though, he thought. Now the bad time is coming and I do not even have the harpoon. The *dentuso* is cruel and able and strong and intelligent. But I was more intelligent than he was. Perhaps not, he thought. Perhaps I was only better armed.

—Excerpted from *The Old Man and the Sea* by Ernest Hemingway

The theme is as follows: "But man is not made for defeat," he said. "A man can be destroyed but not defeated." The old man's comment is a personal statement about the meaning of his own disappointing experience, as well as life's disappointments in general. Through the character of the old man, Hemingway presents a theme that applies to people everywhere: the strength of the human spirit enables an individual to cope with misfortune. A devastating incident ultimately does not ruin a person; he or she is a survivor.

WRITING ACTIVITY 6

In a paragraph, describe an experience in which someone overcomes a personal failure. Use a separate sheet of paper for your description.

Answers will vary.

Inferring Theme

As you discovered in the preceding example, a character's comments may reveal the theme. Usually, however, you have to infer the story's meaning by interpreting the significance of the fictional elements—setting, plot, point of view, characterization, and figurative language. As you read a passage, pay close attention to how the following fictional elements suggest the theme:

- the influence of the setting on the characters and their actions

- the significance of important events

- the characters' observations about life and human behavior

- the author's comments and observations about life and human behavior

- the language the author uses to tell the story

Complete the next set of exercises for further practice in interpreting theme.

EXERCISE 11

Directions: Read the passage below and choose the best answer to each question that follows.

WILL MRS. MALLARD MISS HER HUSBAND?

Knowing that Mrs. Mallard was afflicted with a heart trouble, great care was taken to break to her as gently as possible the news of her husband's death.

5　It was her sister Josephine who told her, in broken sentences, veiled hints that revealed in half concealing. Her husband's friend Richards was there, too, near her. It was he who had been in the newspaper office when intelligence
10　of the railroad disaster was received, with Brently Mallard's name leading the list of "killed." He had only taken the time to assure himself of its truth by a second telegram, and had hastened to forestall any less careful, less
15　tender friend in bearing the sad message.

She did not hear the story as many women have heard the same, with a paralyzed inability to accept its significance. She wept at once, with sudden, wild abandonment, in her sister's
20　arms. When the storm of grief had spent itself she went away to her room alone. She would have no one follow her.

There stood, facing the open window, a comfortable, roomy armchair. Into this she sank,
25　pressed down by a physical exhaustion that haunted her body and seemed to reach into her soul.

She could see in the open square before her house the tops of trees that were all aquiver with
30　the new spring life. The delicious breath of rain was in the air. In the street below a peddler was crying his wares. The notes of a distant song which some one was singing reached her faintly, and countless sparrows were twittering in the eaves.

35　There were patches of blue sky showing here and there through the clouds that had met and piled above the other in the west facing her window.

She sat with her head thrown back upon the
40　cushion of the chair quite motionless, except when a sob came up into her throat and shook her, as a child who has cried itself to sleep continues to sob in its dreams.

She was young, with a fair, calm face, whose
45　lines bespoke repression and even a certain strength. But now there was a dull stare in her eyes, whose gaze was fixed away off yonder on one of those patches of blue sky. It was not a glance of reflection, but rather indicated a
50　suspension of intelligent thought.

There was something coming to her and she was waiting for it, fearfully. What was it? She did not know; it was too subtle and elusive to name. But she felt it, creeping out of the sky, reaching
55　toward her through the sounds, the scents, the color that filled the air.

Now her bosom rose and fell tumultuously. She was beginning to recognize this thing that was approaching to possess her, and she was
60　striving to beat it back with her will—as powerless as her two white slender hands would have been.

When she abandoned herself a little whispered word escaped her slightly parted lips.
65　She said it over and over under her breath: "Free, free, free!" The vacant stare and the look of terror that had followed it went from her eyes. They stayed keen and bright. Her pulses beat fast, and the coursing blood warmed and
70　relaxed every inch of her body. She did not stop to ask if it were not a monstrous joy that held her. A clear and exalted perception enabled her to dismiss the suggestion as trivial.

She knew that she would weep again
75　when she saw the kind, tender hands folded in death; the face that had never looked save with love upon her, fixed and gray and dead. But she saw beyond that bitter moment a long

procession of years to come that would belong
80 to her absolutely. And she opened and spread
her arms out to them in welcome.

—Excerpted from "The Story of an Hour"
by Kate Chopin, 1892

1. What caused the husband's death?

(1) heart disease
(2) a fire in the office where he worked
(3) poison given to him by his wife
(4) old age
(5) a railroad accident

2. How does the woman find out about her husband's death?

(1) Her sister Josephine tells her.
(2) She reads about it in the newspaper.
(3) Her husband's friend Richards sends her a telegram.
(4) The family doctor sends a messenger.
(5) One of her servants comes to her room to tell her.

3. What is the major conflict, or clash between opposing forces, that takes place in the passage?

(1) an argument between the woman and her husband
(2) the husband's fight for his life
(3) the woman's struggle to understand her true feelings
(4) friction between the woman and her family and friends
(5) a psychological battle between the woman and death

4. Which of the following statements best sums up the theme of the story?

(1) It is difficult to adjust to the loss of a loved one.
(2) There is joy to be found in even the saddest situations.
(3) The need for personal freedom is stronger than the need for love.
(4) Most people have a deep-seated fear of the unknown.
(5) Each person has a right to grieve in his or her own way.

5. Why is it fitting that the action takes place in the spring, a time of rebirth and hope?

Because this setting
(1) is needed to lighten the tone of an otherwise sad story
(2) is like the husband, who had an upbeat, sunny personality
(3) indicates that the family will help the woman recover from her loss
(4) reflects how the woman feels about life after her husband's death
(5) helps readers cope with the shocking death of the husband

6. Kate Chopin wrote in the 1890s, when women were considered the property of men.

With which of the following statements would the author of the story be most likely to agree?

(1) Women find it harder to cope with death than men do.
(2) A wife should lead her own life and refuse to live in her husband's shadow.
(3) It takes a year or longer to get over a deep personal loss.
(4) No one knows a person better than her own family and friends.
(5) It's best to look on the bright side of life and forget about life's troubles.

Answers are on page 333.

EXERCISE 12

This selection is a complete short story that is longer than the reading selections on the GED Language Arts, Reading Test. It is included here to give you an opportunity to see how writers use all the elements of fiction that you have studied.

Directions: In the following short story a young man's aunt stays with him while she settles a relative's estate. The young man invites his aunt to a symphony concert. Carefully read the short story and answer the questions that follow.

A Wagner Matinee

I received one morning a letter, written in pale ink on glassy, blue-lined note-paper, and bearing the postmark of a little Nebraska village. This communication, worn and rubbed, looking as though it had been carried for some days in a coat pocket that was none too clean, was from my uncle Howard and informed me that his wife had been left a small legacy by a bachelor relative who had recently died, and that it would be necessary for her to go to Boston to attend to the settling of the estate. He requested me to meet her at the station and render her whatever services might be necessary. On examining the date indicated as that of her arrival, I found it no later than tomorrow. He had characteristically delayed writing until, had I been away from home for a day, I must have missed the good woman altogether.

The name of my Aunt Georgiana called up not alone her own figure, at once pathetic and grotesque, but opened before my feet a gulf of recollection so wide and deep that, as the letter dropped from my hand, I felt suddenly a stranger to all the present conditions of my existence, wholly ill at ease and out of place amid the familiar surroundings of my study. I became, in short, the gangling farmer-boy my aunt had known, scourged with chilblains and bashfulness, my hands cracked and sore from the corn husking. I felt the knuckles of my thumb tentatively, as though they were raw again. I sat again before her parlour organ, fumbling the scales with my stiff, red hands, while she, beside me, made canvas mittens for the huskers.

The next morning, after preparing my landlady somewhat, I set out for the station. When the train arrived I had some difficulty in finding my aunt. She was the last of the passengers to alight, and it was not until I got her into the carriage that she seemed really to recognize me. She had come all the way in a day coach; her linen duster had become black with soot and her black bonnet grey with dust during the journey. When we arrived at my boarding-house the landlady put her to bed at once and I did not see her again until the next morning.

Whatever shock Mrs. Springer experienced at my aunt's appearance, she considerately concealed. As for myself, I saw my aunt's misshapen figure with that feeling of awe and respect with which we behold explorers who have left their ears and fingers north of Franz Josef Land, or their health somewhere along the Upper Congo. My Aunt Georgiana had been a music teacher at the Boston Conservatory, somewhere back in the latter sixties. One summer, while visiting in the little village among the Green Mountains where her ancestors had dwelt for generations, she had kindled the callow fancy of the most idle and shiftless of all the village lads, and had conceived for this Howard Carpenter one of those extravagant passions which a handsome country boy of twenty-one sometimes inspires in an angular, spectacled woman of thirty. When she returned to her duties in Boston, Howard followed her, and the upshot of this inexplicable infatuation was that she eloped with him, eluding the reproaches of her family and the criticisms of her friends by going with him to the Nebraska frontier. Carpenter, who, of course, had no money, had taken a homestead in Red Willow County, fifty miles from the railroad. There they had measured off their quarter section themselves by driving across the prairie in a wagon, to the wheel of which they had tied a red cotton handkerchief, and counting off its revolutions. They built a dugout in the red hillside, one of those cave dwellings whose inmates so often reverted to primitive conditions. Their water they got from the lagoons where the buffalo drank, and their slender stock of provisions was always at the mercy of bands of roving Indians. For thirty years my aunt had not been farther than fifty miles from the homestead.

But Mrs. Springer knew nothing of all this, and must have been considerably shocked at what was left of my kinswoman. Beneath the soiled linen duster which, on her arrival, was the most conspicuous feature of her costume, she wore a black stuff dress, whose ornamentation showed that she had surrendered herself unquestioningly into the hands of a country dressmaker. My poor aunt's figure, however, would have presented astonishing difficulties to any dressmaker.

Originally stooped, her shoulders were now almost bent together over her sunken chest. She wore no stays, and her gown, which trailed unevenly behind, rose in a sort of peak over her abdomen. She wore ill-fitting false teeth, and her skin was as yellow as a Mongolian's from constant exposure to a pitiless wind and to the alkaline water which hardens the most transparent cuticle into a sort of flexible leather.

I owed to this woman most of the good that ever came my way in my boyhood, and had a reverential affection for her. During the years when I was riding herd for my uncle, my aunt, after cooking the three meals—the first of which was ready at six o'clock in the morning—and putting the six children to bed, would often stand until midnight at her ironing board, with me at the kitchen table beside her, hearing me recite Latin declensions and conjugations, gently shaking me when my drowsy head sank down over a page of irregular verbs. It was to her, at her ironing or mending, that I read my first Shakespeare, and her old textbook on mythology was the first that ever came into my empty hands. She taught me my scales and exercises, too—on the little parlour organ which her husband had bought her after fifteen years, during which she had not so much as seen any instrument, but an accordion that belonged to one of the Norwegian farmhands. She would sit beside me by the hour, darning and counting, while I struggled with the "Joyous Farmer," but she seldom talked to me about music, and I understood why. She was a pious woman; she had the consolations of religion and, to her at least, her martyrdom was not wholly sordid. Once when I had been doggedly beating out some easy passages from an old score of *Euryante*[1] I had found among her music books, she came up to me and, putting her hands over my eyes, gently drew my head back upon her shoulder, saying tremulously, "Don't love it so well, Clark, or it may be taken from you. Oh! dear boy, pray that whatever your sacrifice may be, it be not that."

When my aunt appeared on the morning after her arrival, she was still in a semi-somnambulant state. She seemed not to realize that she was in the city where she had spent her youth, the place longed for hungrily half a lifetime. She had been so wretchedly train-sick throughout the journey that she had no recollection of anything but her discomfort, and, to all intents and purposes, there were but a few hours of nightmare between the farm in Red Willow County and my study on Newbury Street. I had planned a little pleasure for her that afternoon, to repay her for some of the glorious moments she had given me when we used to milk together in the straw thatched cowshed and she, because I was more than usually tired, or because her husband had spoken sharply to me, would tell me of the splendid performance of the *Huguenots*[2] she had seen in Paris, in her youth. At two o'clock the Symphony Orchestra was to give a Wagner programme, and I intended to take my aunt; though, as I conversed with her, I grew doubtful about her enjoyment of it. Indeed, for her own sake, I could only wish her taste for such things quite dead, and the long struggle mercifully ended at last. I suggested our visiting the Conservatory and the Common before lunch, but she seemed altogether too timid to wish to venture out. She questioned me absently about various changes in the city, but she was chiefly concerned that she had forgotten to leave instructions about feeding half-skimmed milk to a certain weakling calf, "old Maggie's calf, you know, Clark," she explained, evidently having forgotten how long I had been away. She was further troubled because she had neglected to tell her daughter about the freshly opened kit of mackerel in the cellar, which would spoil if it were not used directly.

I asked her whether she had ever heard any of the Wagnerian operas, and found that she had not, though she was perfectly familiar with their respective situations, and had once possessed the piano score of *The Flying Dutchman*.[3] I began to think it would have been best to get her back to Red Willow County without waking her, and regretted having suggested the concert.

From the time we entered the concert hall, however, she was a trifle less passive and inert, and for the first time seemed to perceive her surroundings. I had felt some trepidation lest she might become aware of the absurdities of her attire, or might experience some painful embarrassment at stepping suddenly into the world to which she had been dead for more than a quarter of a century. But, again, I found how superficially I had judged her. She sat looking about her with eyes as impersonal, almost as stony, as those with which the granite Rameses in a museum watches the froth and fret that ebbs and flows about his pedestal—separated from it by the lonely stretch of centuries. I have seen this same aloofness in old miners who drift into the Brown Hotel at Denver, their pockets full of bullion, their linen soiled, their haggard faces unshaven; standing in the thronged corridors as solitary as though they were still in a frozen camp on the Yukon, conscious that certain experiences have isolated them from their fellows by a gulf no haberdasher could bridge.

We sat at the extreme left of the first balcony, facing the arc of our own and the balcony above us, veritable hanging gardens, brilliant as tulip beds. The matinée audience was made up chiefly of women. One lost the contour of faces and figures, indeed any effect of line what-ever, and there was only the colour of bodices past counting, the shimmer of fabrics soft and firm, silky and sheer; red, mauve, pink, blue, lilac, purple, ecru, rose, yellow, cream, and white, all the colours that an impressionist finds in a sunlit landscape, with here and there the dead shadow of a frock coat. My Aunt Georgiana regarded them as though they had been so many daubs of tube-paint on a palette.

When the musicians came out and took their places, she gave a little stir of anticipation, and looked with quickening interest down over the rail at that invariable grouping, perhaps the first wholly familiar thing that had greeted her eye since she had left old Maggie and her weakling calf. I could feel how all those details sank into her soul, for I had not forgotten how they had sunk into mine when I came fresh from ploughing forever and forever between green aisles of corn, where, as in a treadmill, one might walk from daybreak to dusk with-out perceiving a shadow of change. The clean profiles of the musicians, the gloss of their linen, the dull black of their coats, the beloved shapes of the instruments, the patches of yellow light thrown by the green shaded lamps on the smooth, varnished bellies of the cellos and the bass viols in the rear, the restless, wind-tossed forest of fiddle necks and bows—I recalled how, in the first orchestra I had ever heard, those long bow strokes seemed to draw the heart out of me, as a conjurer's stick reels out yards of paper ribbon from a hat.

The first number was the *Tannhäuser*⁴ overture. When the horns drew out the first strain of the Pilgrim's chorus, my Aunt Georgiana clutched my coat sleeve. Then it was I first realized that for her this broke a silence of thirty years; the inconceivable silence of the plains. With the battle between the two motives, with the frenzy of the Venusberg theme and its ripping of strings, there came to me an overwhelming sense of the waste and wear we are so powerless to combat; and I saw again the tall, naked house on the prairie, black and grim as a wooden fortress; the black pond where I had learned to swim, its margin pitted with sun-dried cattle tracks; the rain gullied clay banks. About the naked house, the four dwarf ash seedlings where the dishcloths were always hung to dry before the kitchen door. The world there was the flat world of the ancients; to the east, a cornfield that stretched to daybreak; to the west, a corral that reached to sunset; between, the conquests of peace, dearer bought than those of war. The overture closed, my aunt released my coat sleeve, but she said nothing. She sat staring at the orchestra through a dullness of thirty years, through the films made little by little by each of the three hundred and sixty-five days in every one of them. What, I wondered, did she get from it? She had been a good pianist in her day I knew, and her musical education had been broader than that of most music teachers of a quarter of a century ago. She had often told me of Mozart's operas and Meyerbeer's, and I could remember hearing her sing, years ago, certain melodies of Verdi's. When I had fallen ill with a fever in her house she used to sit by my cot in the evening—when the cool, night wind blew in through the faded mosquito netting tacked over the window and I lay watching a certain bright star that burned red above the cornfield—and sing "Home to our mountains, O, let us return!" in a way fit to break the heart of a Vermont boy near dead of homesickness already.

I watched her closely through the prelude to *Tristan and Isolde*,⁵ trying vainly to conjecture what that seething turmoil of strings and winds might mean to her, but she sat mutely staring at the violin bows that drove obliquely downward, like the pelting streaks of rain in a summer shower. Had this music any message for her? Had she enough left to at all comprehend this power which had kindled the world since she had left it? I was in a fever of curiosity, but Aunt Georgiana sat silent upon her peak in Darien. She preserved this utter immobility throughout the number from *The Flying Dutchman*, though her fingers worked mechanically upon her black dress, as though, of themselves, they were recalling the piano score they had once played. Poor old hands! They had been stretched and twisted into mere tentacles to hold and lift and knead with; the palm, unduly swollen, the fingers bent and knotted—on one of them a thin, worn band that had once been a wedding ring. As I pressed and gently quieted one of those groping hands, I remembered with quivering eyelids their services for me in other days.

Soon after the tenor began the "Prize Song,"[6] I heard a quick drawn breath and turned to my aunt. Her eyes were closed, but the tears were glistening on her cheeks, and I think, in a moment more, they were in my eyes as well. It never really died, then—the soul that can suffer so excruciatingly and so interminably; it withers to the outward eye only; like that strange moss which can lie on a dusty shelf half a century and yet, if placed in water, grows green again. She wept so throughout the development and elaboration of the melody.

During the intermission before the second half of the concert, I questioned my aunt and found that the "Prize Song" was not new to her. Some years before there had drifted to the farm in Red Willow County a young German, a tramp cow-puncher, who had sung in the chorus at Bayreuth,[7] when he was a boy, along with the other peasant boys and girls. Of a Sunday morning he used to sit on his gingham-sheeted bed in the hands' bedroom which opened off the kitchen, cleaning the leather of his boots and saddle, singing the "Prize Song," while my aunt went about her work in the kitchen. She had hovered about him until she had prevailed upon him to join the country church, though his sole fitness for this step, in so far as I could gather, lay in his boyish face and his possession of this divine melody. Shortly afterward he had gone to town on the Fourth of July, been drunk for several days, lost his money at a *faro* table, ridden a saddled Texas steer on a bet, and disappeared with a fractured collarbone. All this my aunt told me huskily, wanderingly, as though she were talking in the weak lapses of illness.

"Well, we have come to better things than the old *Trovatore*[8] at any rate, Aunt Georgie?" I queried, with a well meant effort at jocularity.

Her lip quivered and she hastily put her handkerchief up to her mouth. From behind it she murmured, "And you have been hearing this ever since you left me, Clark?" Her question was the gentlest and saddest of reproaches.

The second half of the programme consisted of four numbers from the *Ring*,[9] and closed with *Siegfried's*[10] funeral march. My aunt wept quietly, but almost continuously, as a shallow vessel overflows in a rainstorm. From time to time her dim eyes looked up at the lights which studded the ceiling, burning softly under their dull glass globes; doubtless they were stars in truth to her. I was still perplexed as to what measure of musical comprehension was left to her, she who had heard nothing but the singing of Gospel Hymns at Methodist services in the square frame schoolhouse on Section Thirteen for so many years. I was wholly unable to gauge how much of it had been dissolved in soaps suds, or worked into bread, or milked into the bottom of a pail.

The deluge of sound poured on and on; I never knew what she found in the shining current of it; I never knew how far it bore her, or past what happy islands. From the trembling of her face I could well believe that before the last numbers she had been carried out where the myriad graves are, into the grey, nameless burying grounds of the sea; or into some world of death vaster yet, where, from the beginning of the world, hope has lain down with hope and dream with dream and, renouncing, slept.

The concert was over; the people filed out of the hail chattering and laughing, glad to relax and find the living level again, but my kinswoman made no effort to rise. The harpist slipped its green felt cover over his instrument; the flute-players shook the water from their mouthpieces; the men of the orchestra went out one by one, leaving the stage to the chairs and music stands, empty as a winter cornfield.

I spoke to my aunt. She burst into tears and sobbed pleadingly. "I don't want to go, Clark, I don't want to go!"

I understood. For her, just outside the door of the concert hall, lay the black pond with the cattle-tracked bluffs; the tall, unpainted house, with weather-curled boards; naked as a tower, the crook-backed ash seedlings where the dish-cloths hung to dry; the gaunt, moulting turkeys picking up refuse about the kitchen door.

—Willa Cather

Notes to the text:

[1]*Euryanthe:* A now-forgotten opera by Karl Maria von Weber (1786–1826)

[2]*Huguenots:* A popular nineteenth-century opera by Giacomo Meyerbeer (1791–1864)

[3]*The Flying Dutchman:* (1841) One of Wagner's early operas

[4]*Tannhauser:* (1845) Opera by Richard Wagner

[5]*Tristan and Isolde:* (1865) One of Wagner's greatest operas

[6]*"Prize Song":* The song by which one of Wagner's operas concludes

[7]*Bayreuth:* Where Wagner settled after marrying, and where he founded his own theater

[8]*Trovatore:* (1853) Opera by Giuseppi Verdi

[9]*Ring:* (1854–1874) Wagner's cycle of four operas based on Northern European mythology

[10]*Siegfried:* (1871) One of the operas in Wagner's Ring Cycle

1. Who is the main character? _____

2. Who tells this character's story? _____

3. In what city does the story take place? _____

4. Why is this city important to the main character? _____

   _____

5. The narrator tells the story of his aunt's visit to the city where he lives. The events of the story are listed below in jumbled order. Number them according to the sequence in which they are mentioned in the story.

   _____ The narrator recalls his aunt teaching him music.

   _____ Clark and his aunt cry during the singing of "Prize Song."

   _____ The orchestra leaves the stage.

   _____ The narrator takes his aunt to a concert.

   _____ The aunt worries about " old Maggie's calf."

   _____ Aunt Georgiana arrives to settle an estate.

6. The aunt's reactions to the concert are influenced by her past. The first example in the chart below illustrates the cause-and-effect relationship between Georgiana's past (the cause) and her reaction to the concert (the effect). Using the example as a model, identify the reaction that stems from the character's past.

The Incident from the Past (the cause)	The Reaction (the effect)
Georgiana meets Howard Carpenter and moves to his homestead.	Reaction: She falls in love with him and gives up her music work for 30 years.
She had been a good pianist with a broad musical education.	Reaction: _____
She had spent 30 years on the plains without hearing a symphony concert.	Reaction: _____
A Young German who had worked on her farm had sung a chorus from "Prize Song."	Reaction: _____

7. From the narrator's comments, you can infer that he respects his Aunt Georgiana. Identify three incidents that support this inference.

_____

_____

_____

8. What choice best describes the aunt's appearance when she arrives at Mrs. Springer's house?

(1) clean and fashionably dressed
(2) dazed and grossly dressed
(3) proud and lavishly dressed
(4) dusty and plainly dressed
(5) untidy and raggedly dressed

9. Why did the aunt give up her music?

Because
(1) she lost interest in playing
(2) she realized that she wouldn't make much money
(3) she followed the advice of her family and friends
(4) she wanted to follow the man she loved
(5) she became nervous in front of an audience

10. Which of the following choices best expresses the purpose of the passage?

(1) Musicians must continuously practice their playing.
(2) Travel across the country used to be difficult and dangerous.
(3) Cities are the places where culture and art survive.
(4) Music possesses the power to cause the listener pain.
(5) People will make great sacrifices for love.

11. To which of the following television shows would the subject of this short story be best suited?

(1) a soap opera
(2) a situation comedy
(3) a science fiction series
(4) a news program
(5) a courtroom drama

12. Willa Cather is known as a regional writer whose subjects and settings represented prairie life in the early 1900's.

Based on the story, how would Cather describe life on the prairie in the 1900s?

(1) agriculturally booming
(2) culturally successful
(3) physically demanding
(4) financially rewarding
(5) politically unstable

Answers are on page 334.

Go to **www.GEDReading.com** for additional practice and instruction!

Chapter Review

Directions: Read each passage and choose the best answer to the questions that follow.

Questions 1–7 refer to the following excerpt from a novel.

HOW DOES A CROWD BEHAVE AT THE PREMIERE OF A HOLLYWOOD MOVIE?

Although it was still several hours before the celebrities would arrive, thousands of people had already gathered. They stood facing the theatre with their backs toward the gutter in a
5 thick line hundreds of feet long. A big squad of policemen was trying to keep a lane open between the front rank of the crowd and the façade of the theatre.

Tod entered the lane while the policeman
10 guarding it was busy with a woman whose parcel had torn open, dropping oranges all over the place. Another policeman shouted for him to get the hell across the street, but he took a chance and kept going. They had enough to do
15 without chasing him. He noticed how worried they looked and how careful they tried to be. If they had to arrest someone, they joked good-naturedly with the culprit, making light of it until they got him around the corner; then they
20 whaled him with their clubs. Only so long as the man was actually part of the crowd did they have to be gentle.

Tod had walked only a short distance along the narrow lane when he began to get
25 frightened. People shouted, commenting on his hat, his carriage, and his clothing. There was a continuous roar of catcalls, laughter and yells, pierced occasionally by a scream. The scream was usually followed by a sudden movement in
30 the dense mass and part of it would surge forward wherever the police line was weakest. As soon as that part was rammed back, the bulge would pop out somewhere else.

The police force would have to be doubled
35 when the stars started to arrive. At the sight of their heroes and heroines, the crowd would turn demoniac. Some little gesture, either too pleasing or too offensive, would start it moving

and then nothing but machine guns would stop
40 it. Individually the purpose of its members might simply be to get a souvenir, but collectively it would grab and rend.

A young man with a portable microphone was describing the scene. His rapid, hysterical
45 voice was like that of a revivalist preacher whipping his congregation toward the ecstasy of fits.

"What a crowd folks! What a crowd! There must be ten thousand excited, screaming fans
50 outside Kahn's Persian tonight. The police can't hold them. Here, listen to them roar."

—Excerpted from *The Day of the Locust* by Nathanael West, 1939

1. How did the police treat an arrested person after he was separated from the crowd?

   (1) carefully
   (2) gently
   (3) good-naturedly
   (4) jokingly
   (5) violently

2. What is the purpose of the second and third paragraphs?

   To describe
   (1) the movement of the crowd
   (2) Tod's observations of the scene
   (3) the personalities of the policemen
   (4) the effects of a woman's dropping oranges
   (5) the physical appearance of individuals in the crowd

3. According to the passage, which of the following words best describes Tod's feeling toward the crowd?

   (1) excitement
   (2) surprise
   (3) resentment
   (4) fright
   (5) admiration

4. Toward the end of the passage Tod describes the voice of a young man, saying "His rapid, hysterical voice was like that of a revivalist preacher whipping his congregation toward the ecstasy of fits" (lines 44–47). Why does the author use this comparison?

To show that the man
(1) has strong religious convictions
(2) is rehearsing the role of a preacher
(3) enjoys listening to sermons
(4) speaks in an agitated and manipulative manner
(5) wants to lead a congregation

5. In this excerpt, who is telling the story?

(1) Tod
(2) an outside narrator
(3) the man with the microphone
(4) a policeman
(5) a movie star

6. Which statement best expresses the theme of the passage?

(1) When controlling a crowd, police should practice nonviolence.
(2) When a crowd turns into a mob, people lose their individual identities.
(3) Hollywood celebrities like their fans to show devotion.
(4) Law and order at outdoor events should be strictly enforced.
(5) Cities should put extra police on duty when large crowds gather.

7. Where else would the crowd behavior described in this passage be likely to occur?

(1) at a zoo
(2) during a rock concert
(3) in an amusement park
(4) during a religious gathering
(5) at a trade show

Questions 8–12 refer to the following excerpt from a novel.

WHAT DOES PIP NOTICE ABOUT MISS HAVISHAM?

She was dressed in rich materials—satins, and lace, and silks—all of white. Her shoes were white. And she had a long white veil dependent from her
5 hair, and she had bridal flowers in her hair, but her hair was white. Some bright jewels sparkled on her neck and on her hands, and some other jewels lay sparkling on the table. Dresses, less splendid than the dress she wore, and half-packed trunks,
10 were scattered about. She had not quite finished dressing, for she had but one shoe on—the other was on the table near her hand—her veil was but half arranged, her watch and chain were not put on, and some lace for her bosom lay with those
15 trinkets, and with her handkerchief, and gloves, and some flowers, and a Prayer-book, all confusedly heaped about the looking-glass.

It was not in the first few moments that I saw all these things, though I saw more of them in
20 the first moments than might be supposed. But, I saw that everything within my view which ought to be white, had been white long ago, and had lost its lustre, and was faded and yellow. I saw that the bride within the bridal dress had
25 withered like the dress, and like the flowers, and had no brightness left but the brightness of her sunken eyes. I saw that the dress had been put upon the rounded figure of a young woman, and that the figure upon which it now hung loose,
30 had shrunk to skin and bone. . . .

"Who is it?" said the lady at the table.

"Mr. Pumblechook's boy, ma'am. Come—to play."

"Come nearer; let me look at you. Come
35 close."

It was when I stood before her, avoiding her eyes, that I took note of surrounding objects in detail, and saw that her watch had stopped at twenty minutes to nine, and that a clock in the
40 room had stopped at twenty minutes to nine.

—Excerpted from *Great Expectations* by Charles Dickens, 1861

8. Where does the scene take place?

(1) in a parlor
(2) in a living room
(3) in a bedroom
(4) in an attic
(5) in an enclosed porch

9. In this excerpt, how does the author reveal the character of Miss Havisham?

(1) by analyzing her relationship with Pip
(2) by summarizing events from her past
(3) by describing her physical appearance and surroundings
(4) by detailing the reasons for her behavior
(5) by presenting her opinion of herself

10. From lines 1–8 what can you conclude about Miss Havisham?

That she is
(1) wealthy
(2) embarrassed
(3) nervous
(4) beautiful
(5) greedy

11. What do the descriptive details in lines 22–25, suggest about the atmosphere of the setting?

It is one of
(1) decay
(2) disappointment
(3) loneliness
(4) frustration
(5) desperation

12. Later in the novel, we learn that Miss Havisham had been jilted by her lover years before this scene.

What does this information reveal about Miss Havisham's nature?

That Miss Havisham
(1) had stopped waiting for her fiancé to return
(2) thought that Pip was her long-lost love
(3) hoped that Pip would introduce her to Mr. Pumblechook
(4) suffered extreme emotional distress after being jilted
(5) profited financially since being abandoned at the altar

Questions 13–18 refer to the following excerpt from an essay.

WHAT DOES AN AUTHOR SAY ABOUT WRITING?

As I wrote I followed, almost unconsciously, many principles of the novel which my reading of the novels of other writers had made me feel were necessary for the building of a well-
5 constructed book. For the most part the novel is rendered in the present; I wanted the reader to feel that Bigger's story was happening now, like a play upon the stage or a movie unfolding upon the screen. Action follows action, as in a
10 prize fight. Wherever possible, I told of Bigger's life in close-up, slow-motion, giving the feel of the grain in the passing of time. I had long had the feeling that this was the best way to "enclose" the reader's mind in a new world, to
15 blot out all reality except that which I was giving him.

Then again, as much as I could, I restricted the novel to what Bigger saw and felt, to the limits of his feeling and thoughts, even when I
20 was conveying *more* than that to the reader. I had the notion that such a manner of rendering made for a sharper effect, a more pointed sense of the character, his peculiar type of being and

consciousness. Throughout there is but one
25 point of view: Bigger's. This, too, I felt, made for
a richer illusion of reality.

I kept out of the story as much as possible,
for I wanted the reader to feel that there was
nothing between him and Bigger; that the story
30 was a special *première* given in his own private
theater.

I kept the scenes long, made as much
happen within a short space of time as possible;
all of which, I felt, made for greater density and
35 richness of effect.

In a like manner I tried to keep a unified
sense of background throughout the story; the
background would change, of course, but I tried
to keep before the eyes of the reader at all
40 times the forces and elements against which
Bigger was striving.

—Excerpted from "How Bigger Was Born" in the
introduction to *Native Son* by Richard Wright, 1940

13. How does Bigger's story resemble a
prizefight?

(1) Action follows action in the novel.
(2) Bigger constantly faces conflicts.
(3) Bigger often resorts to physical violence.
(4) Bigger is in a win-lose situation.
(5) Bigger competes with other characters.

14. From whose point of view is the novel told?

(1) an outside narrator's
(2) another character's
(3) Bigger's
(4) a spectator's
(5) a movie director's

15. How would you describe the author's
approach to writing?

(1) disorganized
(2) inflexible
(3) deliberate
(4) relaxed
(5) illogical

16. Why does the author want the reader to feel
that "the story was a special *première* given
in his own private theater" (lines 29-31)?

So that the reader can
(1) pretend to own his or her own
playhouse
(2) feel that he or she experiences Bigger's
life
(3) evaluate the story the way a critic might
(4) know what it's like to be important
(5) enjoy the novel in privacy

17. Which of the following phrases best sums up
the content of the excerpt?

(1) similarities between plays and novels
(2) approaches to reading a novel
(3) techniques of novel writing
(4) influences of movies on novel writing
(5) methods for analyzing character

18. If Bigger were real rather than fictional,
which of the following writers would be
most likely to tell his story?

(1) a poet
(2) a movie reviewer
(3) a journalist
(4) a playwright
(5) a songwriter

Answers are on pages 334–335.

Poetry

As you learned in Chapter 6 on prose fiction, the language of poetry distinguishes it from fiction, nonfiction, and drama. Poetry employs fewer words to convey its message, its emotion, or its description. It also employs language that includes the following:

- Similes

- Metaphors

- Personification

However, on the GED Language Arts, Reading Test, you *will not be asked* the term for the technical language used by a poet. You *will be asked* to state the comparison or the poet's purpose in using figurative language.

All writing has a purpose: to communicate facts, observations, opinions, or emotions. For instance, the purpose of newspaper articles is to convey facts about daily events. The journalist's responsibility is to report a truthful and precise account of an incident.

On September 16, 1963, a dynamite explosion in the Sixteenth Street Baptist Church in Birmingham, Alabama, killed four young African American girls. The following excerpt from a news story highlights important details about the incident:

> The four girls killed in the blast had just heard Mrs. Ella C. Demand, their teacher, complete the Sunday School lesson for the day. The subject was "The Love That Forgives."
>
> During the period between the class and an assembly in the main auditorium, they went to the women's lounge in the basement at the northeast corner of the church.
>
> The blast occurred at about 10:25 A.M.
>
> Church members said they found the girls huddled together beneath a pile of masonry debris.
>
> —Excerpted from "Four Negro Girls Killed in Birmingham Church Bombing,"
> *New York Times*

Dudley Randall, a poet, told the story of the bombing in a poem. The events he chose to include in the story are quite different from those reported in the news story. He relates an imaginary conversation between a mother and her daughter, one of the four victims. In his interpretation, the mother mistakenly assumes that going to church is safer than marching in a civil rights demonstration. The poet, unlike the journalist, is not obliged to report the actual circumstances of an event. Often poets are more interested in conveying emotional truths than in reporting facts. Randall's poem, "Ballad of Birmingham," illustrates how poets see real-life experiences in original and imaginative ways.

As you study the poem, compare and contrast its content, style, and structure with those of the newspaper story of the bombing. The comments in the right-hand column will help to guide your reading.

Ballad of Birmingham	Title of the poem
(On the Bombing of a Church in Birmingham, Alabama, 1963)	Poet's reason for writing the poem
"Mother dear, may I go downtown Instead of out to play, And march the streets of Birmingham In a Freedom March today?"	*Stanza 1:* Daughter's spoken words Daughter asks to attend the civil rights demonstration.
5 "No, baby, no, you may not go, For the dogs are fierce and wild, And clubs and hoses, guns and jail Aren't good for a little child."	*Stanza 2:* Mother's spoken words Mother gives reasons for her refusal.
"But, mother, I won't be alone. 10 Other children will go with me, And march the streets of Birmingham To make our country free."	*Stanza 3:* Daughter's spoken words Daughter tries to change her mother's mind.
"No, baby, no, you may not go, For I fear those guns will fire. 15 But you may go to church instead And sing in the children's choir."	*Stanza 4:* Mother's spoken words Mother again denies her daughter's request.
She has combed and brushed her night- dark hair, And bathed rose petal sweet, And drawn white gloves on her small brown hands 20 And white shoes on her feet.	*Stanza 5:* Daughter's physical appearance Mother dresses her daughter.
The mother smiled to know her child Was in the sacred place, But that smile was the last smile To come upon her face.	*Stanza 6:* Mother's feelings Hints suggest that a tragic event will occur.
25 For when she heard the explosion, Her eyes grew wet and wild. She raced through the streets of Birmingham Calling for her child.	*Stanza 7:* Mother's response to the explosion Mother looks for her daughter.
She clawed through bits of glass and brick, 30 Then lifted out a shoe. "O here's the shoe my baby wore, But, baby, where are you?"	*Stanza 8:* Mother's actions and spoken words Mother discovers that her daughter is dead.

—Dudley Randall

Compare some of the characteristics of the newspaper article and the poem. The following chart analyzes the major differences.

Characteristics	Newspaper Article	"Ballad of Birmingham"
Visual Appearance and Arrangement of Word on the Page	Groups sentences into paragraphs	Divides sentences into lines. Four lines are clustered together to form a unit called a stanza.
Sound of the Words	Prose style No rhyme	In the second and fourth lines of each stanza, the last word rhymes. The rhyming words produce a musical effect.
Author's Purpose	To inform the reader	To affect the reader emotionally
Style of Language	Simple, direct statements Examples: "The blast occurred at about 10:25 A.M." "Church members said they found the girls huddled together beneath a pile of masonry debris."	Descriptive language that creates vivid images Examples: "Her eyes grew wet and wild." "She clawed through bits of glass and brick."

Characteristics of Poetry

The observations in the chart can help you form generalizations about poetry. Here are some common characteristics of poems:

- Sentences are divided into lines. Sometimes lines are grouped into stanzas.

- The sounds and sequence of words produce a musical effect.

- Descriptive language, both literal and figurative, creates striking images that may affect the reader emotionally.

- Like the tone of a voice, the tone of a poem reveals the speaker's feelings and attitudes about a subject.

- Poetry imaginatively portrays a wide range of subjects, including both serious topics and everyday experiences and observations.

EXERCISE 1

Directions: Reread the poem "Ballad of Birmingham." Then answer the following questions.

1. The last words in the even-numbered lines of each stanza rhyme. In the spaces provided, write the eight pairs of rhyming words.

Lines 2 and 4:

_____

_____

Lines 6 and 8:

_____

_____

Lines 10 and 12:

_____

_____

Lines 14 and 16:

_____

_____

Lines 18 and 20:

_____

_____

Lines 22 and 24:

_____

_____

Lines 26 and 28:

_____

_____

Lines 30 and 32:

_____

_____

2. Write the specific line or lines from the poem that support(s) each of the following statements:

(1) The streets of Birmingham, Alabama, were dangerous.

_____

_____

_____

(2) The mother was crying.

_____

_____

_____

(3) The mother searched for her daughter at the church.

_____

_____

_____

(4) The mother found evidence that her daughter was dead.

_____

_____

_____

3. Read the following statements. Circle *T* if the statement is true or *F* if it is false.

T F (1) The poet directly states his personal reaction to the bombing.

T F (2) The poem suggests that the girl would have lived if she had attended the "Freedom March."

T F (3) The poet reveals the mother's grief and horror.

T F (4) The words and rhythm of the poem are similar to those of a song.

Answers are on page 335.

WRITING ACTIVITY 1

Find a newspaper article that affects you emotionally. On a separate sheet of paper, write a poem about the story. Imagine the people who were involved in the incident. To make an interesting poem, add descriptive details not reported in the original article. Experiment with different ways of arranging the words on the page.

Answers will vary.

Suggestions for Reading Poetry

How should you read a poem? Two modern poets offer the following advice:

> The best way to begin is by reading the poem several times to get used to the style. After you get a sense of the whole poem, there are some things you can do to help yourself understand anything that's unclear—if anything still is unclear, which often it won't be. There may be a word or two you don't understand, or a reference to a person or a place that you're not familiar with. These you can look up in a dictionary or encyclopedia or ask someone about. There may be a sentence that's so long it's hard to follow, or a sentence that's left incomplete; words may be in an unusual order, or a sentence may be hard to see because it's divided into different lines. For these problems, just go through the poem slowly, seeing where the different sentences begin and end. If you understand part of a poem and not another part, try to use what you do understand to help you see what the rest means.

> —Excerpted from *Sleeping on the Wing* by Kenneth Koch and Kate Farrell

On the following lines, write four suggestions that Koch and Farrell make for reading a poem:

1. _____
2. _____
3. _____
4. _____

Did you include some of these major points?

- Read the poem several times to get accustomed to the poet's style—the way he or she uses language.

- Look up unfamiliar words, places, or people in a dictionary or an encyclopedia.

- Read the poem slowly. Notice where sentences begin and end. (Note: A period usually marks the end of a complete sentence. In some poems, the first word of each line is capitalized. Don't assume that the capitalization signals the beginning of a new sentence.)

- Apply what you already understand about part of the poem to the parts that seem more difficult.

In addition to these suggestions, here are a few more guidelines:

- Read the poem aloud. Listen to the sound and the rhythm of the words.

- Pay attention to the title. The title may provide clues about the topic and the theme of the poem.

- Identify the speaker of the poem. Like the narrator of a short story or a novel, the **speaker** represents a person's voice. The poet invents a voice to narrate the poem. If the poem uses the pronoun *I*, don't assume that *I* refers to the poet personally.

- Grasp the literal meaning of the poem—what the poet directly tells you. Infer the suggested meaning if there is one.

When you interpret poetry, you practice all the reading skills presented in the first four chapters of this textbook. In some poems you also will find the same kinds of elements you find in fiction—for example, setting, plot, characterization, and dialogue.

EXERCISE 2

Directions: In the following poem, a Native American poet writes about a person, a place, and an event. Read the poem and answer the questions that follow.

> I lay my hand
> Upon
> The coldness of the smooth
> White stone,
> 5 My fingers touch the words,
> I read again:
> My father's name,
> Date of birth,
> Date of death,
> 10 Veteran of
> World War I.
> "This is your
> Grandfather's grave,"
> I tell my children,
> 15 Wishing I could tell them,
> That they would understand,

That the man
Who was my father,
Was of that first generation,
20 Born on old land
Newly made reservation,
That at twelve,
He went to Mission School,
To learn to wear shoes,
25 To eat with knife and fork,
To pray to the Catholic God,
To painfully
Learn English words,
English meanings,
30 White ways of thinking,
English words,
To speak,
To think,
To write,
35 English words,
When we,
My children
And I
Know no others.

—Excerpted from "Tribal Cemetery" by Janet Campbell Hale

1. What is the setting for the poem?

(1) an Indian reservation
(2) the Mission School
(3) a graveyard
(4) a funeral parlor
(5) a Catholic church

2. Who is the speaker in the poem?

(1) the father
(2) the father's daughter
(3) the grandchildren
(4) a priest
(5) a schoolteacher

3. Why is the phrase "English words" repeated three times (lines 28, 31, and 35) ?

(1) to praise the superiority of the English language
(2) to emphasize that English was a foreign language for the father to learn
(3) to show that a knowledge of English helps people find good jobs
(4) to stress the importance of studying vocabulary, speech, and grammar
(5) to demonstrate that the father was a poor student

4. How does the daughter feel about her father?

(1) proud
(2) angry
(3) disrespectful
(4) suspicious
(5) annoyed

5. The following inferences are based on statements in the poem. Write *V* if a statement is valid or *I* if it is invalid.

_____ (1) The father was honored with medals for his bravery as a soldier.

_____ (2) Beginning at the age of twelve, the father began to lose touch with his original heritage.

_____ (3) The father practiced only his native religion all his life.

_____ (4) The generations after the father are disconnected from their Native American roots.

_____ (5) The purpose of the father's training at the Mission School was to make him conform to white American culture.

_____ (6) Non-English-speaking immigrants arriving in the United States could probably identify with the father's difficulty in adapting to American society.

Answers are on pages 335–336.

Understanding the Language of Poetry

One of the most striking characteristics of poetry is its attention to language. Poetic language often appeals to the senses—sights, sounds, odors, textures, and tastes.

Poets use both literal statements and figures of speech to express sensations and ideas. In this section, you will learn how poets describe their perceptions through literal and figurative language.

Literal Descriptions

Literal descriptions can help you visualize the physical appearance of a person, place, or thing. The central purpose of purely descriptive poetry is to help you "see" a detailed image.

Use your imagination to picture the man described in the following poem:

The Runner

On a flat road runs the well-train'd runner;
He is lean and sinewy, with muscular legs;
He is thinly clothed—he leans forward as he runs,
With lightly closed fists, and arms partially rais'd.

—Walt Whitman

Can you see a clear image of the runner? Reread the poem and write the specific words or phrases that answer these questions:

1. Where is the man running?

_____

2. What words describe the runner's build?

_____

_____

3. How is the runner dressed?

_____

_____

4. What pose does he strike as he runs?

_____

_____

Here are the correct responses:

1. "on a flat road"

2. "lean"; "sinewy"; "muscular legs"

3. "thinly clothed"

4. "leans forward"; "lightly closed fists"; "arms partially rais'd"

The total effect of these descriptive details creates a vivid portrait of a runner. The words produce an image as distinct as a snapshot.

WRITING ACTIVITY 2

Study the photograph below. On a separate sheet of paper, write a short poem in which you re-create the image of the athletes through descriptive words and phrases. Use Walt Whitman's poem "The Runner" as a model.

Answers will vary.

More Practice with Descriptions

In the preceding poem, Walt Whitman directly conveys what the runner looks like. He offers no comments about the runner's personality. However, you can infer that the poet admires the runner's physical appearance and athletic ability.

As you already know from reading fiction, a character's physical appearance and actions often reveal his or her personality. In the next excerpt from a poem, the speaker describes a migrant worker. Circle the words and phrases that create a picture in your head.

> Calloused hands and sun-chapped skin
> in the fields of ripened harvest
> awakening the dawn
> returning not 'till the sun came down
> 5 The aroma of tossed-up dirt
> fertile soil on your boots
> a familiar scent of labor
> though fatigued and dismayed
> 10 the battle remained within

—Excerpted from "Apa" by Rosalinda Hernandez

You can infer that the subject of this poem is a hard worker. Why? Write the descriptive details that support this inference.

_____

_____

_____

_____

_____

_____

The stanza reveals the worker's labor in the fields. Hard work has calloused the hands, and long hours in the sun have weathered the face. The laborer works from morning until night in soil that clings to the clothes and boots. The worker's sweat and the dirt combine to create the "familiar scent of labor." The words "fatigued and dismayed" in line 8 indicate that the person works a full day to the point of exhaustion. The literal descriptions in the poem provide you with clues about the worker's character. Although this person is a laborer in the fields, the individual values the contribution of a day's labor.

EXERCISE 3

Directions: Read the poem and answer the questions that follow.

The Great Figure

Among the rain
and lights
I saw the figure 5
in gold
on a red
firetruck
moving
tense
unheeded
to gong clangs
siren howls
and wheels rumbling
through the dark city.

—William Carlos Williams

1. What is the focus of the speaker's attention?

    _____

2. In what place did this observation occur?

    _____

3. What does the speaker use the word *tense* to describe?

    (1) the falling of the rain
    (2) the movement of the fire truck
    (3) the victims of the fire
    (4) the firefighter's attitude
    (5) his feelings of uneasiness

4. Copy three descriptions from the poem that refer to sound.

    _____

    _____

    _____

Answers are on page 336.

Figurative Language

Poets also rely on figurative language to describe observations, ideas, and feelings. Recall that figures of speech are comparisons—direct or implied—between two different things. When you read a figure of speech, it helps to visualize the two images being compared. Picturing them in your mind will help you understand the purpose of the comparison.

In this section you will study three types of figurative language—simile, metaphor, and personification. On the GED Language Arts, Reading Test, you will be asked to interpret the meaning of such figures of speech. You will *not* have to identify the figures of speech by name.

Simile and Metaphor

A direct comparison using the words *as, like,* and *than* is called a **simile**.

> O, my luve is like a red, red rose
>
> —Robert Burns

> two socks as soft as rabbits
>
> —Pablo Neruda

> How sharper than a serpent's tooth it is
> To have a thankless child.
>
> —William Shakespeare

A **metaphor**, or implied comparison, states that something *is* something else. The words *as, like,* and *than* are not used in a metaphor.

> You ain't nothin' but a hound dog.
>
> —Jerry Leiber and Mike Stoller

If the lyrics Elvis Presley made famous had read "You act like a hound dog," the comparison would have been a simile. But the comparison is a metaphor because it is implied, not stated directly.

In the following poem, the poet uses five similes and one metaphor to explain the effects of a postponed dream. Read the poem carefully and identify these six figures of speech.

Dream Deferred

What happens to a dream deferred?

Does it dry up
like a raisin in the sun?
Or fester like a sore—
And then run?
Does it stink like rotten meat?
Or crust and sugar over—
like a syrupy sweet?
Maybe it just sags
like a heavy load.

Or does it explode?

—Langston Hughes

A dream deferred is like (*similes*):

1. _____

2. _____

3. _____

4. _____

5. _____

In the last line the speaker implies that a dream deferred is a (*metaphor*):

6. _____

    Did you state that the speaker directly compares "a dream deferred" to
(1) a raisin, (2) a sore, (3) rotten meat, (4) a sweet, and (5) a heavy load?
The concluding line of the poem implies a metaphor. From the word *explodes*,
you can assume that "a dream deferred" *is* a bomb, not is *like* a bomb.

    Did you notice that through these figures of speech, the speaker of the
poem conveys his frustration over having the fulfillment of a dream delayed?
The final metaphor—an exploding bomb—illustrates a violent reaction.

Personification

A figure of speech that represents nonliving things as humans or animals is called **personification**. In the following example, the poet shows the sun speaking like a person. Like a real human being, the sun reveals its personality through dialogue. As you read the excerpt, think about the personality the poet has created for the sun.

> The Sun woke me this morning loud
> and clear, saying "Hey I've been
> trying to wake you up for fifteen
> minutes. Don't be so rude, you are
> 5 only the second poet I've ever chosen
> to speak to personally
>   so why
> aren't you more attentive? If I could
> burn you through the window I would
> 10 to wake you up. I can't hang around
> here all day."
>   "Sorry, Sun, I stayed
> up late last night talking to Hal."

—Excerpted from "A True Account of Talking to the Sun at Fire Island" by Frank O'Hara

Which word best describes the sun's behavior as it is revealed in its remarks to the speaker?

(1) apologetic

(2) polite

(3) sleepy

(4) impatient

(5) shy

You were correct if you said *impatient*. Examine the clues that support this inference. The sun has been trying to wake up the poet for fifteen minutes. In lines 10–11, the sun states, "I can't hang around / here all day." From these details you can conclude that the sun is expressing its impatience.

Why might the poet have chosen to personify the sun? Portraying the sun as an impatient person is a good way to communicate what it is like to be awakened prematurely by the bright morning light.

WRITING ACTIVITY 3

What would a tree full of birds say if it could talk? What would the first flower of spring say? the last leaf of autumn? Using the Frank O'Hara excerpt as a model, create a brief conversation between you and a tree, a flower, a leaf, or another nonhuman object, living or not living. Write your conversation in paragraph form on a separate sheet of paper.

Answers will vary.

EXERCISE 4

In this exercise you will read two versions of a poem. In Version 1, you will read the poem in its original format. In Version 2, you will read the same lines of poetry in the balloons of a comic strip. Notice how the comic-strip version uses illustrations to show the poetic images and figures of speech.

Directions: After you study the two versions, answer the questions that follow.

Version 1

I Wandered Lonely as a Cloud

I wandered lonely as a cloud
That floats on high o'er vales and hills,
When all at once I saw a crowd,
A host, of golden daffodils,
5 Beside the lake, beneath the trees,
Fluttering and dancing in the breeze.

Continuous as the stars that shine
And twinkle on the milky way,
They stretched in never-ending line
10 Along the margin of a bay:
Ten thousand saw I at a glance,
Tossing their heads in sprightly dance.

The waves beside them danced; but they
Out-did the sparkling waves in glee:
15 A poet could not but be gay,
In such a jocund company:
I gazed—and gazed—but little thought
What wealth the show to me had brought:

For oft, when on my couch I lie
20 In vacant or in pensive mood,
They flash upon that inward eye
Which is the bliss of solitude;
And then my heart with pleasure fills,
And dances with the daffodils.

—William Wordsworth, 1804

Version 2

1. From what viewpoint does the speaker of the poem observe nature?

    From that of
    (1) a flower
    (2) a cloud
    (3) a hill
    (4) the wind
    (5) the lake

2. To what does the poet compare the arrangement of the daffodils in the second stanza?

    (1) stars in the Milky Way
    (2) waves in the ocean
    (3) leaves on a tree
    (4) grass on a hillside
    (5) ballerinas in a performance

3. In which of the following descriptions does the poet attribute human traits to something nonhuman?

    (1) "I saw . . . daffodils/Beside the lake, beneath the trees
    (2) "[The line of daffodils was as] continuous as the stars that shine"
    (3) "[The daffodils] stretched in never-ending line"
    (4) "Ten thousand [daffodils] saw I at a glance"
    (5) "[The daffodils were] tossing their heads in sprightly dance"

4. Which of the following words best describes the speaker's feelings about nature?

    (1) negative
    (2) indifferent
    (3) joyous
    (4) respectful
    (5) critical

Answers are on page 336.

The Subjects of Poetry

What kinds of subjects attract poets' attention? Poets imaginatively portray a wide variety of subjects, from the tragic to the humorous, from the unusual to the ordinary.

In this section you will study poems on four different subjects—family relationships, love, a person's work, and memories. Answer the questions after each poem to develop your skills in interpreting poetry.

EXERCISE 5

Directions: Read the following excerpt from a poem. Notice how the speaker in the poem portrays the members of her family. Then answer the questions that follow.

My sister in her well-tailored silk blouse hands me
the photo of my father
in naval uniform and white hat.
I say, "Oh, this is the one which Mama used to have on her dresser."

5 My sister controls her face and furtively looks at my mother,
a sad rag bag of a woman, lumpy and sagging everywhere,
like a mattress at the Salvation Army, though with no holes or tears,
and says, "No."

I look again,
10 and see that my father is wearing a wedding ring,
which he never did
when he lived with my mother. And that there is a legend on it,
"To my dearest wife,
        Love
15   Chief"
And I realize the photo must have belonged to his second wife,
whom he left our mother to marry.

—Excerpted from "The Photos" by Diane Wakoski

1. List the five family members referred to in the poem.

   _____

   _____

   _____

   _____

   _____

2. To what does the speaker compare her mother in line 6?

   _____

   _____

3. To what does the speaker compare her mother in line 7?

   _____

   _____

4. In lines 10–15, what object does the speaker notice in her father's photograph? What does this object tell you about both his marriages?

   _____

   _____

5. In a few sentences, summarize the content of this poem in your own words.

   _____

   _____

   _____

   _____

   _____

Answers are on page 336.

EXERCISE 6

Directions: In the following excerpt from a love poem, the poet expresses his feelings about a woman. The word *you* in the poem refers to the woman the speaker loves. As you read the poem, pay attention to the poet's awareness of her physical appearance. Then answer the questions that follow.

Shiny record albums scattered over
the livingroom floor, reflecting light
from the lamp, sharp reflections that hurt
my eyes as I watch you, squatting among the platters,
5 the beer foam making mustaches on your lips.

And, too,
the shadows on your cheeks from your long lashes
fascinate me—almost as much as the dimples:
in your cheeks, your arms and your legs:
10 dimples . . . dimples . . . dimples . . .

You
hum along with Mathis—how you love Mathis!
with his burnished hair and quicksilver voice that dances
among the stars and whirls through canyons
15 like windblown snow. Sometimes I think that Mathis
could take you from me if you could be complete
without me. I glance at my watch. It is now time.

—Excerpted from "As You Leave Me" by Etheridge Knight

1. Where is the woman?

_____

2. What objects are scattered around her?

_____

3. Why does the poet repeat the word *dimples* three times in line 10?

_____

4. Why does the poet imagine that he is jealous of popular singer Johnny Mathis?

_____

_____

5. Why does the poet say that Mathis's voice "dances / among the stars and whirls through canyons / like windblown snow"?

In order to
(1) suggest that Mathis's reputation as a singer is overblown
(2) show that Mathis is a star who has reached the height of his career
(3) compare the power of Mathis's voice to a violent blizzard
(4) describe the rhythm, the softness, and the beauty of Mathis's voice
(5) suggest that Mathis howls and whistles when he sings

Answers are on page 336.

EXERCISE 7

Directions: The following poem describes a man performing his job. As you read, picture the man and his actions. Then answer the questions that follow.

Hay for the Horses

He had driven half the night
From far down San Joaquin
Through Mariposa, up the
Dangerous mountain roads,
5 And pulled in at eight A.M.
With his big truckload of hay
    behind the barn.
With winch and ropes and hooks
We stacked the bales up clean
10 To splintery redwood rafters
High in the dark, flecks of alfalfa
Whirling through shingle-cracks of light,
Itch of haydust in the
    sweaty shirt and shoes.
15 At lunchtime under Black oak
Out in the hot corral,
—The old mare nosing lunchpails,
Grasshoppers crackling in the weeds—
"I'm sixty-eight," he said,
20 "I first bucked hay when I was seventeen.
I thought, that day I started,
I sure would hate to do this all my life.
And dammit, that's just what
I've gone and done."

—Gary Snyder

1. According to the poem the man began stacking hay at
   _____ and took a break at

   _____

2. What two images from the poem describe a texture (how something feels)?

   _____

   _____

3. What image from the poem describes a sound?

   _____

4. How old was the man when he first bucked hay? _____

   How old is he now? _____

5. How did the man originally feel about doing this job?

   _____

Answers are on page 336.

 Go to **www.GEDReading.com** for additional practice and instruction!

WRITING ACTIVITY 4

In this exercise you will be writing a poem about memories. The following excerpt is from a book-length poem. Joe Brainard, the poet, lists his memories. As the excerpt illustrates, each line of the poem begins with the words "I remember," followed by an image.

> I remember that Eskimos kiss with their noses. (?)
>
> I remember that the only friends my parents had who owned a swimming pool also owned a funeral parlor.
>
> I remember laundromats at night all lit up with nobody in them.
>
> I remember a very clean Catholic book-gift shop with practically nothing in it to buy.
>
> I remember rearranging boxes of candy so it would look like not so much was missing.
>
> I remember brown and white shoes with little decorative holes cut out of them.
>
> I remember certain group gatherings that are hard to get up and leave from.
>
> I remember alligators and quicksand in jungle movies. (Pretty scary)
>
> —Excerpted from "I Remember" by Joe Brainard

Using the poem as a model, write your own poem on a separate sheet of paper. List memorable experiences and observations. Your poem may or may not rhyme. Here are some ideas to write about:

- TV shows
- Hollywood films
- movie stars
- fashion styles
- relatives
- friends
- objects
- places
- vacations

Answers will vary.

Chapter Review

Directions: Read each poem below and choose the best answer to the questions that follow.

Questions 1–8 refer to the following excerpt from a poem.

WHAT KIND OF PERSON IS FLICK?

Flick stands tall among the idiot pumps—
Five on a side, the old bubble-head style,
Their rubber elbows hanging loose and low.
One's nostrils are two S's, and his eyes
5 An E and O. And one is squat, without
A head at all—more of a football type.

Once, Flick played for the high school team,
the Wizards.
He was good: in fact, the best. In '46,
10 He bucketed three hundred ninety points,
A county record still. The ball loved Flick.
I saw him rack up thirty-eight or forty
In one home game. His hands were like
wild birds.

15 He never learned a trade; he just sells gas,
Checks oil, and changes flats. Once in a
while,
As a gag, he dribbles an inner tube,
But most of us remember anyway.
20 His hands are fine and nervous on the
lug wrench.
It makes no difference to the lug
wrench, though.

Off work, he hangs around Mae's
25 Luncheonette.
Grease-grey and kind of coiled, he plays
pinball,
Sips lemon cokes, and smokes those thin
cigars;
30 Flick seldom speaks to Mae, just sits and
nods
Beyond her face towards the bright
applauding tiers
Of Necco Wafers, Nibs, and Juju Beads.

—Excerpted from "Ex-Basketball Player"
by John Updike, 1957

1. How does Flick currently earn his living?

   As a
   (1) car salesman
   (2) professional basketball player
   (3) busboy and cook
   (4) high school coach
   (5) gas station attendant

2. What is the poet describing in the phrase "rubber elbows hanging loose and low" (line 3)?

   (1) an auto mechanic's tools
   (2) the hoses on the gas pumps
   (3) the stance of a football player
   (4) Flick's long, flexible arms
   (5) Flick's injured elbows

3. What is the main idea expressed in lines 7–14?

   (1) Flick scored 390 points during the 1946 season.
   (2) Flick's high school team was named the Wizards.
   (3) Fans applauded Flick's athletic performance.
   (4) Flick was an outstanding high school basketball player.
   (5) Flick broke a county record.

4. What is the purpose of the comparison "His hands were like wild birds" (line 12)?

   To show that Flick
   (1) seemed to fly on the basketball court
   (2) was an aggressive basketball player
   (3) lacked control in making jump shots
   (4) lapped and waved his hands
   (5) quickly and agilely handled the basketball

5. What can you conclude is the major point of the third stanza?

That Flick
(1) skillfully uses a lug wrench
(2) misses playing basketball
(3) pretends the inner tube is a basketball
(4) has fans who remember his achievements
(5) likes to amuse himself at work

6. What is the underlying purpose of the poem?

To show
(1) that a high school athlete's fame is often short-lived
(2) that untrained people are stuck in boring jobs
(3) how high schools develop their students' talents
(4) how teenagers choose their careers
(5) why fans admire athletes

7. Which of the following magazines would be most likely to publish an article about high school graduates whose situation is similar to Flick's?

(1) *Personal Computing*
(2) *Sports Illustrated*
(3) *Car and Driver Magazine*
(4) *Science Digest*
(5) *Business Week*

8. The author wrote a novel in which his main character, "Rabbit" Angstrom, relived his days as a basketball star while failing as an adult to accept his responsibilities as a husband, father, and worker.

What similarity can you infer exists between Flick and Rabbit?

They are both
(1) unsuccessful professional basketball players
(2) successful businessmen
(3) adults who never grew up emotionally
(4) grownups who learned from their youthful mistakes
(5) individuals who married too young

Questions 9–14 refer to the following poem.

WHAT DO YOU LEARN ABOUT RICHARD CORY?

Richard Cory

Whenever Richard Cory went down town,
We people on the pavement looked at him:
He was a gentleman from sole to crown,
Clean favored, and imperially slim.

5 And he was always quietly arrayed,
And he was always human when he talked;
But still he fluttered pulses when he said,
"Good-morning," and he glittered when he
     walked.

10 And he was rich—yes, richer than a king—
And admirably schooled in every grace:

In fine, we thought that he was everything
To make us wish that we were in his place.

So on we worked, and waited for the light,
15 And went without the meat, and cursed the
     bread;

And Richard Cory, one calm summer night,
Went home and put a bullet through his
     head.

—Edwin Arlington Robinson, 1897

9. Who are "we people" (line 2)?

(1) the wealthy and satisfied
(2) the poor and hardworking
(3) the lazy and unemployed
(4) the middle-class and successful
(5) the concerned and politically active

10. What event occurs at the end of the poem?

Richard Corey
(1) is assassinated
(2) receives a death threat
(3) dies of natural causes
(4) dies in an accidental shooting
(5) commits suicide

11. What can you infer from Richard Cory's actions?

That he
(1) resents the townspeople
(2) knows he is going bankrupt
(3) conceals serious personal problems
(4) behaves like a coward
(5) wishes he had closer friends

12. What is meant by the phrase *waited for the light* (line 14)?

The people
(1) hoped for better times
(2) wanted new lamps
(3) looked forward to the sunrise
(4) expected an inheritance
(5) prayed for sparkling jewels

13. What would the title be if the major theme of the poem were stated as the title of a magazine article?

(1) "People Learn to Cope with Poverty"
(2) "Society Frowns on Suicide"
(3) "Wealth Impresses People"
(4) "Money Doesn't Ensure Happiness"
(5) "People Reveal Their True Feelings"

14. Many of the poet's characters are social outcasts, misunderstood and confused people who doubt their own value and lead unhappy lives.

From this information, what can you infer was the reaction of the townspeople at the end of the poem?

(1) They wished that they had been aware of his problems.
(2) They were angry about his selfish actions.
(3) They felt unsympathetic because of his gifts.
(4) They were not surprised because he was so quiet.
(5) They believed that his family should have known.

Questions 15–20 refer to the following poem.

WHAT IS IT LIKE TO HOE AN ONION FIELD?

Daybreak

In this moment when the light starts up
In the east and rubs
The horizon until it catches fire,

We enter the fields to hoe,
5   Row after row, among the small flags of
        onion,
Waving off the dragonflies
That ladder the air.

And tears the onions raise
Do not begin in your eyes but in ours,
10 In the salt blown
From one blister into another;

They begin in knowing
You will never waken to hear
The hour timed to a heart beat,
15 The wind pressing us closer to the ground.

When the season ends,
And the onions are unplugged from their
        sleep,
We won't forget what you failed to see,
20 And nothing will heal
Under the rain's broken fingers.

—Gary Soto, 1977

15. What is described in the first stanza?

(1) a campfire
(2) an early sunrise
(3) a blazing field
(4) a person striking a match
(5) a forest fire

16. What is signaled by the break between stanza 4 (lines 12–15) and stanza 5 (lines 16–20)?

A change in
(1) topic, from the present situation to a prediction about the future
(2) rhyme, from one pattern to another
(3) speakers, from a farm worker to the owner of a farm
(4) tone, from loud and angry to quiet and forgiving
(5) setting, from an onion field to a farmhouse

17. What image is suggested in lines 10–11?

(1) the heat forming blisters on the soil
(2) insects creating blisters on the onion's surface
(3) the intensity of the hot sun
(4) the onion pickers' emotional wounds
(5) the painful, blistered hands of the onion pickers

18. What is the meaning of the figure of speech, "And the onions are unplugged from their sleep" (line 17)?

(1) The onions look like electrical sockets.
(2) The farm workers are drowsy.
(3) The onions are uprooted from the soil.
(4) The onions are dead.
(5) Electrical machines pick the onions.

19. What is described by the phrase "the rain's broken fingers" in line 20?

The way the raindrops
(1) brutally strike the ground
(2) form huge puddles
(3) damage the onion crop
(4) beat on the farm workers' heads
(5) soak into the soft earth

20. What is the purpose of the poem?

To reveal the
(1) conflicts between farm workers
(2) beauty and splendor of nature
(3) process of picking onions
(4) hardships of the field workers
(5) characteristics of an onion field

Answers are on pages 336–337.

CHAPTER 8

Drama

You may not think of drama as a form of literature, because most plays are intended to be performed rather than read. The ideal way to experience a play is in a theater, where actors recite lines of dialogue and perform their roles in the play's events. When you watch a theatrical performance onstage, you see the story unfold before your eyes. This experience is similar to viewing a television show or a movie, except that there is a sense of immediacy—of being part of the action—that may be missing from TV or movies. When you watch a play, you directly witness the characters and their actions.

On the GED Language Arts, Reading Test, you will be asked questions about passages from drama. This chapter will help you acquire the reading skills needed to interpret the content of drama and analyze its elements. You will learn how to

- recognize the parts of a script

- read and interpret dialogue

- analyze elements such as setting, plot, and theme

Comparing Drama and Prose

Studying drama as a work of literature is similar to reading a short story or a novel. Playwrights and fiction writers both tell a story. They create imaginary settings in which characters act out the events of the plot. However, their methods of presentation differ.

The passages on the following pages illustrate some of the similarities and differences between drama and novels. The first excerpt is from John Steinbeck's novel *Of Mice and Men*. In the second excerpt Steinbeck rewrote the scene from the novel in play form. Study the novel version and the play version carefully. Find the similarities and differences by answering these two questions: (1) What methods of storytelling are used? (2) How do the visual appearance and arrangement of the words on the printed page differ?

Novel Version

Lennie got up on his knees and looked down at George. "Ain't we gonna have no supper?"

"Sure we are, if you gather up some dead willow sticks. I got three cans of beans in my bindle. You get a fire ready. I'll give you a
5 match when you get the sticks together. Then we'll heat the beans and have supper."

Lennie said, "I like beans with ketchup."

"Well, we ain't got no ketchup. You go get wood. An' don't you fool around. It'll be dark before long."

10 Lennie lumbered to his feet and disappeared in the brush. George lay where he was and whistled softly to himself. There were sounds of splashings down the river in the direction Lennie had taken. George stopped whistling and listened. "Poor bastard," he said softly, and then went on whistling again.

15 In a moment Lennie came crashing back through the brush. He carried one small willow stick in his hand. George sat up. "Awright," he said brusquely, "Gi'me that mouse!"

But Lennie made an elaborate pantomime of innocence. "What mouse, George? I ain't got no mouse."

20 George held out his hand. "Come on. Give it to me. You ain't puttin' nothing over."

Lennie hesitated, backed away, looked wildly at the brush line as though he contemplated running for his freedom. George said coldly, "You gonna give me that mouse or do I have to sock you?"

25 "Give you what, George?"

"You know God damn well what. I want that mouse."

Lennie reluctantly reached into his pocket. His voice broke a little. "I don't know why I can't keep it. It ain't nobody's mouse. I didn't steal it. I found it lyin' right beside the road."

30 George's hand remained outstretched imperiously. Slowly, like a terrier who doesn't want to bring a ball to its master, Lennie approached, drew back, approached again. George snapped his fingers sharply, and at the sound Lennie laid the mouse in his hand.

"I wasn't doin' nothing bad with it, George. Jus' stroking it."

35 George stood up and threw the mouse as far as he could into the darkening brush, and then he stepped to the pool and washed his hands. "You crazy fool. Don't you think I could see your feet was wet where you went acrost the river to get it?" He heard Lennie's whimpering cry and wheeled about. "Blubberin' like a baby! Jesus
40 Christ! A big guy like you." Lennie's lip quivered and tears started in his eyes. "Aw, Lennie!" George put his hand on Lennie's shoulder. "I ain't takin' it away jus' for meanness. That mouse ain't fresh, Lennie; and besides, you've broke it pettin' it. You get another mouse that's fresh and I'll let you keep it a little while."

—Excerpted from *Of Mice and Men* (novel) by John Steinbeck

Play Version

LENNIE: *[Gets up on his knees and looks down at GEORGE, plaintively.]* Ain't we gonna have no supper?

GEORGE: Sure we are. You gather up some dead willow sticks. I got three cans of beans in my bindle. I'll open 'em up while you get a
5 fire ready. We'll eat 'em cold.

LENNIE: *[Companionably.]* I like beans with ketchup.

GEORGE: Well, we ain't got no ketchup. You go get the wood, and don't you fool around none. Be dark before long. *[LENNIE lumbers to his feet and disappears into the brush. GEORGE gets out the*
10 *bean cans, opens two of them, suddenly turns his head and listens. A little sound of splashing comes from the direction that LENNIE has taken. GEORGE looks after him; shakes his head. LENNIE comes back carrying a few small willow sticks in his hand.]* All right, give me that mouse.

15 LENNIE: What, George? I ain't got no mouse.

GEORGE: *[Holding out his hand.]* Come on! Give it to me! You ain't putting nothing over. *[LENNIE hesitates, backs away, turns and looks as if he were going to run. Coldly.]* You gonna give me that mouse or do I have to take a sock at you?

20 LENNIE: Give you what, George?

GEORGE: You know goddamn well, what! I want that mouse!

LENNIE: *[Almost in tears.]* I don't know why I can't keep it. It ain't nobody's mouse. I didn't steal it! I found it layin' right beside the road. *[GEORGE snaps his fingers sharply, and LENNIE lays the*
25 *mouse in his hand.]* I wasn't doin' nothing bad with it. Just stroking it. That ain't bad.

GEORGE: *[Stands up and throws the mouse as far as he can into the brush, then he steps to the pool, and washes his hands.]* You crazy fool! Thought you could get away with it, didn't you? Don't you
30 think I could see your feet was wet where you went into the water to get it? *[LENNIE whimpers like a puppy.]* Blubbering like a baby. Jesus Christ, a big guy like you! *[LENNIE tries to control himself, but his lips quiver and his face works with effort. GEORGE puts his hand on LENNIE'S shoulder for a moment.]* Aw, Lennie, I ain't takin' it
35 away just for meanness. That mouse ain't fresh. Besides, you broke it pettin' it. You get a mouse that's fresh and I'll let you keep it a little while.

—Excerpted from *Of Mice and Men* (play) by John Steinbeck

Examine how the novel and the play present the same scene. The following chart compares and contrasts two characteristics mentioned earlier—storytelling methods and format.

How *Of Mice and Men* Is Told

Novel Version	*Play Version*
Storytelling Method An outside narrator who doesn't participate in the action tells the story. The narrator comments on the characters and describes plot details. The narrator uses past-tense verbs to show that the action has already occurred. Example: Lennie got up on his knees and looked down at George.	**Storytelling Method** No narrator is present. Instead **stage directions**—words, phrases, and sentences in italicized print and enclosed in brackets—explain to the actors what their tone of voice, facial expressions, and gestures should be. The stage directions use present-tense verbs to show that the action is happening now. Example: LENNIE: *[Gets up on his knees and looks down at GEORGE, plaintively.]*
Format Sentences are grouped into paragraphs. The characters' dialogue is enclosed in quotation marks. When the conversation switches to another speaker, a new paragraph begins. Words not enclosed in quotation marks identify the speaker, comment on the characters, or describe actions. Example: But Lennie made an elaborate pantomime of innocence. "What mouse, George? I ain't got no mouse."	**Format** The play is written in script form consisting of dialogue and stage directions. The character's dialogue appears next to his or her name. The stage directions correlate the character's speech with his or her emotions and physical movements. Stage directions also guide the actor who portrays the character. Example: LENNIE: *[With elaborate pantomime of innocence.]* What, George? I ain't got no mouse.

EXERCISE 1

Directions: Reread the play version of *Of Mice and Men* on page 251 and answer the questions below.

1. Write the stage directions that describe each of the following actions. Remember, the stage directions are italicized words enclosed in brackets.

    (1) Lennie looks as though he is about to cry.

    _____

    _____

    (2) George gets rid of the mouse.

    _____

    _____

    (3) George tries to comfort Lennie.

    _____

    _____

2. Write the dialogue that supports each of the following statements:

    (1) George says that Lennie is acting childish.

    _____

    _____

    (2) Lennie lies to George.

    _____

    _____

    (3) George knows where Lennie went to get the mouse.

    _____

    _____

3. Write *V* if a statement is valid or *I* if it is invalid.

    _____ (1) George is insensitive to Lennie's feelings.

    _____ (2) Lennie and George use formal language in their speech.

    _____ (3) George dominates Lennie.

    _____ (4) Lennie has a mental handicap.

Answers are on pages 337–338.

WRITING ACTIVITY 1

Following are two versions of a fictional scene. The first version is in story form. The second version is the same scene rewritten in the form of a play. Using the script for Excerpt 1 as a model, continue rewriting the story as a play. On a separate sheet of paper, create a play script for Excerpt 2. If you want, go one step further and create your own ending for the scene.

Story Version: Excerpt 1

Shadesha lowered her voice and said to her sister, "Did you hear something just now—something outside?"

"Not really," said Pam, matter-of-factly. "Well, I sort of heard a kind of clicking sound. Is that what you heard? It's probably just the evergreen brushing against the kitchen window. You know it's pretty windy out there tonight."

"Quiet!" whispered Shadesha, sitting up in her bed. "Listen!"

Play Version: Excerpt 1

SHADESHA: *[Lowering her voice]* Did you hear something just now—something outside?

PAM: *[Matter-of-factly]* Not really. Well, I sort of heard a kind of clicking sound. Is that what you heard? It's probably just the evergreen brushing against the kitchen window. You know, it's pretty windy out there tonight.

SHADESHA: *[Whispering, with genuine fear in her voice]* Quiet! *[SHADESHA sits up in her bed.]* Listen!

Story Version: Excerpt 2

Pam held her breath and listened intently. She heard a rattling sound, as if someone were turning the knob of the back door. Was someone testing it to see if the door was locked? "I think someone's on the back porch," she whispered to her sister.

Shadesha said in a frightened voice, "I heard it too!"

Both sisters heard the kitchen door creak as it was being opened. Then they heard the sound of muffled footsteps, as if someone were tiptoeing, trying not to be heard.

"Get up! Get out of here!" Shadesha cried. She leapt out of bed and grabbed her sister by the arm. Pam lay paralyzed with fear.

Answers will vary.

Recognizing the Parts of a Script

The excerpt from the play *Of Mice and Men* illustrates how drama tells a story in script form. This section will discuss the parts of a script in more detail. Your ability to read and interpret a play will improve once you recognize the distinctive features of a script.

Acts and Scenes: Structuring the Plot

Long plays are organized into major sections called **acts**. Sometimes acts are divided into **scenes**—specific episodes from the story set in one place and occurring during a fixed time period. For example, here is the organization of Dr. Endesha Ida Mae Holland's play *From the Mississippi Delta*.

Scenes

Act I

Scene 1 Memories

Scene 2 Ain't Baby

Scene 3 Calm, Balmy Days

Scene 4 Second Doctor Lady

Scene 5 The Delta Queen

Intermission

Act II

Scene 6 The Water Meter

Scene 7 The Whole Town's Talking

Scene 8 The Funeral

Scene 9 From the Mississippi Delta

Scene 10 A Permit to Parade

Scene 11 Letter to Alice Walker:
Request from the Mississippi Delta

When you pay attention to the shifts in acts and scenes, you may find clues about how the plot of the play is structured. Furthermore, you may also gather clues about the events or scenes that are about to unfold.

A Cast List: Introducing the Characters

The first page of most scripts lists the characters who perform in the play. As you will notice in the example that follows, the cast list includes the following information about the main characters:

• name

• age

- occupation
- physical description or personality traits

Cast

NOLA BARNES is thirty. She is a single mother who divides her time between her son and her career as a social worker. Proud and determined, she commands respect from those around her.

SAM MILLER, thirty-four, is Nola's ex-husband. A star athlete in high school, Sam relies too much on his physical strength and appearance to impress people. He is a steelworker who would like to spend more time with Nola and David.

DAVID, Nola's eleven-year-old son, is thinner and smaller than his classmates. He is working to overcome a learning disability that has slowed his progress in school. He is a loner who shares his feelings more with his tutor at school than with his father.

DWIGHT PARKS, David's tutor, is twenty-eight. He laughs easily, is a good listener, and cares more about his students than he admits. He has never met Nola, but when she comes to pick up David, Dwight watches for her by the window.

JUAN MORALES lives in Nola's building. He is seventeen and has been arrested several times for petty theft and trespassing. He has a deep scar on his chin and looks out at the world through black, expressionless eyes.

BEATRICE LUIS, Juan's grandmother, has taken care of Juan since he was a child. Now in declining health, she worries about her grandson and would like to ask Nola for help.

LUCITA

ESMERALDA

LU-KEE   } Nola and David's neighbors

JOE

EXTRAS

Stage Directions: Establishing the Setting

As you have already learned, playwrights use **stage directions** to suggest a character's tone of voice, feelings, facial expressions, gestures, and actions. Stage directions also explain the setting—where and when the action takes place.

Terms such as *stage right*, *stage left*, and *down right* inform the actors of where events should take place onstage. The wing refers to the area on either side of the stage that is not visible to the audience.

Stage directions are given for the benefit of the actors, who face the audience from the stage. Therefore, action which occurs *stage right*—to the actors' right as they face the audience—takes place on the audience's left.

The following passage shows how the setting should appear in a script. As you read the stage directions, try to picture in your mind what this setting looks like. Notice the arrangement of furniture, windows, and doors, and the stage directions for sound. Remember that the actors will perform their roles in this imaginary place.

Scene 1

Sound of traffic passing by on the street. Early evening.

The Ruiz family's apartment. A balcony with two white plastic chairs and a small table, and a small living/dining room where dinner is laid out on a table. Three places are set. In the background a stereo is playing jazz music. A chandelier is lit over the table. Elena Ruiz and her sister Silvia are seated on the balcony holding drinks. Suddenly, the music stops, the lights go out, and a man's voice is heard shouting from inside the apartment.

WRITING ACTIVITY 2

Imagine a room in your house or apartment as the setting for a play. Using the preceding example as a model, write a paragraph or two of stage directions explaining the physical appearance of the room. Describe the furniture and how it is arranged. Also include noticeable features of the room, such as the size, the condition, the color of the walls and floor, etc. Use a separate sheet of paper for this description.

Answers will vary.

Dialogue: Revealing Character and Advancing Plot

A script consists mainly of **dialogue**—conversations among the characters. Dramatic dialogue, however, differs from everyday conversations with people. The playwright carefully chooses dialogue that reveals character and advances the plot. The action progresses as the characters recite their lines and participate in the events of the story. When you read a play, focus on interpreting the characters' spoken words in the context of the dramatic situation. Here are some other suggestions for reading the dialogue in a script:

1. Notice the punctuation. Playwrights sometimes use a dash (—) or an ellipsis (. . .) to indicate pauses or interruptions in the characters' speech.

2. Study the stage directions printed before and after the characters' dialogue. Look for clues that explain how the characters deliver their lines. Descriptions of voice, attitude, or actions heighten the meaning of the spoken words.

Apply these suggestions as you read the dialogue between a woman named Trina and her brother, who everyone calls Uncle Chris.

TRINA: *(with desperate courage)* Uncle Chris . . . Uncle Chris . . . I must speak to you.

UNCLE CHRIS: I have business.

TRINA: But, Uncle Chris. . . . I want to get married.

UNCLE CHRIS: Well, then, *get* married. *(He starts off again.)*

TRINA: No, wait, I . . . I want to marry Mr. Thorkelson. Here. *(She produces him from behind her.)* Peter, this is Uncle Chris. Uncle Chris, this is Mr. Thorkelson.

UNCLE CHRIS: *(staring at him)* So?

MR. THORKELSON: How are you, sir?

UNCLE CHRIS: Busy. *(He turns again.)*

TRINA: Please, Uncle Chris. . . .

UNCLE CHRIS: What is? You want to marry him? All right, marry him. I have other things to think about.

TRINA: *(eagerly)* Then . . . then you give your permission?

UNCLE CHRIS: Yes, I give my permission. If you want to be a fool, I cannot stop you.

—Excerpted from *I Remember Mama* by John van Druten, adapted from *Mama's Bank Account* by Kathryn Forbes

The ellipses (. . .) or the dash (—) show pauses or interruptions in speech in a dialogue. How does Trina speak when she says "Uncle Chris . . . I must speak to you"? If you said *hesitantly* or *nervously*, you correctly interpreted how the stage directions correspond to the statement.

The play, *I Remember Mama*, is the story of a Norwegian immigrant family in the early 1900s. It is told from the point of view of one of the daughters of the Hanson family. The play centers around the Hanson children, their parents, their three aunts, and their gruff Uncle Chris. The conversation above gives you some insight into the characters in the play. You can infer that the other characters seem to be afraid of Uncle Chris. You can also infer that he seems to be in charge in the family.

EXERCISE 2

Directions: Read the passage below and answer the questions that follow.

CAN THIS FRIENDSHIP BE SAVED?

FELIX: What's wrong? *[Crosses back to tray, puts down glasses, etc.]*

OSCAR: There's something wrong with this system, that's what's wrong. I don't think
5 that two single men living alone in a big eight-room apartment should have a cleaner house than my mother.

FELIX: *[Gets rest of dishes, glasses and coasters from table.]* What are you talking
10 about? I'm just going to put the dishes in the sink. You want me to leave them here all night?

OSCAR: *[Takes his glass which FELIX has put on tray and crosses to bar for refill.]* I don't care if you take them to bed with you. You
15 can play Mr. Clean all you want. But don't make *me* feel guilty.

FELIX: *[Takes tray into kitchen, leaving swinging door open.]* I'm not asking you to do it, Oscar. You don't have to clean up.

20 OSCAR: *[Moves up to door]* That's why you make me feel guilty. You're always in my bathroom hanging up my towels. . . . Whenever I smoke you follow me around with an ashtray. Last night I found you washing the
25 kitchen floor shaking your head and moaning, "Footprints, footprints"! *[Paces Right]*

FELIX: *[Comes back to the table with silent butler into which he dumps the ashtrays; then wipes them carefully]* I didn't say they
30 were yours.

OSCAR: *[Angrily; sits Down Right in wing chair.]* Well, they were mine, damn it. I have feet and they make prints. What do you want me to do, climb across the cabinets?

35 FELIX: No! I want you to walk on the floor.

OSCAR: I appreciate that! I really do.

FELIX: *[Crosses to telephone table and cleans ashtray there]* I'm just trying to keep
40 the place livable. I didn't realize I irritated you that much.

—Excerpted from "The Odd Couple"
by Neil Simon, 1966

1. Where does the scene take place?

   (1) in a house
   (2) in a hotel
   (3) in a dormitory
   (4) in an apartment
   (5) in a bar

2. What do the stage directions referring to Felix reveal about him?

   (1) his tone of voice
   (2) his facial expressions
   (3) his actions
   (4) his emotions
   (5) his clothing

3. What is Oscar's tone in lines 31–34?

   (1) guilty
   (2) angry
   (3) comic
   (4) insincere
   (5) selfish

4. What does Felix do while talking with Oscar?

   (1) tidies up the surroundings
   (2) refills his glass of beer
   (3) smokes a cigarette
   (4) hangs up Oscar's towels
   (5) relaxes in a wing chair

5. What causes tension between the men?

   (1) They are both unmarried.
   (2) They have different housekeeping habits.
   (3) Oscar smokes and Felix doesn't.
   (4) Oscar is overly attached to his mother.
   (5) Felix wants to be a butler.

Answers are on page 338.

Story Elements of Drama

In plays you will find many of the story elements that were described in Chapter 6 on prose fiction. Review the definitions of these elements as they apply to drama.

Setting: The place, the time, and the atmosphere in which dramatic situations occur. Setting in plays is conveyed by the stage directions and the characters' comments about the physical surroundings.

Plot: The series of events tracing the action of a story. The plot of a play relies almost entirely on the characters' performance—the way they immediately respond to ongoing situations. Therefore, the plot stems from the characters, whose purpose is to act out events. Characters involved in conflicts create moments of tension in the plot. Plays usually contain scenes showing conflicts among the characters. For example, the conflict in the scene from *Of Mice and Men* (page 251) results when George discovers that Lennie has snatched a mouse and unintentionally killed it. George's initial reaction is anger; George scolds Lennie. George resolves the conflict by telling Lennie to "get a mouse that's fresh."

Characterization: The methods of revealing character—appearance, personality, and behavior. Because plays are written in script form, you learn about the characters from reading the dialogue and the stage directions. As you read, look for clues in the dialogue and stage directions that suggest character traits. Your understanding of characterization is based largely on the inferences you make.

Theme: A general statement that explains the underlying meaning of a story. As a rule, you have to read the entire play, rather than an excerpt, to determine the significance of the dramatic action. However, the dialogue in some scenes expresses beliefs or opinions about life and human behavior. The topic of conversation and the characters' statements about that topic may reveal the major or minor theme of the play.

EXERCISE 3

Directions: The following excerpt is from the play *The Tumult and the Shouting*. In this scene Professor Sheldon and his wife Willa must deal with the illness of their son. As you read the passage, try to imagine the actors saying their lines. Then answer the questions that follow.

WHY DOES A SON'S ILLNESS WORRY THE FATHER?

SHELDON: David, you and Julian wait outside. *[DAVID and JULIAN leave, go down the hall and enter their room]*

DOCTOR: Hand me my bag, Mrs. Sheldon.
5 *[WILLA hands him the bag. The DOCTOR removes a hypodermic needle.]* I'm going to give him a sedative. *[He holds the syringe up to the light, squeezes it, then places it on the table in a piece of cotton. He then removes a*
10 *bottle of alcohol and a swab of cotton and begins to clean BILLY'S arm. He then makes the injection. BILLY flinches slightly.]* Now he'll sleep. *[He puts the cotton, alcohol and hypodermic needle back into the bag.]*

15 WILLA: Doctor, what's wrong with him?

DOCTOR: Tonsillitis and he's got a very high fever, Mrs. Sheldon. His tonsils are badly infected as I told you. They'll have to come out soon or his heart may be damaged. I just
20 hope we haven't put it off too long.

SHELDON: Will that stop the asthma too?

DOCTOR: That I can't say. But it certainly won't make it any worse. I'm going to give you a prescription for the fever and
25 something to reduce the inflammation. Where can I write?

SHELDON: Downstairs in the living room, doctor. *[JULIAN and DAVID appear in the hallway. The DOCTOR goes down.]*

30 DAVID: Daddy?

SHELDON: Yes, David.

DAVID: Can we go in?

SHELDON: No. You better not. *[he starts down]*

35 JULIAN: Daddy?

SHELDON: Yes? *[a bit impatient]*

JULIAN: How is he?

SHELDON: Don't bother me now boys. I'm busy.

40 DAVID *[calling after him]* Is he going to be all right? *[SHELDON does not answer. JULIAN and DAVID turn and go back down the hall. SHELDON enters the living room.]*

DOCTOR: He'll be all right now, Professor.
45 *[hands him the prescription]* Here you are. Have this filled right away. I think he'll be all right now but if you need me, don't hesitate to call. *[glancing around]* You have a telephone, don't you?

50 SHELDON: There's a pay phone in Old Main. I can get the night watchman to let me in.

DOCTOR: Fine. *[He shakes hands with SHELDON and leaves. SHELDON accompanies him to the front door.]* Uh,
55 Professor.

SHELDON: Yes, doctor.

DOCTOR: I mean it.

SHELDON: What will an operation cost?

DOCTOR: Let's not talk about that now. The
60 main thing is Billy's health.

SHELDON: Thank you, doctor.

DOCTOR: Well, good night. *[He goes. SHELDON stands there examining the two prescriptions as WILLA comes down the stairs.]*

65 WILLA: He's asleep.

SHELDON: *[showing her the prescriptions]* I'm going to get these filled.

WILLA: Mister—

SHELDON: Yes?

70 WILLA: What about the operation?

SHELDON: I don't know—

WILLA: [exasperated] You don't know what?

SHELDON: I don't know where the money's
75 coming from—that's all.

[He puts on his hat and coat and goes out
the front door as the lights fade.]

—Excerpted from *The Tumult and the Shouting* by
Thomas Pawley, 1969

1. How does Willa feel about Billy's operation?

  (1) She doesn't know where the money will
     come from.
  (2) She worries that this crisis will be too
     much for Sheldon.
  (3) She knows Billy must have the
     operation no matter the cost.
  (4) She fears that her other sons will come
     down with the illness.
  (5) She trusts that the doctor has cured
     Billy of his health problem.

2. Why does the doctor tell Sheldon, "I mean
it" (line 57)?

  (1) to make sure he can get to a phone
  (2) to remind him to get the prescriptions
  (3) to conceal the truth from Willa
  (4) to emphasize the need for the
     operation
  (5) to try to reduce Sheldon's anxiety

3. What word best describes Sheldon in this
scene?

  (1) hopeful
  (2) conflicted
  (3) grief-stricken
  (4) insensitive
  (5) composed

4. Which word best describes how David and
Julian feel about their brother?

  (1) jealous
  (2) playful
  (3) hysterical
  (4) indifferent
  (5) concerned

5. What is the purpose of this scene?

  (1) to reveal how a family must overcome a
     crisis
  (2) to suggest that professors do not earn
     much money
  (3) to demonstrate the importance of good
     medical care
  (4) to complain about the high cost of
     prescription drugs
  (5) to illustrate how people will help those
     in need

Answers are on page 338.

Characters: Performers of Drama

In drama the characters participate in the ongoing events of the story. Their performance is the central focus of your attention. Why? Because scripts consist almost entirely of characters' dialogue and actions. The roles the characters play develop these elements of drama—plot, characterization, and theme.

Unlike prose fiction, plays usually do not have a narrator who comments on the characters and summarizes events. Instead, you directly observe the characters performing the action. You see how they respond to past or present situations. You also "hear" their remarks about themselves or other characters.

Based on your observations, you make inferences about the characters' dramatic role in a play. Do they cause conflicts? Do they influence events? Do they make decisions that affect the outcome of the play?

You also form opinions about the characters' personalities and relationships with other people. Do they communicate honestly, or do their words disguise their true feelings? Does their dialogue show an understanding of another character's viewpoint?

In the next exercise you will closely examine these aspects of the characters' performance:

- comments about themselves

- comments about other people

- responses to each other's comments

- reactions to events

EXERCISE 4

Directions: Read the passage below, in which Nora confronts her husband, Torvald Helmer. Then answer the questions that follow.

NORA: Sit down. This'll take some time. I have a lot to say.

HELMER: *[sitting at the table directly opposite her]* You worry me, Nora. And I don't understand you.

NORA: No, that's exactly it. You don't understand me. And I've
5 never understood you either—until tonight. No, don't interrupt. You can just listen to what I say. We're closing out accounts, Torvald.

HELMER: How do you mean that?

NORA: *[after a short pause]* Doesn't anything strike you about our sitting here like this?

10 HELMER: What's that?

NORA: We've been married now eight years. Doesn't it occur to you that this is the first time we two, you and I, man and wife, have ever talked seriously together?

15 HELMER: What do you mean—seriously?

NORA: In eight whole years—longer even—right from our first acquaintance, we've never exchanged a serious word on any serious thing.

HELMER: You mean I should constantly go and involve you in 20 problems you couldn't possibly help me with?

NORA: I'm not talking of problems. I'm saying that we've never sat down seriously together and tried to get to the bottom of anything.

HELMER: But dearest, what good would that ever do you?

NORA: That's the point right there: you've never understood me. 25 I've been wronged greatly, Torvald—first by Papa, and then by you.

HELMER: What! By us—the two people who've loved you more than anyone else?

NORA: [shaking her head] You never loved me. You've thought it fun to be in love with me, that's all.

30 HELMER: Nora, what a thing to say!

NORA: Yes, it's true now, Torvald. When I lived at home with Papa, he told me all his opinions, so I had the same ones too; or if they were different I hid them, since he wouldn't have cared for that. He used to call me his doll-child, and he played with me the way I 35 played with my dolls. Then I came into your house—

HELMER: How can you speak of our marriage like that?

NORA: [unperturbed] I mean, then I went from Papa's hands into yours. You arranged everything to your own taste, and so I got the 40 same taste as you—or I pretended to; I can't remember. I guess a little of both, first one, then the other. Now when I look back, it seems as if I'd lived here like a beggar—just from hand to mouth. I've lived by doing tricks for you, Torvald. But that's the way you wanted it. It's a great sin what you and Papa did to me. You're to blame that nothing's become of me.

45

HELMER: Nora, how unfair and ungrateful you are! Haven't you been happy here?

NORA: No, never. I thought so—but I never have.

HELMER: Not—not happy!

NORA: No, only lighthearted. And you've always been so kind to me. But our home's been nothing but a playpen. I've been your doll-
50 wife here, just as at home I was Papa's doll-child. And in turn the children have been my dolls. I thought it was fun when you played with me, just as they thought it fun when I played with them. That's been our marriage, Torvald.

HELMER: There's some truth in what you're saying—under all the
55 raving exaggeration. But it'll all be different after this. Playtime's over; now for the schooling.

NORA: Whose schooling—mine or the children's?

HELMER: Both yours and the children's, dearest.

NORA: Oh, Torvald, you're not the man to teach me to be a good
60 wife to you.

HELMER: And you can say that?

NORA: And I—how am I equipped to bring up children?

HELMER: Nora!

NORA: Didn't you say a moment ago that that was no job to trust
65 me with?

HELMER: In a flare of temper! Why fasten on that?

NORA: Yes, but you were so very right. I'm not up to the job. There's another job I have to do first. I have to try to educate myself. You can't help me with that. I've got to do it alone. And
70 that's why I'm leaving you now.

—Excerpted from *A Doll's House* by Henrik Ibsen

1. Where are Nora and Helmer seated during their conversation?

_____

2. What does Nora mean by the phrase "closing out accounts" (line 6)?

    (1) paying the household bills
    (2) transferring the savings account to another bank
    (3) filing for bankruptcy
    (4) discussing financial investments
    (5) ending the marriage

3. What does Nora mean when she says, "I've been your doll-wife here, just as at home I was Papa's doll-child" (lines 49–50)?

   (1) She has always been as pretty as a doll.
   (2) She has a cute and playful personality.
   (3) Neither her husband nor her father has treated her like a human being.
   (4) Her husband and father collect lifelike dolls.
   (5) Nora toys with her father's and Helmer's affection.

4. According to this passage, what is the significance of the title *A Doll's House*?

   _____

   _____

   _____

5. Circle *T* if the statement is true or *F* if it is false.

   T F (1) Helmer discusses serious issues with Nora.

   T F (2) Helmer is satisfied with the marriage.

   T F (3) Nora and Helmer disagree about the definition of love.

   T F (4) Helmer considers Nora his equal.

   T F (5) Helmer understands his wife's point of view.

   T F (6) Helmer has not physically abused Nora.

6. In a short paragraph, write your opinion of either Nora or Helmer. Explain your feelings about the character's behavior and role as either a wife or a husband.

   _____

   _____

   _____

   _____

   _____

   _____

Answers are on pages 338–339.

Reading a Complete Scene from a Play

In this section you will read an entire scene from a play. Unlike a shorter passage, a complete scene presents a more detailed development of character and plot.

Use the following questions as study aids for understanding the literal meanings, the suggested meanings, and the structural elements of drama:

- Where and when does the scene occur?

- What is the topic of conversation?

- What is the literal meaning of the speaker's statements?

- What is the relationship between the stage directions and the dialogue? Do the speaker's tone of voice and actions emphasize or change the literal meaning of the spoken words?

- What do other characters say in response to the first speaker? Based on these responses, what inferences can you make about the relationships of the characters involved in the conversation?

- Does the dialogue show a conflict between the characters? Is the conflict resolved?

- Do the characters in the scene discuss other people? What do the characters' comments reveal about those people?

- Does the dialogue reveal the speaker's personality, behavior, or background?

- What specific incidents of plot are depicted in the scene?

- Do characters express their beliefs or opinions about life or human behavior? If so, do their comments suggest a theme—a general statement explaining the significance of the dramatic action?

EXERCISE 5

This excerpt is longer than those you'll see on the GED Language Arts, Reading Test. However, when you read the entire scene, you will see how all of the elements of drama work together.

Directions: The play *Death of a Salesman* tells the story of Willy Loman, a sixty-year-old sales representative who is approaching the end of his career. In the following scene from Act II, Willy meets with his boss, Howard. Willy proposes a change in his position with the firm. Read the script and answer the questions that follow.

[HOWARD WAGNER, thirty-six, wheels in a small typewriter table on which is a wire-recording machine and proceeds to plug it in. This is on the left forestage. . . . HOWARD is intent on threading the machine and only glances over his shoulder as WILLY appears.]

5 WILLY: Pst! Pst!

HOWARD: Hello, Willy, come in.

WILLY: Like to have a little talk with you, Howard.

HOWARD: Sorry to keep you waiting. I'll be with you in a minute.

WILLY: What's that, Howard?

10 HOWARD: Didn't you ever see one of these? Wire recorder.

WILLY: Oh. Can we talk a minute?

HOWARD: Records things. Just got delivery yesterday. Been driving me crazy, the most terrific machine I ever saw in my life. I was up all night with it.

15 WILLY: What do you do with it?

HOWARD: I bought it for dictation, but you can do anything with it. Listen to this. I had it home last night. Listen to what I picked up. The first one is my daughter. Get this. *[He flicks the switch and "Roll out the Barrel" is heard being whistled.]* Listen to that kid whistle.

20 WILLY: That is lifelike, isn't it?

HOWARD: Seven years old. Get that tone.

WILLY: Ts, ts. Like to ask a little favor of you . . .

[The whistling breaks off, and the voice of HOWARD'S DAUGHTER is heard.]

25 HIS DAUGHTER: "Now you, Daddy."

HOWARD: She's crazy for me! *[Again the same song is whistled.]* That's me! Ha! *[He winks.]*

WILLY: You're very good!

[The whistling breaks off again. The machine runs silent for a
30 *moment.]*

HOWARD: Sh! Get this now, this is my son.

HIS SON: "The capital of Alabama is Montgomery; the capital of Arizona is Phoenix; the capital of Arkansas is Little Rock; the capital of California is Sacramento . . . " *[And on, and on]*

35 HOWARD: *[holding up five fingers]* Five years old, Willy!

WILLY: He'll make an announcer some day!

THE SON: *[continuing]* "The capital . . . "

HOWARD: Get that—alphabetical order! *[The machine breaks off suddenly.]* Wait a minute. The maid kicked the plug out.

40 WILLY: It certainly is a—

HOWARD: Sh, for God's sake!

HIS SON: "It's nine o'clock, Bulova watch time. So I have to go to sleep."

WILLY: That really is—

45 HOWARD: Wait a minute. The next is my wife. *[They wait.]*

HOWARD'S VOICE: "Go on, say something." [Pause.] "Well, you gonna talk?"

HIS WIFE: "I can't think of anything."

HOWARD'S VOICE: "Well, talk—it's turning."

50 HIS WIFE: *[shyly, beaten]* "Hello." *[Silence.]* "Oh, Howard, I can't talk into this . . . "

HOWARD: *[snapping the machine off]* That was my wife.

WILLY: That is a wonderful machine. Can we—

HOWARD: I tell you, Willy, I'm gonna take my camera, and my
55 bandsaw, and all my hobbies, and out they go. This is the most fascinating relaxation I ever found.

WILLY: I think I'll get one myself.

HOWARD: Sure, they're only a hundred and a half. You can't do without it. Supposing you wanna hear Jack Benny, see? But you
60 can't be at home at that hour. So you tell the maid to turn the radio on when Jack Benny comes on, and this automatically goes on with the radio.

WILLY: And when you come home you—

HOWARD: You can come home twelve o'clock, one o'clock, any time
65 you like, and you get yourself a Coke and sit yourself down, throw the switch, and there's Jack Benny's program in the middle of the night!

WILLY: I'm definitely going to get one. Because lots of time I'm on the road, and I think to myself, what I must be missing on the radio!

70 HOWARD: Don't you have a radio in the car?

WILLY: Well, yeah, but who ever thinks of turning it on?

HOWARD: Say, aren't you supposed to be in Boston?

WILLY: That's what I want to talk to you about, Howard. You got a minute? [He draws a chair in from the wing.]

75 HOWARD: What happened? What're you doing here?

WILLY: Well . . .

HOWARD: You didn't crack up again, did you?

WILLY: Oh, no. No . . .

HOWARD: Geez, you had me worried there for a minute. What's the
80 trouble?

WILLY: Well, to tell you the truth, Howard, I've come to the decision that I'd rather not travel any more.

HOWARD: Not travel! Well, what'll you do?

WILLY: Remember, Christmas time, when you had the party here?
85 You said you'd try to think of some spot for me here in town.

HOWARD: With us?

WILLY: Well, sure.

HOWARD: Oh, yeah, yeah. I remember. Well, I couldn't think of anything for you, Willy.

90 WILLY: I tell ya, Howard. The kids are all grown up, y'know. I don't need much any more. If I could take home—well, sixty-five dollars a week, I could swing it.

HOWARD: Yeah, but Willy, see I —

WILLY: I tell ya why, Howard. Speaking frankly and between the two
95 of us, y'know—I'm just a little tired.

HOWARD: Oh, I could understand that, Willy. But you're a road man, Willy, and we do a road business. We've only got a half-dozen salesmen on the floor here.

WILLY: God knows, Howard, I never asked a favor of any man. But I
100 was with the firm when your father used to carry you in here in his arms.

HOWARD: I know that, Willy, but—

WILLY: Your father came to me the day you were born and asked me what I thought of the name of Howard, may he rest in peace.

105 HOWARD: I appreciate that, Willy, but there just is no spot here for you. If I had a spot I'd slam you right in, but I just don't have a single, solitary spot.

[He looks for his lighter. WILLY has picked it up and gives it to him. Pause.]

110 WILLY: [*with increasing anger*] Howard, all I need to set my table is fifty dollars a week.

HOWARD: But where am I going to put you, kid?

WILLY: Look, it isn't a question of whether I can sell merchandise, is it?

115 HOWARD: No, but it's a business, kid, and everybody's gotta pull his own weight.

WILLY: [*desperately*] Just let me tell you a story, Howard—

HOWARD: 'Cause you gotta admit, business is business.

WILLY: [*angrily*] Business is definitely business, but just listen for a
120 minute. You don't understand this. When I was a boy—eighteen, nineteen—I was already on the road. And there was a question in my mind as to whether selling had a future for me. Because in those days I had a yearning to go to Alaska. See, there were three gold strikes in one month in Alaska, and I felt like going out. Just for the
125 ride, you might say.

HOWARD: [*barely interested*] Don't say.

WILLY: Oh, yeah, my father lived many years in Alaska. He was an adventurous man. We've got quite a little streak of self-reliance in our family. I thought I'd go out with my older brother and try to
130 locate him, and maybe settle in the North with the old man. And I was almost decided to go, when I met a salesman in the Parker House. His name was Dave Singleman. And he was eighty-four years old, and he'd drummed merchandise in thirty-one states. And old Dave, he'd go up to his room, y'understand, put on his green velvet
135 slippers—I'll never forget—and pick up his phone and call the buyers, and without ever leaving his room, at the age of eighty-four, he made his living. And when I saw that, I realized that selling was the greatest career a man could want. 'Cause what could be more satisfying than to be able to go, at the age of eighty-four, into
140 twenty or thirty different cities, and pick up a phone, and be

remembered and loved and helped by so many different people? Do you know? When he died—and by the way he died the death of a salesman, in his green velvet slippers in the smoker of the New York, New Haven, and Hartford, going into Boston—when he died,
145 hundreds of salesmen and buyers were at his funeral. Things were sad on a lotta trains for months after that. *[He stands up. HOWARD has not looked at him.]* In those days there was personality in it, Howard. There was respect, and comradeship, and gratitude in it. Today, it's all cut and dried, and there's no chance for bringing
150 friendship to bear—or personality. You see what I mean? They don't know me any more.

HOWARD: *[moving away, to the right]* That's just the thing, Willy.

WILLY: If I had forty dollars a week—that's all I'd need. Forty dollars, Howard.

155 HOWARD: Kid, I can't take blood from a stone, I—

WILLY: *[desperation is on him now]* Howard, the year Al Smith was nominated, your father came to me and—

HOWARD: *[starting to go off]* I've got to see some people, kid.

WILLY: *[stopping him]* I'm talking about your father! There were
160 promises made across this desk! You mustn't tell me you've got people to see—I put thirty-four years into this firm, Howard, and now I can't pay my insurance! You can't eat the orange and throw the peel away—a man is not a piece of fruit! *[After a pause.]* Now pay attention. Your father—in 1928 I had a big year. I averaged a
165 hundred and seventy dollars a week in commissions.

HOWARD: *[impatiently]* Now, Willy, you never averaged—

WILLY: *[banging his hand on the desk]* I averaged a hundred and seventy dollars a week in the year of 1928! And your father came to me—or rather, I was in the office here—it was right over this desk—
170 and he put his hand on my shoulder—

HOWARD: *[getting up]* You'll have to excuse me, Willy, I gotta see some people. Pull yourself together. *[Going out]* I'll be back in a little while.

[On HOWARD'S exit, the light on his chair grows very bright and
175 *strange.]*

WILLY: Pull myself together! What the hell did I say to him! My God, I was yelling at him! How could I! *[WILLY breaks off, staring at the light, which occupies the chair, animating it. He approaches this chair, standing across the desk from it.]* Frank, Frank, don't you
180 remember what you told me that time? How you put your hand on

my shoulder, and Frank . . . *[He leans on the desk and as he speaks the dead man's name he accidentally switches on the recorder, and instantly—]*

HOWARD'S SON: " . . . of New York is Albany. The capital of Ohio is
185 Cincinnati, the capital of Rhode Island is . . . " *[The recitation continues.]*

WILLY: *[leaping away with fright, shouting]* Ha! Howard! Howard! Howard!

HOWARD: *[rushing in]* What happened?

190 WILLY: *[pointing at the machine, which continues nasally, childishly, with the capital cities]* Shut it off! Shut it off!

HOWARD: *[pulling the plug out]* Look, Willy . . .

WILLY: *[pressing his hands to his eyes]* I gotta get myself some coffee. I'll get some coffee . . .

195 *[WILLY starts to walk out. HOWARD stops him.]*

HOWARD: *[rolling up the cord]* Willy, look . . .

WILLY: I'll go to Boston.

HOWARD: Willy, you can't go to Boston for us.

WILLY: Why can't I go?

200 HOWARD: I don't want you to represent us. I've been meaning to tell you for a long time now.

WILLY: Howard, are you firing me?

HOWARD: I think you need a good long rest, Willy.

WILLY: Howard—

205 HOWARD: And when you feel better, come back, and we'll see if we can work something out.

WILLY: But I gotta earn money, Howard. I'm in no position—

HOWARD: Where are your sons? Why don't your sons give you a hand?

210 WILLY: They're working on a very big deal.

HOWARD: This is no time for false pride, Willy. You go to your sons and tell them that you're tired. You've got two great boys, haven't you?

WILLY: Oh, no question, no question, but in the meantime . . .

HOWARD: Then that's that, heh?

215 WILLY: All right. I'll go to Boston tomorrow.

HOWARD: No, no.

WILLY: I can't throw myself on my sons. I'm not a cripple!

HOWARD: Look, kid, I'm busy this morning.

WILLY: *[grasping HOWARD'S arm]* Howard, you've got to let me go
220 to Boston!

HOWARD: *[hard, keeping himself under control]* I've got a line of people to see this morning. Sit down, take five minutes, and pull yourself together, and then go home, will ya? I need the office, Willy. *[He starts to go, turns, remembering the recorder, starts to push off*
225 *the table holding the recorder.]* Oh, yeah. Whenever you can this week, stop by and drop off the samples. You'll feel better, Willy, and then come back and we'll talk. Pull yourself together, kid, there's people outside.

[HOWARD exits, pushing the table off left. WILLY stares into space,
230 *exhausted.]*

—Excerpted from *Death of a Salesman* by Arthur Miller

1. As the scene opens, why does Howard insistently play with the wire recorder?

    (1) to show his enthusiasm for new machines
    (2) to avoid talking to Willy
    (3) to explain how a wire recorder operates
    (4) to introduce his family to Willy
    (5) to persuade Willy to buy a wire recorder

2. When Willy says, "I've come to the decision that I'd rather not travel any more" (lines 81–82) what action occurs as a result of this statement?

    (1) a friendly conversation
    (2) a job interview
    (3) a heated argument
    (4) a fair debate
    (5) a fistfight

3. What is the major point of Willy's long speech (lines 127–151)?

   (1) Hundreds of salesmen and buyers attended Dave Singleman's funeral.
   (2) Willy's father was an adventurous man who lived in Alaska.
   (3) The advantages of a sales career outweigh the disadvantages.
   (4) Salesmen used to value respect and friendships as well as commissions.
   (5) Willy decided not to settle in the North.

4. How long has Willy worked for the firm? _____

5. Write two of Howard's statements that indirectly say to Willy, "You are fired."

   _____

   _____

6. From Willy's and Howard's actions, what judgments can you make about their personalities and behavior?

   _____

   _____

7. Which of the following descriptions apply to Willy? Choose three.

   _____ (1) desperate

   _____ (2) proud

   _____ (3) greedy

   _____ (4) ambitious

   _____ (5) grateful

   _____ (6) composed

   _____ (7) frustrated

8. Which of the following descriptions apply to Howard? Choose three.

   _____ (1) concerned

   _____ (2) respectful

   _____ (3) bored

   _____ (4) impatient

   _____ (5) generous

   _____ (6) appreciative

   _____ (7) insensitive

9. The author wrote an essay in which he said that in tragedies of the past, kings, queens, and nobles were the tragic heroes. Now it is the *common man* whose daily struggles raise the character to a tragic hero.

Based on this excerpt, in what way is Willie Loman a modern hero?

(1) He tries to sell products that are inferior.
(2) He struggles tirelessly to provide an income for his family.
(3) He remembers the past as a better time.
(4) He fights the use of technology in replacing workers.
(5) He has to take orders from his boss's son.

Answers are on page 339.

WRITING ACTIVITY 3

On a separate sheet of paper, write a short scene in script form portraying a conflict between a boss and an employee. Write down the following information before you begin writing the dialogue:

- time

- characters

- place

- conflict

Answers will vary.

Go to **www.GEDReading.com** for additional practice and instruction!

Chapter Review

Questions 1–4 refer to the following excerpt from a play.

ARE MAY AND EDDIE IN LOVE?

EDDIE: I'm not leavin'. I don't care what you think anymore. I don't care what you feel. None a' that matters. I'm not leavin'. I'm stayin' right here. I don't care if a hundred
5 "dates" walk through that door—I'll take every one of 'em on. I don't care if you hate my guts. I don't care if you can't stand the sight of me or the sound of me or the smell of me. I'm never leavin'. You'll never get rid
10 of me. You'll never escape me either. I'll track you down no matter where you go. I know exactly how your mind works. I've been right every time. Every single time.

MAY: You've gotta' give this up, Eddie.

15 EDDIE: I'm not giving it up! *[Pause]*

MAY: *[calm]* Okay. Look. I don't understand what you've got in your head anymore. I really don't. I don't get it. *Now* you desperately need me. *Now* you can't live
20 without me. *Now* you'll do anything for me. Why should I believe it this time?

EDDIE: Because it's true.

MAY: It was supposed to have been true every time before. Every other time. Now
25 it's true again. . . . Fifteen years I've been a yo-yo for you. I've never been split. I've never been two ways about you. I've either loved you or not loved you. And now I just plain don't love you. Understand? Do you
30 understand that? I don't love you. I don't need you. I don't want you. Do you get that? Now if you can still stay, then you're either crazy or pathetic.

*[She crosses down left to table, sits in
35 upstage chair facing audience, takes slug of tequila from bottle, slams it down on table.]*

—Excerpted from *Fool for Love* by Sam Shepard, 1983

1. According to lines 4–6, what is the emotional basis for Eddie's attachment to May?

   (1) loneliness and depression
   (2) pity and guilt
   (3) obligation and commitment
   (4) love and respect
   (5) jealousy and possessiveness

2. From this excerpt, what can you infer about May and Eddie's relationship?

   It is
   (1) unhealthy
   (2) caring
   (3) stable
   (4) unemotional
   (5) casual

3. Which of the following words best describes May's impression of Eddie's behavior?

   (1) brave
   (2) unpredictable
   (3) calm
   (4) mature
   (5) sympathetic

4. May "takes slug of tequila from bottle, slams it down on table" (lines 35–36). Why does the playwright include this stage direction?

   To show May's
   (1) alcoholism
   (2) clumsiness
   (3) thirst
   (4) anger
   (5) strength

Directions: Read the passages below and choose the best answer to the questions that follow.

Questions 5–10 refer to the following excerpt from a play.

WHY IS MARGARET ANGRY?

[At the rise of the curtain someone is taking a shower in the bathroom, the door of which is half open. A pretty young woman, with anxious lines in her face, enters the
5 *bedroom and crosses to the bathroom door.]*

MARGARET: *[shouting above roar of water]* One of those no-neck monsters hit me with a hot buttered biscuit so I have t'change!

10 *[MARGARET'S voice is both rapid and drawling, in her long speeches she has the vocal tricks of a priest delivering a liturgical chant, the lines are almost sung, always continuing a little beyond her breath so she*
15 *has to gasp for another. Sometimes she intersperses the lines with a little wordless singing, such as "Da-da-daaaa!"]*

[Water turns off and BRICK calls out to her, but is still unseen. A tone of politely feigned
20 *interest, masking indifference, or worse, is characteristic of his speech with MARGARET.]*

BRICK: Wha'd you say, Maggie? Water was on s' loud I couldn't hear ya. . . . .

25 MARGARET: Well, I!—just remarked that!— one of th' no-neck monsters messed up m' lovely lace dress so I got t'—cha-a-ange . . . .

[She opens and kicks shut drawers of the dresser.]

30 BRICK: Why d'ya call Gooper's kiddies no-neck monsters?

MARGARET: Because they've got no necks! Isn't that a good enough reason?

BRICK: Don't they have any necks?

35 MARGARET: None visible. Their fat little heads are set on their fat little bodies without a bit of connection.

BRICK: That's too bad.

MARGARET: Yes, it's too bad because you
40 can't wring their necks if they've got no necks to wring! Isn't that right, honey?

[She steps out of her dress, stands in a slip of ivory satin and lace.]

Yep, they're no-neck monsters, all no-neck
45 people are monsters.

[Children shriek downstairs.]

Hear them? Hear them screaming? I don't know where their voice-boxes are located since they don't have necks. I tell you I got
50 so nervous at that table tonight I thought I would throw back my head and utter a scream you could hear across the Arkansas border an' parts of Louisiana an' Tennessee. I said to your charming sister-in-law, Mae,
55 honey, couldn't you feed those precious little things at a separate table with an oilcloth cover? They make such a mess an' the lace cloth looks so pretty! She made enormous eyes at me and said, "Ohhh,
60 noooooo! On Big Daddy's birthday? Why, he would never forgive me!"

—Excerpted from *Cat on a Hot Tin Roof*
by Tennessee Williams, 1954

5. Which of the following words best describes Brick's attitude toward Margaret's remarks?

(1) interested
(2) indifferent
(3) critical
(4) excited
(5) impolite

6. Who is Gooper?

   (1) Brick's father
   (2) Brick's nephew
   (3) Brick's uncle
   (4) Brick's brother-in-law
   (5) Brick's brother

7. For what special occasion is the family gathered?

   (1) the Fourth of July
   (2) Margaret and Brick's wedding anniversary
   (3) Christmas Eve
   (4) Big Daddy's birthday
   (5) Mae's graduation

8. What is the main topic of Margaret's conversation?

   (1) the children's appearance and behavior
   (2) her fondness for Big Daddy
   (3) the birthday celebration
   (4) her low opinion of her sister-in-law
   (5) the description of her dress

9. If this scene were adapted to a movie, on whom would the camera focus?

   (1) Brick
   (2) the children
   (3) Big Daddy
   (4) Margaret
   (5) Mae

10. As the play progresses, we learn that Margaret is the "cat on a hot tin roof" fighting to win the affections of her husband.

    Based on this information and the excerpt, what can you infer is the underlying reason for Margaret's resentment of Gooper's children?

    (1) The children will inherit Big Daddy's fortune.
    (2) Big Daddy likes Gooper and Mae more than Brick and Margaret.
    (3) Margaret and Brick have no children of their own.
    (4) Margaret finds the children physically and socially repulsive.
    (5) Brick makes excuses for the children's rude behavior to Margaret.

Questions 11–16 refer to the following excerpt from a play.

WHAT DO YOU LEARN ABOUT BIG WALTER?

RUTH: *[Studying her mother-in-law furtively and concentrating on her ironing, anxious to encourage without seeming to]* Well, Lord knows, we've put enough rent into this here

5 rat trap to pay for four houses by now . . .

MAMA: *[Looking up at the words "rat trap" and then looking around and leaning back and sighing—in a suddenly reflective mood—]* "Rat trap"—yes, that's all it is.

10 *[Smiling]* I remember just as well the day me and Big Walter moved in here. Hadn't been married but two weeks and wasn't planning on living here no more than a year. *[She shakes her head at the dissolved dream.]* We

15 was going to set away, little by little, don't you know, and buy a little place out in Morgan Park. We had even picked out the house. *[Chuckling a little]* Looks right dumpy today. But Lord, child, you should know all

20 the dreams I had 'bout buying that house and fixing it up and making me a little garden in the back—*[She waits and stops smiling.]* And didn't none of it happen. *[Dropping her hands in a futile gesture]*

25 RUTH: *[Keeps her head down, ironing]* Yes, life can be a barrel of disappointments, sometimes.

MAMA: Honey, Big Walter would come in here some nights back then and slump down

30 on that couch there and just look at the rug, and look at me and look at the rug and then back at me—and I'd know he was down then . . . really down. *[After a second very long and thoughtful pause; she is seeing

35 back to times that only she can see]* And then, Lord, when I lost that baby—little Claude—I almost thought I was going to lose Big Walter too. Oh, that man grieved hisself! He was one man to love his children.

45 RUTH: Ain't nothin' can tear at you like losin' your baby.

MAMA: I guess that's how come that man finally worked hisself to death like he done. Like he was fighting his own war with this

50 here world that took his baby from him.

RUTH: He sure was a fine man, all right. I always liked Mr. Younger.

MAMA: Crazy 'bout his children! God knows there was plenty wrong with Walter

50 Younger—hard-headed, mean, kind of wild with women—plenty wrong with him. But he sure loved his children. Always wanted them to have something—be something. That's where Brother gets all these notions, I

55 reckon. Big Walter used to say, he'd get right wet in the eyes sometimes, lean his head back with the water standing in his eyes and say, "Seem like God didn't see fit to give the black man nothing but dreams—

60 but He did give us children to make them dreams seem worthwhile." *[She smiles.]* He could talk like that, don't you know.

RUTH: Yes, he sure could. He was a good man, Mr. Younger.

65 MAMA: Yes, a fine man—just couldn't never catch up with his dreams, that's all.

—Excerpted from *A Raisin in the Sun* by Lorraine Hansberry, 1959

11. Which of the following words best describes Mama and Ruth's attitude toward Big Walter?

(1) frustration
(2) respect
(3) disappointment
(4) resentment
(5) guilt

12. What was the major cause of Big Walter's grief?

    (1) his baby's death
    (2) financial troubles
    (3) shabby surroundings
    (4) war experiences
    (5) a demanding job

13. From Mama's comments about her husband, Big Walter, what kind of wife can you infer she was?

    (1) hot-tempered
    (2) pampered
    (3) selfish
    (4) insensitive
    (5) understanding

14. According to Mama, what overall goal was Big Walter unable to accomplish?

    (1) growing a garden
    (2) buying a house
    (3) fulfilling his dreams
    (4) financing his children's education
    (5) earning a high salary

15. Why does the playwright include the gesture "Keeps her head down, ironing" (line 25) before Ruth's line of dialogue?

    (1) to show that Ruth is concerned only about her housework
    (2) to emphasize that Ruth, too, understands life's disappointments
    (3) to hint that Ruth is afraid to look directly at Mama
    (4) to reveal Ruth's hardworking personality
    (5) to stress that Ruth is bored with the conversation

16. If Big Walter were still alive, which of the following statements would he most likely support?

    (1) Children are a burden to their parents.
    (2) Children should behave as maturely as adults.
    (3) Parents should ignore their children.
    (4) Children represent the hopes for the future.
    (5) Parents should spoil their children.

Answers are on pages 339–340.

Language Arts, Reading

Directions: This Language Arts, Reading Posttest will give you the opportunity to evaluate your readiness for the actual GED Language Arts, Reading Test.

The Posttest contains 40 questions. These questions are based on passages of fiction and nonfiction prose, poetry, and drama.

You should take approximately 65 minutes to complete this test. At the end of 65 minutes, stop and mark your place. Then finish the test. This will give you an idea of whether you can finish the real GED Test in the time allotted. Try to answer as many questions as you can. A blank will count as a wrong answer, so make a reasonable guess for questions you are not sure of.

When you are finished with the test, turn to the evaluation chart on page 299. Use the chart to evaluate whether you are ready to take the actual GED Test and, if not, what areas need more work.

Posttest Answer Grid

1 ① ② ③ ④ ⑤	15 ① ② ③ ④ ⑤	29 ① ② ③ ④ ⑤
2 ① ② ③ ④ ⑤	16 ① ② ③ ④ ⑤	30 ① ② ③ ④ ⑤
3 ① ② ③ ④ ⑤	17 ① ② ③ ④ ⑤	31 ① ② ③ ④ ⑤
4 ① ② ③ ④ ⑤	18 ① ② ③ ④ ⑤	32 ① ② ③ ④ ⑤
5 ① ② ③ ④ ⑤	19 ① ② ③ ④ ⑤	33 ① ② ③ ④ ⑤
6 ① ② ③ ④ ⑤	20 ① ② ③ ④ ⑤	34 ① ② ③ ④ ⑤
7 ① ② ③ ④ ⑤	21 ① ② ③ ④ ⑤	35 ① ② ③ ④ ⑤
8 ① ② ③ ④ ⑤	22 ① ② ③ ④ ⑤	36 ① ② ③ ④ ⑤
9 ① ② ③ ④ ⑤	23 ① ② ③ ④ ⑤	37 ① ② ③ ④ ⑤
10 ① ② ③ ④ ⑤	24 ① ② ③ ④ ⑤	38 ① ② ③ ④ ⑤
11 ① ② ③ ④ ⑤	25 ① ② ③ ④ ⑤	39 ① ② ③ ④ ⑤
12 ① ② ③ ④ ⑤	26 ① ② ③ ④ ⑤	40 ① ② ③ ④ ⑤
13 ① ② ③ ④ ⑤	27 ① ② ③ ④ ⑤	
14 ① ② ③ ④ ⑤	28 ① ② ③ ④ ⑤	

POSTTEST

Directions: Read each passage and choose the best answer to the questions that follow.

Questions 1–6 refer to the following excerpt from a short story.

WHAT ARE THE CHARACTERS' IMPRESSIONS OF A JOCKEY NAMED BITSY BARLOW?

The three men at the corner table were a trainer, a bookie, and a rich man. The trainer was Sylvester—a large, loosely built fellow with a flushed nose and slow blue
5 eyes. The bookie was Simmons. The rich man was the owner of a horse named Seltzer, which the jockey had ridden that afternoon. The three of them drank whiskey with soda, and a white-coated waiter had
10 just brought on the main course of the dinner.

It was Sylvester who first saw the jockey. He looked away quickly, put down his whiskey glass, and nervously mashed the tip
15 of his red nose with his thumb. "It's Bitsy Barlow," he said. "Standing over there across the room. Just watching us."

"Oh, the jockey," said the rich man. He was facing the wall and he half turned his
20 head to look behind him. "Ask him over."

"God no," Sylvester said.

"He's crazy," Simmons said. The bookie's voice was flat and without inflection. He had the face of a born gambler, carefully
25 adjusted, the expression a permanent deadlock between fear and greed.

"Well, I wouldn't call him that exactly," said Sylvester. "I've known him a long time. He was O.K. until about six months ago. But
30 if he goes on like this, I can't see him lasting another year. I just can't."

"It was what happened in Miami," said Simmons.

"What?" asked the rich man.

35 Sylvester glanced across the room at the jockey and wet the corner of his mouth with his red, fleshy tongue. "An accident. A kid got hurt on the track. Broke a leg and a hip. He was a particular pal of Bitsy's. A Irish kid.
40 Not a bad rider, either."

"That's a pity," said the rich man.

—Excerpted from "The Jockey"
by Carson McCullers, 1936

1. Where does the scene occur?

   (1) in a local tavern
   (2) at a racetrack
   (3) in a locker room
   (4) in Miami Beach
   (5) in a restaurant

2. What is the author's purpose in the arrangement of details in the first paragraph?

   (1) to reveal the jockey's behavior
   (2) to establish a conflict in the plot
   (3) to introduce three characters
   (4) to create an atmosphere of suspense
   (5) to show the drinking habits of alcoholics

3. How did Sylvester react when he first noticed the jockey?

   (1) He invited the jockey to the table.
   (2) He looked away quickly.
   (3) He glanced across the room.
   (4) He ordered another round of drinks.
   (5) He criticized the jockey's career.

POSTTEST

4. According to the passage, what is the effect of Bitsy Barlow on Sylvester and Simmons?

(1) He arouses their sympathy.
(2) He makes them feel nervous.
(3) He angers them.
(4) They admire him.
(5) They show affection toward him.

5. Whose situation is similar to Bitsy's?

(1) an injured football player who makes a fast recovery
(2) a gambler who has occasional losing streaks
(3) a politician who wins a major election
(4) a boxer who loses his confidence
(5) a salesman who can't make a sale

6. When did a change occur in Bitsy Barlow's character?

When he
(1) drank too much whiskey and soda
(2) broke his leg and hip
(3) lost a race and went crazy
(4) saw a close friend get injured on the track
(5) lost his money in a gambling bet

POSTTEST

Questions 7–12 refer to the following excerpt from a play.

WHY IS CHELSEA COMPLAINING TO HER MOTHER?

ETHEL: Can't you be home for five minutes without getting started on the past?

CHELSEA: This house seems to set me off.

5 ETHEL: Well, it shouldn't. It's a nice house.

CHELSEA: I act like a big person everywhere else. I do. I'm in charge in Los Angeles. I guess
10 I've never grown up on Golden Pond. Do you understand?

ETHEL: I don't think so.

CHELSEA: It doesn't matter. There's just something about coming back
15 here that makes me feel like a little fat girl.

ETHEL: Sit down and tell me about your trip.

CHELSEA: *[An outburst]* I don't want to sit
20 down. Where were you all that time? You never bailed me out.

ETHEL: I didn't know you needed bailing out.

CHELSEA: Well, I did.

25 ETHEL: Here we go again. You had a miserable childhood. Your father was overbearing, your mother ignored you. What else is new? Don't you think everyone looks
30 back on their childhood with some bitterness or regret about something? You are a big girl now, aren't you tired of it all?

35 You have this unpleasant chip on your shoulder which is very unattractive. You only come home when I beg you to, and when you get here all you can do
40 is be disagreeable about the past. Life marches by, Chelsea, I suggest you get on with it. *[ETHEL stands and glares at CHELSEA.]*

—Excerpted from *On Golden Pond* by Ernest Thompson, 1979

7. How does Chelsea feel when she visits Golden Pond?

(1) like a grown-up
(2) like a little fat girl
(3) like a houseguest
(4) like a released prisoner
(5) like an unwelcome stranger

8. What is the tone of Chelsea's dialogue?

(1) calm
(2) insensitive
(3) horrifying
(4) mature
(5) emotional

9. What is the main point of Ethel's dialogue in lines 25–42, "Here we go again . . . "?

(1) Chelsea has an overbearing father and a neglectful mother.
(2) Chelsea avoids visiting her parents at Golden Pond.
(3) Chelsea should stop dwelling on the past.
(4) Chelsea should pay more attention to events in her past.
(5) Chelsea's unhappiness as an adult stems from her miserable childhood.

10. With what statement would Ethel probably agree?

(1) Parents ruin their children's lives.
(2) People shouldn't bear grudges.
(3) Mothers don't confront the past.
(4) Children are forced to grow up too quickly.
(5) Relationships with parents improve over time.

11. What is Ethel's tone in lines 25–42?

(1) pleading
(2) angry
(3) solemn
(4) sarcastic
(5) friendly

12. What is the nature of the conflict between the two women?

(1) Chelsea blames her weight problem on Ethel.
(2) Ethel refuses to listen to Chelsea's problems.
(3) Chelsea is unwilling to grow up emotionally.
(4) Ethel resents Chelsea's leaving home.
(5) Chelsea doesn't like the home on Golden Pond.

POSTTEST

Questions 13–19 refer to the following excerpt from a review of a play.

WHAT IS SPECIAL ABOUT THIS PLAY?

Joy is in short supply on Broadway these days. If you luck into any, you should seize and cherish it. Joy comes with the first beats of the Steppenwolf Theatre
5 Company's "The Song of Jacob Zulu" at the Plymouth, when the rusting corrugated backdrop, which simulates a township fence, rises up and Ladysmith Black Mambazo, a nine-man a-cappella group
10 that serves here as a chorus, march into view, in their white tunics, and then down the raked stage toward us. "*Lalelani, lalelani,*" they chant, in the mournful, sonorous harmonies that have made them
15 world famous as the backup group for Paul Simon's "Graceland" album. The words of the song, and of the English ones that follow, are projected on a screen above the proscenium, so the audience can follow
20 their South African English patois, but it hardly matters. The heart knows what they're saying, and it inexplicably lifts at their sound. We are in the presence of something pure and wholly original.
25 Ladysmith Black Mambazo step in place, idling as their song continues

The fire is burning.
It lights up the sky. . . .
It is taking the children
30 *It is eating the future.*

The Zulu word for music—*sicathamiya*—comes from dancing and means "tiptoe." To Western eyes, the group's step is something between a hitch kick and a karate kick; but
35 the movement, so beautiful to see, is neither frivolous nor aggressive. It bears the stamp of all Zulu gesture—economical, elegant, and starkly dramatic. Freedom needs a song, and Ladysmith Black Mambazo give

40 voice and body to both the struggle and the longing.

—Excerpted from "The Forest and the Trees" by John Lahr, *The New Yorker*, April 12, 1993

13. What is the rusty, corrugated backdrop in the scene supposed to look like?

  (1) an abandoned city
  (2) a township fence
  (3) a worn-out stage
  (4) a neighborhood school
  (5) an old building

14. What is the author's purpose in the first three sentences?

  (1) to outline the plot of the play
  (2) to provide background information on Zulu music
  (3) to introduce the actors cast in leading roles
  (4) to explain why the audience will enjoy the play
  (5) to describe the costumes and scenery

15. What is the Zulu word for music?

  (1) mambazo
  (2) lalelani
  (3) patois
  (4) ladysmith
  (5) sicathamiya

16. What is the reviewer's attitude toward the total production?

  He believes it is
  (1) inconsistent
  (2) inspiring
  (3) disturbing
  (4) overwhelming
  (5) gloomy

POSTTEST

17. What conclusion does the reviewer reach about the significance of *The Song of Jacob Zulu?*

(1) The chorus will become a world-famous recording group.
(2) The play speaks to the heart of the struggle for freedom.
(3) The experience will motivate people to learn more about the South African Zulus.
(4) The music and dance will change traditional views of black South Africans.
(5) The audience may react in a negative way to this new kind of musical.

18. Which group of people especially might have identified with the characters in this play?

(1) Oriental karate experts
(2) English country dancers
(3) French missionaries
(4) American slaves
(5) Spanish explorers

19. The songs in this production were created during a time when the Blacks of South Africa were subject to the system of apartheid. This system denied them the right to vote and limited where they could live, study, and work.

Based on this information, what does the word "fire" in the song lines refer to?

(1) justice
(2) freedom
(3) poverty
(4) enslavement
(5) illness

POSTTEST

Questions 20–24 are from an excerpt from a novel.

WHAT ARE A PERSON'S TREASURES?

"You like my treasures?" the rabbi said, and Michael's heart slipped.

"What?"

"My books," the rabbi said, his own
5   hand touching the books on the second shelf, below the photograph of the dark-haired woman. "Is all I have, but treasure, yes?"

Michael's heart steadied as he peered
10 more closely at the books. Their titles were in languages he did not know or letters that he did not recognize.

"You like books?" the rabbi asked.

"Yes," Michael said. "I love books. But—
15 are these books written in Jewish?"

The rabbi pointed at the leather bindings of the thickest books.

"Not Jewish, *Hebrew*, these here," he said. And then he touched some smaller
20 books, with worn paper bindings. "These are Yiddish."

"What's the difference?"

"Hebrew is, eh, the eh . . . " His eyes drifted to the dictionary. "Language of
25 Yisreal."

The word came out *lan-goo-age*, the last syllable rhyming with *rage*. Michael pronounced it correctly for the rabbi, who nodded, his bushy black eyebrows rising in
30 appreciation.

"Eh, language." He said it correctly. "Good, I need your help. Please tell me when I make mistake. Language, language. Good. Anyway, Hebrew is language of Torah
35 and Talmud—"

"*The* language," Michael said, remembering the endless drills in grammar class. "The *the*? It's called an article," Michael explained. "A definite article, they
40 call it. *The* language, *the* table, *the* stove."

The rabbi smiled. "The tea!"

He went to the stove and lifted the boiling water and poured it into a pot.

"We soon have *the* tea!"

45 "What are those other books?" Michael said. "You started to say—"

"Yiddish," the rabbi said. "The language of the people. The ordinary people. Not the rabbis. The ordinary people."

50 "What are the books about?"

The rabbi stood before the bookcase.

"They are about everything," he said lifting a volume. "Religion. The history of the Jews." He hefted a volume. "But also
55 Balzac. You know Balzac?"

"No."

"Very good, Balzac. A very smart Frenchman. You should read the Balzac. He knows everything. And this is Henrich Heine.
60 Very good poetry. And here, Tolstoy, very great."

Michael squatted down, took a dusty book off a bottom shelf, and opened it.

—Excerpted from *Snow in August* by Pete Hamill, 1997

20. What language was used for the rabbi's religious books?

(1) Jewish
(2) English
(3) Yiddish
(4) French
(5) Hebrew

POSTTEST

21. What relationship would be similar to that of Michael and the rabbi?

   (1) parent and child
   (2) employer and employee
   (3) student and teacher
   (4) counselor and patient
   (5) attorney and client

22. According to the passage, what do Michael and the rabbi share?

   (1) religious beliefs
   (2) language
   (3) educational background
   (4) attitude toward books
   (5) ability to read in several languages

23. What is meant by the line, "Is all I have, but treasure, yes?"

   (1) The rabbi's books were expensive.
   (2) The rabbi's books were important to him.
   (3) The rabbi was poor.
   (4) The rabbi thought Michael wanted his books.
   (5) The rabbi has gold and jewels.

24. Earlier in the story one of Michael's friends tells him about the treasure of gold, diamonds, and jewels that many believed the rabbis had hidden away.

Which of the following is Michael most likely to do?

   (1) complain to his friend for leading him to expect that the rabbi would have gold
   (2) demand that the rabbi stop hiding his gold
   (3) become friendly with the rabbi because of his appreciation of the rabbi's books
   (4) become friendly with the rabbi in order to find out where his real treasure is
   (5) steal the rabbi's books and sell them for gold

POSTTEST

Questions 25–29 are based on the following business-related document.

HOW IS THE COMPANY'S E-MAIL NETWORK TO BE USED?

Company Property

The computer system is the property of the company and should be used for company business only. Employee use of the network is considered consent to the policy and to management's right to review e-mail (or listen to telephone conversations or voice mail).

5 ### Business Use Only

The company requires that e-mail be sent only if it has a valid business or work-related reason. E-mail should not be used to solicit or to advocate non-company or purely personal interests. Foul, offensive, defamatory, pornographic or other inappropriate communication is prohibited. *This prohibition is critically important because the company as the employer can be held liable*
10 *for anything that can be construed as harassment that takes place over the e-mail network.*

Right to Monitor

The employer reserves the right to monitor the e-mail network and to access and examine information in an employee's e-mail mailbox at any time, without prior notice, to ensure that the system is being used for company purposes only and to ensure that employer policies prohibiting
15 harassment are being followed.

Not Private

Employees must understand that they do not have a personal privacy right in any matter created, received, or sent from the e-mail system. We remind employees that e-mail can be read or intercepted by others, including inadvertent disclosure, accidental transmission to third parties,
20 or purposeful transmission to another employee's internal mailing list. Management may enter an employee's e-mail mailbox or computer files for business purposes, and for this reason, employees must disclose their personal passwords to the employer. During new employee orientation, HR representatives will advise newcomers that e-mail is "as private as a postcard."

Need to Know

25 Employees should disclose information or messages from the e-mail network only to authorized employees and managerial staff. E-mail is limited to those with a need to know. This applies to both company proprietary information or confidential material protected by attorney-client privilege. In some cases, sensitive information should not be sent via e-mail.

Policy Violations

30 E-mail policy violations will subject an employee to disciplinary action, including possible discharge. All employees will sign a form indicating that they have read and reviewed the policy. In addition to discussion at the new employee orientation, the personnel manual contains this policy, and a reminder e-mail notice will appear on the computer screen the first time an employee logs on to the network.

POSTTEST

35 **On-screen Prompt**

To minimize any after-the-fact privacy claims, *every time* an employee logs on to the computer terminal, this on-screen message will appear:

"This system is to be used for official company business only. You have no privacy rights in e-mail messages or any other data files. This account is subject to monitoring to determine if it complies
45 *with business use. If you understand and agree to these terms, press ENTER."*

—Based on an e-mail statement from *HRnext.com*

25. According to this policy statement, what is the company's primary concern?

    (1) unfair competition
    (2) employee distractions
    (3) security leaks
    (4) unwanted business solicitation
    (5) legal compliance

26. What is the purpose of the "On-screen Prompt" described in the final paragraph?

    (1) to advise employees of the penalties for using e-mail for personal interests
    (2) to suggest ways to avoid monitoring
    (3) to remind employees of their responsibilities
    (4) to define what is not a business-related use
    (5) to discourage employees from using e-mail

27. According to the passage, who has the ultimate responsibility for adhering to the policy?

    (1) employees
    (2) the company
    (3) supervisors and administrators
    (4) e-mail network monitors
    (5) human-resource trainers

28. Which choice best describes the overall purpose of the policy?

    (1) disciplinary
    (2) cautionary
    (3) critical
    (4) polite
    (5) vague

29. An employee at this company sends a fellow employee an e-mail which contains the e-mail addresses of potential clients the second employee needs to contact in the course of work.

Which choice best describes the employee's actions?

The employee
    (1) has violated policy for transmitting nonbusiness information
    (2) must justify to management the business nature of the e-mail
    (3) has properly disclosed information on a need-to-know basis
    (4) should have delivered the addresses personally to avoid interception
    (5) has put the employer at risk for possible harassment

Questions 30–34 are from the following excerpt from a short story.

WHY DOES CARTER DRUSE GO TO WAR?

The sleeping sentinel in the clump of laurel was a young Virginian named Carter Druse. He was the son of wealthy parents, an only child, and had known such ease and
5   cultivation and high living as wealth and taste were able to command in the mountain country of western Virginia. His home was but a few miles from where he now lay. One morning he had risen from the
10 breakfast-table and said, quietly but gravely: "Father, a Union regiment has arrived at Grafton. I am going to join it."

The father lifted his leonine head, looked at the son a moment in silence, and
15 replied: "Well, go, sir, and whatever may occur do what you conceive to be your duty. Virginia, to which you are a traitor, must get on without you. Should we both live to the end of the war, we will speak further of the
20 matter. Your mother, as the physician has informed you, is in a most critical condition; at the best she cannot be with us longer than a few weeks, but that time is precious. It would be better not to disturb her."

25 So Carter Druse, bowing reverently to his father, who returned the salute with a stately courtesy that masked a breaking heart, left the home of his childhood to go soldiering. By conscience and courage, by
30 deeds of devotion and daring, he soon commended himself to his fellows and officers; and it was to these qualities and to some knowledge of the country that he owed his selection for his present perilous
35 duty at the extreme outpost. Nevertheless, fatigue had been stronger than resolution and he had fallen asleep. What good or bad angel came in a dream to rouse him from his state of crime, who shall say? Without a
40 movement, without a sound, in the profound silence and the languor of the afternoon, some invisible messenger of fate touched with unsealing finger the eyes of his consciousness—whispered into the ear of
45 his spirit the mysterious awakening word which no human lips ever have spoken, no human memory ever has recalled. He quietly raised his forehead from his arm and looked between the masking stems of the laurels,
50 instinctively closing his right hand about the stock of his rifle.

His first feeling was a keen artistic delight. On a colossal pedestal, the cliff,— motionless at the extreme edge of the
55 capping rock and sharply outlined against the sky,—was an equestrian statue of impressive dignity. The figure of the man sat the figure of the horse, straight and soldierly, but with the repose of a Grecian
60 god carved in the marble which limits the suggestion of activity.

—Excerpted from "A Horseman in the Sky"
by Ambrose Bierce

30. What does the father's attitude toward his son appear to be?

One of
(1) hatred
(2) suspicion
(3) amusement
(4) respect
(5) disbelief

31. According to the excerpt, how does Carter Druse perform as a soldier?

He is
(1) fierce and terrifying
(2) dedicated and brave
(3) foolish and cowardly
(4) brutal and menacing
(5) obedient and attentive

POSTTEST

32. What is the purpose of the third paragraph?

(1) to reveal his cowardice in combat
(2) to introduce an important event
(3) to describe a soldier's routine
(4) to explain Druse's regret at leaving home
(5) to suggest the impact of his mother's death

33. On the basis of the father's character as revealed in the passage, which of the following would he most likely do if Carter deserted the Union Army because of cowardice?

(1) welcome Carter home happily
(2) insist that Carter join the army of Virginia
(3) be ashamed because Carter had not done his duty as he saw it
(4) lie if necessary to keep his friends from learning about his son's actions
(5) tell Carter that he had done the right thing

34. At the end of the story, Druse shoots the horseman on the cliff, knowing that the horseman is his father.

On the basis of this information, which choice offers the best explanation for the author's purpose for the story?

(1) to explain the son's anger toward his father
(2) to reveal one of the causes of the war
(3) to suggest how families suffered during the war
(4) to explain how the Civil War affected Virginians
(5) to state that doing one's duty involves difficult choices

POSTTEST

Questions 35–40 refer to the following poem.

WHAT ADVICE DOES A MOTHER GIVE HER SON?

Well, son, I'll tell you:
Life for me ain't been no crystal stair.
It's had tacks in it,
And splinters,
5 And boards torn up,
And places with no carpet on the floor—
Bare.
But all the time
I'se been a-climbin' on,
10 And reachin' landin's,
And turnin' corners,
And sometimes goin' in the dark
Where there ain't been no light.
So boy, don't you turn back.
15 Don't you set down on the steps
'Cause you finds it's kinder hard.
Don't you fall now—
For I'se still goin', honey,
I'se still climbin',
20 And life for me ain't been no crystal stair.

—"Mother To Son" by Langston Hughes

35. What does the mother mean by "crystal stair" (lines 2 and 20)?

A life that is
(1) hard and challenging
(2) short and happy
(3) easy and smooth
(4) painful and long
(5) long and winding

36. What is meant by line 14, "So boy, don't you turn back"?

(1) Look for the easy way.
(2) Don't return to poverty.
(3) Get a good education.
(4) Choose your friends wisely.
(5) Never stop trying to improve.

37. Which of the following is the best description of the way the mother has dealt with hardship?

(1) complaining
(2) persevering
(3) surrendering
(4) slowing down
(5) fantasizing

38. Which situation would be similar to the mother's in this poem?

That of
(1) a counselor who advises a patient
(2) an employer who must reprimand a worker
(3) a doctor who gives good news to a patient
(4) an artist who loses the inspiration to work
(5) a scientist who makes an important discovery

39. How does the mother hope to convince her son?

(1) with gifts
(2) with threats
(3) with sympathy
(4) by example
(5) with guilt

40. Which choice best represents the meaning of the poem?

(1) The mother resents all the sacrifices she has made.
(2) The son does not appreciate his mother's hard work.
(3) The mother has held herself back from better jobs.
(4) The mother wants her son to see the value in not giving up.
(5) The son needs an education to earn a high paying job.

Answer Key

1. (5) The following statement supports this inference: "A white-coated waiter had just brought on the main course of the dinner" (lines 9–11).

2. (3) The first paragraph introduces Sylvester, the trainer; Simmons, the bookie; and the rich man.

3. (2) Lines 12–13 directly state, "It was Sylvester who first saw the jockey. He looked away quickly."

4. (2) When Sylvester saw Bitsy, he "looked away quickly", and objected to the rich man's suggestion of inviting Bitsy over with "God no." Simmons claimed, "He's crazy."

5. (4) Just as the accident with his friend weakened Bitsy's confidence, a boxer who lost his confidence in the ring would endanger his career.

6. (4) Sylvester, the trainer, states the reason for Bitsy Barlow's behavior change: "An accident. A kid got hurt on the track. Broke a leg and a hip. He was a particular pal of Bitsy's" (lines 37–39).

7. (2) Chelsea directly states, "There's just something about coming back here that makes me feel like a little fat girl" (lines 13–16).

8. (5) The stage direction [An outburst] (line 19) indicates that Chelsea is delivering her lines emotionally.

9. (3) The main point of Ethel's speech is "Don't you think everyone looks back on their childhood with some bitterness or regret . . . ?" (lines 29–31). The remaining lines of dialogue imply that Chelsea's situation is not unique, and that she should move on with her life.

10. (2) From the very beginning of the scene, you can infer that Ethel finds Chelsea's complaining about the past to be annoying and senseless. Therefore, Ethel would probably agree that people shouldn't bear grudges because they should place their past experiences behind them.

11. (4) Ethel is exaggerating Chelsea's childhood problems.

12. (3) Ethel reminds Chelsea several times that she dwells too much on the past. "Life marches by, Chelsea, I suggest you get on with it." (lines 41–42)

13. (2) Lines 7–8 state that the backdrop simulates a township fence.

14. (4) The reviewer creates an aura of expectation. The words he chooses to describe the play's opening scene cause the reader to feel that something special is happening: For example, in lines 3–5, he says, "Joy comes with the first beats of the Steppenwolf Theatre Company's 'The Song of Jacob Zulu'.

15. (5) Lines 31–32 directly translate the Zulu word for music—sicathamiya.

16. (2) From the first paragraph, the author speaks of the joy found in the total production. He also says that the heart "knows what they're saying, and it inexplicably lifts at their sound."

17. (2) The reviewer describes how, in song and dance, Ladysmith Black Mambazo evokes the struggle and longing for freedom.

18. (4) The Song of Jacob Zulu embodies the same struggle for freedom as the historical longing for freedom of slaves in America.

19. (4) The performance is about the South Africans' struggle for freedom. The "fire" *takes* children and *eats* the future. Enslavement is the denial of freedom for the children's future.

20. (5) The rabbi tells Michael that "Hebrew is the language of Torah and Talmud."

21. (3) Michael and the rabbi teach one another. Michael teaches the rabbi proper English, and the rabbi teaches Michael about his books.

22. (4) The rabbi calls books his treasures, and Michael states, "I love books."

23. (2) The conversation that follows shows that the rabbi sees his books as very important, as treasures.

24. (3) Michael's questions about the rabbi's books indicate that he is interested in learning more about them.

25. (5) The wording of the policy statement is carefully chosen to be in legal compliance by spelling out the employer/employee responsibilities for use of the e-mail network.

26. (3) The on-screen prompt makes it clear to the employee what the policy is and forces the employee to acknowledge the policy before using the computer.

27. (1) The focus of the entire policy statement is the employee's responsibility to adhere to the policy's provisions.

28. (2) The policy warns or cautions the employee about how the e-mail network is to be used.

29. (4) Because the e-mail addresses of potential clients are sensitive information that could be intercepted and misused, the employee should deliver them to the fellow employee in a manner that ensures the privacy of the potential clients.

30. (4) Although father and son differ in their views, the father respects the son's convictions.

31. (2) Paragraph 3 states that Carter Druse commended himself "by conscience and courage, by deeds of devotion and daring."

32. (2) The paragraph states that "some invisible messenger of fate" woke him from his sleep. When he awoke, he spotted the horseman on the cliff.

33. (3) His father agreed that Carter should join the Union Army if he feels that is his duty, so he would be disappointed if Carter did not stick to that duty.

34. (5) The entire passage focuses on Carter Druse's sense of duty and honor. The fact that he must shoot his own father conveys his strong belief in his service to the Union cause.

35. (3) The mother describes her life as difficult, with "tacks," "splinters," and "boards torn up." By "crystal stair," she means a life very different from her own.

36. (5) The mother describes the hardships she has faced and *continues* to face, and she keeps trying, struggling.

37. (2) The mother has been "climbin'," "reachin'," and "turnin'" all her life.

38. (1) Just as a counselor helps a patient cope with a problem, the mother tries to encourage her son to meet the challenges of life.

39. (4) Lines 15–20 reveal that the mother has never stopped trying but continues to work for a better life. Her life is an example for her son.

40. (4) Line 15 reveals the mother's advice directed at her son: "Don't you set down on the steps"; you keep going.

POSTTEST

Evaluation Chart

Use the following chart to determine the reading skills areas in which you need to do the most work. For the GED Language Arts, Reading Test, you are required to answer the following types of questions: comprehension, application, analysis, and synthesis. These reading skills, covered on pages 15–105 of this book, are absolutely essential for success on the test. Circle any items that you got wrong and pay particular attention to areas in which you missed half or more of the questions.

Skill Area/Content Area	Comprehension (pages 15–37)	Application (pages 39–46)	Analysis (pages 47–88)	Synthesis (pages 89–105)
Nonfiction Prose (pages 109–164)	13, 15, 25	19	14, 16, 26, 27	17, 18, 28, 29
Prose Fiction (pages 165–215)	3, 6, 20, 31	5, 21, 33	1, 2, 23, 30, 32	4, 22, 24, 34
Poetry (pages 217–247)	37, 39	38	35, 36	40
Drama (pages 249–281)	7, 9	10	8, 11	12

Language Arts, Reading

Directions: This Language Arts, Reading Practice Test will give you a second opportunity to evaluate your readiness for the actual GED Language Arts, Reading Test.

The Practice Test contains 40 questions. These questions are based on passages of fiction and nonfiction prose, poetry, and drama.

You should take approximately 65 minutes to complete this test. At the end of 65 minutes, stop and mark your place. Then finish the test. This will give you an idea of whether or not you can finish the real GED Test in the time allotted. Try to answer as many questions as you can. A blank will count as a wrong answer, so make a reasonable guess for questions that you are not sure of.

When you are finished with the test, turn to the evaluation chart on page 318. Use the chart to evaluate whether you are ready to take the actual GED Test and, if not, what areas need more work.

Practice Test Answer Grid

1 ① ② ③ ④ ⑤		15 ① ② ③ ④ ⑤		29 ① ② ③ ④ ⑤
2 ① ② ③ ④ ⑤		16 ① ② ③ ④ ⑤		30 ① ② ③ ④ ⑤
3 ① ② ③ ④ ⑤		17 ① ② ③ ④ ⑤		31 ① ② ③ ④ ⑤
4 ① ② ③ ④ ⑤		18 ① ② ③ ④ ⑤		32 ① ② ③ ④ ⑤
5 ① ② ③ ④ ⑤		19 ① ② ③ ④ ⑤		33 ① ② ③ ④ ⑤
6 ① ② ③ ④ ⑤		20 ① ② ③ ④ ⑤		34 ① ② ③ ④ ⑤
7 ① ② ③ ④ ⑤		21 ① ② ③ ④ ⑤		35 ① ② ③ ④ ⑤
8 ① ② ③ ④ ⑤		22 ① ② ③ ④ ⑤		36 ① ② ③ ④ ⑤
9 ① ② ③ ④ ⑤		23 ① ② ③ ④ ⑤		37 ① ② ③ ④ ⑤
10 ① ② ③ ④ ⑤		24 ① ② ③ ④ ⑤		38 ① ② ③ ④ ⑤
11 ① ② ③ ④ ⑤		25 ① ② ③ ④ ⑤		39 ① ② ③ ④ ⑤
12 ① ② ③ ④ ⑤		26 ① ② ③ ④ ⑤		40 ① ② ③ ④ ⑤
13 ① ② ③ ④ ⑤		27 ① ② ③ ④ ⑤		
14 ① ② ③ ④ ⑤		28 ① ② ③ ④ ⑤		

PRACTICE TEST

Directions: Read each passage and choose the best answer to the questions that follow.

Questions 1–6 refer to the following excerpt from an autobiography.

IS THERE A WAY TO DEFEAT A GHOST?

"You will not win, Boulder," she spoke to the ghost. "You do not belong here. And I will see to it that you leave. When morning comes, only one of us will control this room,
5 Ghost, and that one will be me. I will be marching its length and width; I will be dancing, not sliding and creeping like you. I will go right out that door, but I'll come back. Do you know what gift I will bring
10 you? I'll get fire, Ghost. You made a mistake haunting a medical school. We have cabinets full of alcohol, laboratories full. We have a communal kitchen with human-sized jars of oil and cooking fat, enough to burn for a
15 month without our skipping a single fried meal. I will pour alcohol into my washbucket, and I'll set fire to it. Ghost, I will burn you out. I will swing the bucket across the ceiling. Then from the kitchen my friends will
20 come with the lard; when we fire it, the smoke will fill every crack and corner. Where will you hide, Ghost? I will make this room so clean, no ghost will ever visit here again.

"I do not give in," she said. "There is no
25 pain you can inflict that I cannot endure. You're wrong if you think I'm afraid of you. You're no mystery to me. I've heard of you Sitting Ghosts before. Yes, people have lived to tell about you. You kill babies, you
30 cowards. You have no power over a strong woman. You are no more dangerous than a nesting cat. My dog sits on my feet more heavily than you can. You think this is suffering? I can make my ears ring louder by
35 taking aspirin. Are these all the tricks you have, Ghost? Sitting and ringing? That is nothing. A Broom Ghost can do better. You

cannot even assume an interesting shape. Merely a boulder. A hairy butt boulder. You
40 must not be a ghost at all. There are no such things as ghosts."

—Excerpted from *The Woman Warrior*
by Maxine Hong Kingston, 1977

1. How does the ghost described in the excerpt upset the woman?

    (1) by setting fire to alcohol in her washbucket
    (2) by sitting on her feet and making her ears ring
    (3) by burning her with jars of oil and cooking fat
    (4) by throwing stones and scaring her cat
    (5) by giving her aspirin to make her stomach ache

2. Where does the haunting take place?

    (1) in a school
    (2) in a closet
    (3) in a castle
    (4) in a graveyard
    (5) in a library

3. Which choice best describes the woman?

    (1) friendly
    (2) shy
    (3) contented
    (4) cautious
    (5) determined

4. Why does the woman speak angrily to the ghost?

   (1) to show the ghost that she is more powerful than it is
   (2) to entertain the ghost so that it will not harm her
   (3) to drown out the ghost's voice so that she won't hear it
   (4) to keep the ghost from haunting someone else
   (5) to make the ghost as angry as she is

5. How does the author reveal the woman's personality?

   (1) through her friends' statements about her
   (2) through the ghost's reaction to her
   (3) through her speech to the ghost
   (4) through her statements about herself
   (5) through her interaction with other characters

6. What would the woman be most likely to do if someone tried to rob her?

   (1) faint in fright
   (2) run away
   (3) call for help
   (4) refuse to cooperate
   (5) hand over her purse

Questions 7–12 refer to the following excerpt from a short story.

DO DREAMS SOMETIMES HAVE TO WAIT FOR ANOTHER SUMMER?

This idea of selling ice cream during the summer seems ridiculous, pointless. I'd much rather be close to the water. The waves. Where I can hear them tumble in and
5 then roll out, and see the tiny bubbles left behind on the sand pop one by one. Or feel the undercurrents warm this time of year. Swimming. Watching the girls in bikinis with sand stuck to the backs of their thighs walk
10 up and down the boardwalk. At this time of the morning, the surfers are out riding the waves.

Instead I'm inside an ice cream truck with my father, selling, cruising the streets.
15 The pumps suck oil out of the ground rapidly with the creaking sounds of iron biting iron in a fenced lot at the end of the street. They look like giant rocking horses.

Father turns at the corner, then,
20 suddenly, he points to another ice cream truck.

"There's the competition," he says. "If the economy doesn't improve soon, these streets'll be full of them."

25 He's smoking, and the smoke floats back my way and chokes me. I can't stand it. Some of the guys on the swim team smoke. I don't understand how they can smoke and do their best when it's time for competition.
30 I wouldn't smoke. To do so would be like cheating myself out of winning.

All morning he's been instructing me on how to sell ice cream.

"Tonio," he says now, "come empty your
35 pockets."

I walk to the front of the truck, stick my hands deep into my pockets and grab a handful of coins—what we've made in change all morning. The coins fall, overlap
40 and multiply against the sides of the grease-smudged change box. I turn my pockets inside-out until the last coin falls. He picks the pieces of lint and paper from the coins.

When he begins to explain the truck's
45 quirks, "the little problems," as he calls the water leaks, burning oil, and dirty carburetor, I return to the back of the truck and sit down on top of the wood counter next to the window.

50 "Be always on the lookout for babies," father says. "The ones in Pampers. They pop out of nowhere. Check your mirrors all the time."

A CAUTION CHILDREN cardboard sign
55 hangs from the rearview mirror. Running over children is a deep fear that seems to haunt him.

All I need, I keep reminding myself, is to pass the CPR course, get certified, and look
60 for a job as a beach lifeguard.

—Excerpted from "A Perfect Hotspot"
by Virgil Suárez, 1992

7. What is the main idea of this excerpt?

(1) A son wants a life different from his father's.
(2) A father trains his son in the art of selling.
(3) A son hopes to improve his father's business.
(4) A father and son cope with a failing economy.
(5) A son passes a CPR course to help his father.

8. Which of the following activities would Tonio be most likely to enjoy?

(1) smoking cigarettes with his friends
(2) working at a beach or pool
(3) helping his father's business succeed
(4) teaching road safety to youngsters
(5) spending the summer selling ice cream

9. What does the father fear most?

(1) losing money in the oil business
(2) having things go wrong with the truck
(3) competing with other ice-cream vendors
(4) injuring very young children
(5) developing an illness from smoking

10. Where does the situation described in the excerpt take place?

(1) in a congested business district
(2) on an oceanside beach
(3) in a residential neighborhood
(4) on a deserted oil field
(5) in a small farming community

11. What behavior of his father's does Tonio find most annoying?

(1) his cautions to watch for children
(2) his smoking while on the truck
(3) his views on the failing economy
(4) his instructions on caring for the truck
(5) his directions for selling ice cream

12. How are the first two paragraphs organized?

(1) time order (details presented in the order in which they happened)
(2) comparison and contrast (one idea placed after a contrasting idea to show how they differ)
(3) classification (similar ideas grouped together on the basis of what they have in common)
(4) order of importance (ideas presented in order of their significance or effectiveness)
(5) cause and effect (ideas grouped as either reasons or outcomes)

PRACTICE TEST

Questions 13–17 refer to the following excerpt from a play.

IS THERE SOMETHING MORE VALUABLE THAN POSSESSIONS?

DERELICT: I got no place to go. This here is my home. But that don't bother me. What does though—is how cold this place is getting to be. And I ain't talking about the
5   weather. . . . Seems to me we going through a New Ice Age where everything is cold, frozen, and dead.

Now it wasn't always like that. There used to be a time when these streets were
10 warm, people was civil—and Harlem was a different place. A place where the living came to enjoy life.

You still hear the old music sometimes— see the old photographs, but it's gone. All
15 gone . . .

I seen it all and more. Mixed with everybody. Stayed up till the moon went down and the sun came out shining. Drove around in fast cars, but somehow got left
20 behind when the whole parade turned the corner. . . . Why?. . . I don't know. Maybe I got too old.

Louis Armstrong, Billie Holiday, Ethel Waters, Duke Ellington, Bo Jangles, and all
25 them others walked these streets and blessed this area with the music of their soul. This is a holy ground, if you know what I mean. This place should be a shrine to the talent and life that was spent here.
30 Somebody should anoint it as the Black man's Capital, the way Rome is for Catholics and DC is for the Nation, before this new cold spell passes and takes it all away. But what can you do? Maybe it's too late already
35 . . . . and who am I to be telling you what you should, and shouldn't, be doing? Just another dirty derelict, shuffling through the streets looking for a handout. Ain't that so?

Well, I ain't one to argue. After all, I still
40 got my memories. What've you got?

—Excerpted from *New Ice Age* by Gus Edwards, 1985

13. In the excerpt, what does the word *derelict* refer to?

(1) a person who is looking for a job
(2) a man who is past retirement age
(3) a musician who plays in clubs
(4) a homeless person who begs for handouts
(5) an individual who lives in the past

14. Why does the derelict feel that Harlem is "holy ground"?

(1) because it is famous for its many beautiful old churches
(2) because it is a warm and friendly place
(3) because the area was a center of African-American life and culture
(4) because the neighborhood resembles Rome, the seat of Roman Catholicism
(5) because the derelict used to play religious music there as a young man

15. What activity would be most likely to interest the derelict?

(1) restoring an old dilapidated building
(2) observing a parade from a street corner
(3) listening to a jazz concert in a Harlem club
(4) attending a church revival in Washington, D.C.
(5) taking a bus tour to see how Harlem has changed

PRACTICE TEST

16. In the play, what does the derelict represent?

    (1) old Harlem music and photographs
    (2) a Harlem parade turning a corner
    (3) poor people who live in Harlem
    (4) Harlem's famous musicians
    (5) Harlem's past and present

17. Why does the derelict feel superior to other people?

    Because he
    (1) doesn't have to work
    (2) has wonderful memories
    (3) is friends with famous people
    (4) enjoys an active nightlife
    (5) drives a fast car

PRACTICE TEST

Questions 18–22 refer to the following excerpt from a review of a play.

DOES THE REVIEWER LIKE THE PLAY?

In the second act of Scott McPherson's "Marvin's Room," Bessie, the play's heroine, learns by phone that there is no help for her in her battle against leukemia.

5 She hangs up the receiver, breaks the news to the family members gathered around her in the kitchen and tries to put a brave face on the bad news.

But then, as she makes a nervous
10 gesture, she tips over a small container and out spill all of her pills, dozens of small white pellets that roll noisily over the floor, now scattered and useless, like the hopes she has been keeping for her recovery.

15 There's a terrible moment of silence, and then Bessie kneels and frantically starts throwing the pills back into the container one by one, as if by quickly returning them she could also restore her chances for life.

20 It's a shocking and moving moment of drama, one of many such scenes in a play whose tremendous emotional power lies in the fact that it is filled with such brilliantly realized passages.

25 Of course, "Marvin's Room" deals with the potent and basic theme of family relationships, and beyond that, with the equally powerful subjects of the necessity of love and the inevitability of death in our
30 lives.

But what makes the play so remarkable is that these subjects are dramatized in that rare and special way of theater in which literature and action are joined in a perfect,
35 natural union of word and image.

From the everyday environment of a suburban home to the fantasy land of Disney World, McPherson found the exact scene, the perfect dialogue and the precise
40 image to express his American tragicomedy. There's nothing artificial or mechanical about it; everything, the most bizarre incident or darkest bit of humor, seems at home.

—Excerpted from "'Marvin's Room' Still a Winner" by Richard Christiansen, *Chicago Tribune*, March 24, 1993

18. According to the review, what story does the play *Marvin's Room* tell?

    The story of a
    (1) family's struggle to get along with each other
    (2) teenager's attempt to overcome drug addiction
    (3) brother and sister's final trip to Disney World
    (4) scientist's development of a pill to cure cancer
    (5) woman's battle against a deadly disease

19. What does the reviewer mean when he says that Bessie attempts to "put a brave face on the bad news" (lines 7–8)?

    (1) She refuses to listen to the bad news.
    (2) She doesn't realize that the news is bad.
    (3) She schemes to cover up the news with lies.
    (4) She acts bravely upon hearing the news.
    (5) She pretends the news isn't as bad as it is.

20. Which of the following phrases best describes what the reviewer thinks of the play?

    (1) brilliant and moving
    (2) artificial and mechanical
    (3) bizarre and shocking
    (4) frantic and funny
    (5) long and boring

21. Why does the reviewer give a detailed account of a dramatic moment from Act II?

   (1) to give an example of the kind of scene that he feels makes the play remarkable

   (2) to interpret for readers what a confusing event in the play means

   (3) to inform people about who the heroine and other main characters are

   (4) to let readers picture where the second act takes place

   (5) to explain why the playwright chose to cover certain subjects

22. How is the reviewer's writing style characterized?

By his
   (1) reliance on slang and other informal language

   (2) use of long, flowing sentences

   (3) lack of description and vivid words

   (4) development of a bitter, negative tone

   (5) attempt to be objective and unbiased

Questions 23–29 refer to an excerpt from a short story.

WHAT KIND OF PERSON IS DR. HEIDEGGER?

If all the stories were true, Dr. Heidegger's study must have been a very curious place. It was a dim, old-fashioned chamber, festooned with cobwebs and
5   besprinkled with antique dust. Around the walls stood several oaken bookcases, the lower shelves of which were filled with rows of gigantic folios[1] and black-letter quartos,[2] and the upper with little parchment-covered
10   duodecimos.[3] Over the central bookcase was a bronze bust of Hippocrates,[4] with which, according to some authorities, Dr. Heidegger was accustomed to hold consultations in all difficult cases of his
15   practice. In the obscurest corner of the room stood a tall and narrow oaken closet, with its door ajar, within which doubtfully appeared a skeleton. Between two of the bookcases hung a looking glass, presenting
20   its high and dusty plate with a tarnished gilt frame. Among many wonderful stories related of this mirror, it was fabled that the spirit of all the doctor's deceased patients dwelt within its verge and would stare him in
25   the face whenever he looked thitherward. The opposite side of the chamber was ornamented with the full-length portrait of a young lady, arrayed in the faded magnificence of silk, satin, and brocade and
30   with a visage as faded as her dress. Above half a century ago, Dr. Heidegger had been on the point of marriage with this young lady; but being affected with some slight disorder, she had swallowed one of her
35   lover's prescriptions and died on the bridal evening. The greatest curiosity of the study remains to be mentioned; it was a ponderous folio volume, bound in black leather, with massive silver clasps. There

40   were no letters on the back, and nobody could tell the title of the book. But it was well known to be a book of magic; and once, when a chambermaid had lifted it, merely to brush away the dust, the skeleton
45   rattled in its closet, the picture of the young lady had stepped one foot upon the floor, and several ghastly faces had peeped forth from the mirror; while the brazen head of Hippocrates frowned and said, "Forbear!"

50   Such was Dr. Heidegger's study. On the summer afternoon of our tale, a small round table, as black as ebony, stood in the center of the room, sustaining a cut-glass vase of beautiful form and elaborate workmanship.
55   The sunshine came through the window, between the heavy festoons of two faded damask curtains, and fell directly across this vase; so that a mild splendor was reflected from it on the ashen visages of the five old
60   people who sat around. Four champagne glasses were also on the table.

"My dear old friends," repeated Dr. Heidegger, "may I reckon on your aid in performing an exceedingly curious
65   experiment?"

[1] **folios:** books from 12 to 20 inches in height

[2] **quartos:** books about 9 1/2 inches wide by 12 1/2 inches high

70   [3] **duodecimos:** small volumes, about 5 inches wide by 8 inches high

[4] **Hippocrates:** a Greek physician (460?–370? B.C.)

—Excerpted from "Dr. Heidegger's Experiment" by Nathaniel Hawthorne

PRACTICE TEST

23. What is the narrator's attitude toward the stories told about Dr. Heidegger?

The narrator feels that the stories are
(1) terrifying
(2) humorous
(3) flattering
(4) rumors
(5) scientific fact

24. Which of the following words best describes the study?

(1) sterile
(2) mysterious
(3) lavish
(4) antiquated
(5) comfortable

25. According to the passage, which choice provides the best meaning for "Forbear" (line 49)?

(1) read
(2) continue
(3) clean
(4) stop
(5) listen

26. How did the young lady whose portrait was in the study die?

(1) The doctor poisoned her to avoid marrying her.
(2) She died of a broken heart when the doctor refused to marry her.
(3) One of the doctor's prescriptions killed her.
(4) She died after a long illness.
(5) The doctor cast a spell on her that trapped her spirit in the mirror.

27. What type of entertainment might Dr. Heidegger enjoy?

(1) a carnival sideshow
(2) stand-up comedy
(3) a Broadway musical
(4) a professional sports event
(5) a fishing trip

28. What can you infer about the people sitting in Dr. Heidegger's study from the line "a mild splendor was reflected from it on the ashen visages of the five old people who sat around." (lines 58–60)?

The four people were
(1) enthusiastic
(2) mild-mannered
(3) pale
(4) mysterious
(5) attractive

29. In the story Dr. Heidegger offers his guests the chance of being young again by drinking water from the Fountain of Youth.

Given this information, what object in the doctor's study takes on a practical significance?

(1) the mirror
(2) the folios and quartos
(3) the skeleton
(4) the portrait of a lady
(5) the champagne glasses

Questions 30–34 refer to the following excerpt from a short story.

WHAT DOES IT MEAN TO BE RICH?

Begin with an individual, and before you know it you find that you have created a type, begin with a type, and you find that you have created—nothing. That is because
5 we are all queer fish, queerer behind our faces and voices than we want any one to know or than we know ourselves. When I hear a man proclaiming himself an "average, honest, open fellow," I feel pretty sure that
10 he has some definite and perhaps terrible abnormality which he has agreed to conceal—and his protestation of being average and honest and open is his way of reminding himself of his misprision [error].

15 There are no types, no plurals. There is a rich boy, and this is his and not his brothers' story. All my life I have lived among his brothers but this one has been my friend. Besides, if I wrote about his brothers I
20 should have to begin by attacking all the lies that the poor have told about the rich and the rich have told about themselves—such a wild structure they have erected that when we pick up a book about the rich, some
25 instinct prepares us for unreality. Even the intelligent and impassioned reporters of life have made the country of the rich as unreal as fairy-land.

Let me tell you about the very rich. They
30 are different from you and me. They possess and enjoy early, and it does something to them, makes them soft where we are hard, and cynical where we are trustful, in a way that, unless you were born rich, it is very
35 difficult to understand. They think, deep in their hearts, that they are better than we are because we had to discover compensations and refuges of life for ourselves. Even when they enter deep into our world or sink below

40 us, they still think that they are better than we are. They are different. The only way I can describe young Anson Hunter is to approach him as if he were a foreigner and cling stubbornly to my point of view. If I
45 accept his for a moment I am lost—I have nothing to show but a preposterous movie.

—Excerpted from "The Rich Boy"
by F. Scott Fitzgerald, 1925

30. What is the purpose of the passage?

(1) to praise the narrator's friend for his honesty
(2) to criticize the how the rich view average people
(3) to suggest that stereotyping individuals is wrong
(4) to apologize for attacking his friend's honesty
(5) to describe young Anson Hunter

31. According to the passage, what makes the rich different from other people?

(1) their culture
(2) their arrogance
(3) their honesty
(4) their intelligence
(5) their privilege

32. With what statement would the narrator most likely agree?

(1) Every person, rich or poor, is unique and original.
(2) Class distinctions are a result of culture and intelligence.
(3) People judge others by the friends they have.
(4) Average individuals are more honest and open than wealthy ones.
(5) Rich people do not see themselves as different.

33. What is the purpose of the third paragraph?

The narrator
(1) reveals his disgust for the wealthy lifestyle
(2) suggests that the rich prevent the poor's success
(3) proposes to make a movie of his friend's life
(4) understands the average person's envy of the rich
(5) explains why he can't accept Anson's point of view

34. Fitzgerald wrote in his other fiction that the rich had a "heightened sensitivity to the promises of life."

According to the excerpt, which of the following offers the best explanation for this statement?

The rich
(1) have the resources to do what others only dream about
(2) belong to a class that supports music, art, and culture
(3) associate only with those who equal them in status
(4) follow a lifestyle characterized by honesty and intelligence
(5) live a lifestyle that has been exaggerated by others

PRACTICE TEST

Questions 35–40 refer to the following poem.

HOW DOES THE SPEAKER FEEL ABOUT THE POET EMILY DICKINSON?

EMILY DICKINSON

Like you, I belong to yesterday,
to the bays where
day is anchored to
wait for its hour.

5 Like me, you belong to today,
the progression of that hour
when what is unborn
begins to throb.

We are cultivators of
10 the unsayable, weavers
of singulars,[1] migrant
workers in search of
floating gardens as yet
unsown, as yet unharvested.

[1]**weavers of singulars:** in Spanish, *singulars*
means "unique things," or "creations."

—Lucha Corpi

35. How is the poem organized?

  (1) as a review of the subjects of Emily Dickinson's poetry.

  (2) as a request by the speaker for Dickinson to inspire her work

  (3) as an argument against those critics who attacked Dickinson

  (4) as an imaginary conversation between the speaker and the poet

  (5) as a list of Emily Dickinson's accomplishments in her poetry

36. What situation would be similar to the speaker's?

  (1) a researcher discovering a long lost document

  (2) a baseball player autographing photographs for fans

  (3) an adult having a conversation with a childhood hero

  (4) two writers arguing about the meaning of a novel

  (5) a sculptor making a copy of a famous statue

37. What is meant by the line "when what is unborn/begins to throb" (lines 7–8)?

  (1) An artist is inspired.

  (2) The poet is born.

  (3) A new day begins.

  (4) The speaker meets the poet.

  (5) The poet's career begins.

38. Why does the speaker feel that she and Emily Dickinson are similar?

  (1) Both were born in the same time period.

  (2) Both create works that are fresh and new.

  (3) Both write poetry that everyone enjoys.

  (4) Both enjoy performing household tasks.

  (5) Both wish to travel around the world.

39. What is the purpose of the third stanza (lines 9–14)?

  (1) to describe the speaker's search to find the poet

  (2) to praise the work of farmers and gardeners

  (3) to define the poet's search for originality

  (4) to demonstrate the difficulties in writing poetry

  (5) to make a link between the past and the present

40. What is the meaning of stanzas 1 (lines 1–4) and 2 (lines 5–8)?

(1) Emily Dickinson and the speaker write poetry for all times.

(2) Both poets share an interest in the sea and in children.

(3) The speaker feels that Emily Dickinson dwells in the past.

(4) The modern reader does not appreciate Dickinson's poetry.

(5) Dickinson was not appreciated in her time but is enjoyed now.

Answer Key

1. (2) The woman says to the ghost, "My dog sits on my feet more heavily than you can" (lines 32–33). She also says, "I can make my ears ring louder by taking aspirin" (lines 34–35).

2. (1) In lines 10–11, the woman says to the ghost, "You made a mistake haunting a medical school."

3. (5) The woman's belligerent speech to the ghost indicates that she is determined to conquer it.

4. (1) The woman's way of conquering the ghost is to taunt it into believing that she is more powerful than it.

5. (3) The excerpt consists mainly of the woman's speech to the ghost. What she says to it reveals what kind of person she is.

6. (4) From the woman's response to the ghost, one can reasonably assume that in another threatening situation she might again refuse to cooperate with the force trying to overcome her.

7. (1) Tonio's opening statements sum up the main idea, or theme, of the excerpt: "This idea of selling ice cream during the summer seems ridiculous, pointless. I'd much rather be close to the water."

8. (2) In the last sentence, Tonio says, "All I need is to pass the CPR course, get certified, and look for a job as a beach lifeguard."

9. (4) In lines 55–57, Tonio says, "Running over children is a deep fear that seems to haunt him."

10. (3) Note the references to toddlers wandering into the street and the appearance of another ice-cream truck.

11. (2) In paragraph 5, Tonio says of his father's smoking, "I can't stand it."

12. (2) The first paragraph describes what Tonio would like to be doing; the second, what Tonio is actually doing.

13. (4) In lines 36–38 the speaker says that he's "just another dirty derelict, shuffling through the streets looking for a handout."

14. (3) In lines 23–26 the derelict says, "Louis Armstrong, Billie Holiday, Ethel Waters, Duke Ellington, Bo Jangles, and all them others walked these streets and blessed this area with the music of their soul."

15. (3) In paragraph 5 the derelict speaks highly of the singers and musicians who made Harlem a center for jazz.

16. (5) The speaker's life mirrors the rise and fall of Harlem. Just as the once-vibrant man is now a derelict sustained by memories, the once-vibrant Harlem is now poverty stricken but sustained by its glorious past.

17. (2) In the last two lines of the excerpt, the derelict says, "After all, I still got my memories. What've you got?"

18. (5) The first sentence of the review states, "Bessie, the play's heroine, learns by phone that there is no help for her in her battle against leukemia."

19. (5) The reviewer suggests that Bessie tries to break the bad news gently to her family but betrays her true feelings when she upsets the pill bottle.

20. (1) In lines 20–24 the reviewer says that the play is "moving," with "brilliantly realized passages."

21. (1) In lines 20–24 the reviewer describes the scene from Act II as "shocking and moving . . . one of many such scenes in a play . . . filled with such brilliantly realized passages."

22. (2) The sentence structure of the review tends to be sophisticated. Most of the sentences are complex, and even simple sentences contain many qualifying phrases.

23. (4) In paragraph 1 the narrator says, "If all the stories were true," and later in the paragraph, "it was fabled" to indicate that

he heard the details secondhand and they may not be true.

24. (2) The description of the study in paragraph 1 includes faces of dead patients in the mirror, a young lady who steps from her portrait, a book of magic, and a talking bust.

25. (4) When the chambermaid lifted the book of magic, she was warned to stop.

26. (3) Lines 33–35 state that "being affected with some slight disorder, she had swallowed one of her lover's prescriptions and died."

27. (1) The doctor's interest in magic and spirits might lure him to a carnival sideshow with its bizarre creatures, magic, and illusions.

28. (3) Described as "ashen" figures, the four old people would resemble ash, meaning pale and sickly.

29. (5) The addition of information on waters from the Fountain of Youth suggests the need for the glasses to drink from in order to carry out the doctor's "exceedingly curious experiment."

30. (3) From paragraph 1 the narrator builds a case against typing people. "There are no types, no plurals."

31. (5) The narrator states that the rich are different because "they possess and enjoy early."

32. (1) The narrator states in lines 15–17, "There is a rich boy, and this is his and not his brothers' story."

33. (5) The narrator reveals in the paragraph, "If I accept his [point of view] for a moment I am lost—I have nothing to show but a preposterous movie."

34. (1) Paragraph 3 states, "They possess and enjoy early." Fitzgerald suggests that their wealth opens up many creative possibilities denied those without wealth.

35. (4) The poem is a conversation between the speaker and the deceased poet Emily Dickinson.

36. (3) The poem reveals the speaker's admiration for Dickinson and also her recognition of similarities between the two.

37. (1) The poem contains many references to artistic inspiration or creating anew subjects previously untreated in poetry.

38. (2) The reference in lines 7–8 to the "unborn" and in the last line "unsown, as yet unharvested" refer to ideas imminent but not yet present.

39. (3) Both the speaker and Dickinson sought to create something new, fresh, and original.

40. (1) The speaker compares herself to Dickinson in the two stanzas, suggesting that their works are for the past and the present.

Evaluation Chart

Use the following chart to determine the reading skill areas in which you need the most work. For the GED Language Arts, Reading Test, you are required to answer the following types of questions: comprehension, application, analysis, and synthesis. These reading skills, covered on pages 15–105 of this book, are absolutely essential for success on the test. Circle any items that you got wrong and pay particular attention to areas in which you missed half or more of the questions.

Skill Area/Content Area	Comprehension (pages 15–37)	Application (pages 39–46)	Analysis (pages 47–88)	Synthesis (pages 89–105)
Nonfiction Prose (pages 109–164)	1, 2, 18, 19	6	4, 5, 21	3, 20, 22
Prose Fiction (pages 165–215)	8, 10, 11, 26, 28, 31, 32	27	9, 23, 25, 33	7, 12, 24, 29, 30, 34
Poetry (pages 217–247)		36	37, 38, 39	35, 40
Drama (pages 249–281)	13, 14	15	17	16

Answer Key

CHAPTER 1

Exercise 1, page 19

Any six of the following are correct:
1. the sky
2. the earth
3. the sun
4. the stars
5. the wind
6. bird's nests
7. the moon
8. tepees
9. the seasons
10. the life of a man

GED PRACTICE
Exercise 2, page 21

1. (5) In the second sentence Coleman says that he slices lemons.
2. (2) In line 4, Coleman corrects her by saying, "I'm the man who [slices lemons]."
3. (2) Lines 22–25 state that you won't be respected "if you do work that others don't respect even if you have a Ph.D. It isn't education that counts, but the job in which you land."

Exercise 3, page 25

1. An Indian's name tells the world what kind of person he or she is. This statement summarizes the main idea of the passsage.
2. An Indian's first name describes some circumstance surrounding his or her birth.
3. The Indian woman who was helping his mother heard a wolf howling across the river. When she told his mother what had happened, the mother decided to call her son "Howling-in-the-Middle-of-the-Night."

Exercise 4, pages 28–29

1. (1) Ellison was born.
   (2) He moved to New York City.
   (3) His novel *Invisible Man* was published.
   (4) He won the National Book Award for Fiction.
2. music and composing
3. Richard Wright
4. White America had to recognize blacks as human beings.
5. *Shadow and Act*

Exercise 5, page 33

1. **waifs:** homeless children
2. **charisma:** a magnetic and charming personality
3. **subpoena:** a legal document requiring a person to testify in court
4. **extraterrestrial:** a creature from another planet
5. **convoluted:** complicated; full of twists and turns
6. **toxic:** poisonous
7. **tuition reimbursement:** payment for the cost of a class
8. **panhandling:** begging

GED PRACTICE
Chapter Review, pages 34–37

1. (5) **Comprehension (Supporting Details)**
   In the seventh paragraph Rheaume says, "It's normal to be the number three goalie, because I'm just 20 years old. The two other goaltenders are 24 and 25, and they have a lot more experience than me."
2. (5) **Comprehension (Supporting Details)**
   In line 50 the excerpt states that Rheaume is "working hard"; she is described throughout as being cooperative and enjoying the chance to play.
3. (2) **Comprehension (Context Clues)**
   Hockey has traditionally been an all-male sport. The gender barrier always excluded females. In lines 1–3, the author states, "Maybe it's understandable that nobody noticed the girl until she played against the boys." Lines 8–12 state that "Manon

Rheaume . . . has broken a gender barrier [and] shattered another misconception about the limits of female athletes."

4. (1) **Comprehension (Main Idea of a Passage)**
The excerpt as a whole describes how Manon Rheaume's performance as a goalie is helping female athletes in general.

5. (4) **Comprehension (Supporting Details)**
The topic sentence says that Rheaume's "detractors say she didn't deserve the NHL tryout." The rest of the sentences in the paragraph present reasons why the detractors feel as they do.

6. (2) **Comprehension (Main Idea of a Passage)**
The entire passage discusses the young boys' game of imitating a bullfight.

7. (3) **Comprehension (Context Clues)**
Line 8 refers to "fans or aficionados." Fans is the English word for *aficionados*.

8. (4) **Comprehension (Main Idea of a Paragraph)**
The second paragraph describes in detail how a boy disguised himself as a bull by using the bleached skull of a steer with horns, and a cactus leaf.

9. (2) **Comprehension (Supporting Details)**
As lines 30–34 state directly, if the bull suspected that he was poked in a sensitive spot on purpose, a free-for-all, or a fight, would follow.

10. (3) **Comprehension (Main Idea of a Passage)**
This passage describes the miners' faces, walks, builds, and other noticeable features.

11. (2) **Comprehension (Supporting Details)**
Lines 3–5 directly state that their faces are pale from breathing in foul air.

12. (5) **Comprehension (Supporting Details)**
The author summarizes the reasons for this condition in lines 21–24.

13. (4) **Comprehension (Context Clues)**
The word *cheeses* immediately follows the word *Roquefort*. This is a clue that *Roquefort* is a type of cheese.

CHAPTER 2

GED PRACTICE
Chapter Review, pages 42–46

1. (3) **Application**
The passage indicates that Miss Daisy likes things to be nice but does not want to be seen as rich.

2. (1) **Application**
Miss Daisy's agitated reaction to Hoke's unexpected action indicates that she would not take other unplanned events calmly. Her reserve in public—suggested by her embarrassment at being seen as rich—would keep her from starting conversations with strangers. Her eventual acceptance of Hoke's giving her a ride suggests that in spite of her complaining, she would not get out of the car and walk.

3. (3) **Application**
Hoke has shown himself talkative and comfortable with someone as uncooperative as Miss Daisy, so he would not hesitate to talk with other drivers, with whom he has something in common.

4. (3) **Application**
In the passage Hoke states, " 'Cause if I ever was to get ahold of what you got I be shakin' it around for everybody in the world to see."

5. (2) **Application**
From Miss Daisy's comments about her past, it seems she puts value on working hard. She seems to have definite opinions, which makes answers (1), (3), and (5) unlikely. In lines 40–41, her reference to being a teacher is followed by, "I did without plenty of times," which implies that she didn't have money at that time, which makes answer (4) unlikely.

6. (5) **Comprehension**
This statement summarizes the central focus of the passage. All of the paragraphs describe the personalities and the distinctive characteristics of the men.

7. (2) **Comprehension**
The author uses this figurative language to give readers a sense of the boomers as wandering adventurers. He implies this comparison to reveal the character of the construction workers. The statement is not literally true.

8. (1) **Comprehension**
   Lines 17–21 explain the meaning of the figurative name *boomers*.

9. (3) **Comprehension**
   The supporting details are related directly to this statement. The fourth paragraph presents several examples of the dangers that construction workers face.

10. (2) **Comprehension**
    You can conclude from the details describing the construction workers' life and behavior that they would not choose to settle down to a safe life.

11. (1) **Application**
    The unsettled lifestyle and the tasks related to building railroads most closely matches the construction workers' job skills and outlook on life.

12. (3) **Comprehension**
    The author uses this comparison to show how a creative idea is similar to a pregnancy. He carries within him a story that he can bring to life.

13. (2) **Comprehension**
    The paragraph describes in detail the way his father told stories, and compares it to the way he, as a writer, tells stories.

14. (2) **Comprehension**
    Becoming a writer seems to be a mixed blessing. The phrase "cursed my fate" suggests the difficulties and struggles that the author experiences.

15. (4) **Application**
    Because a painter produces original work, he or she would most closely identify with the author's struggle for creative expression.

CHAPTER 3

Exercise 1, page 48

1. **Clues:** The referee blows his whistle to stop the game. The quarterback, unable to move, must be carried away on a stretcher.

2. **Clues:** Companies usually call successful job applicants and send letters of refusal to applicants whom they do not plan to hire. The director says, "Congratulations!"

3. **Clues:** An alarm goes off. The sweater that falls from underneath the woman's coat is obviously stolen merchandise.

4. **Clues:** Loud claps and cheers and the expression "Bravo!" indicate the audience's enjoyment.

5. **Clues:** A black limousine is often used as a hearse, a car for transporting a body. Cars follow the limousine. Cars in a funeral procession usually have their headlights turned on.

Exercise 2, pages 51–52

1. (4)

2. **Clues:** There are "no fish in the river" because fish cannot survive in a polluted river. Other clues include garbage on the bank and in the river.

3. (1)

4. **Clues:** The rope attached to the cross-beam and the noose around the man's neck indicate that a hanging is the central event.

GED PRACTICE
Exercise 3, page 55

1. (2) **Analysis (Inference, Conclusions)**
   Descriptive details that support this response include "elevator doors," "glass doors at the end of the lobby," and "revolving doors." Also, the time is 5:18. Office workers usually leave their jobs at about five o'clock.

2. (4) **Analysis (Inference, Conclusions)**
   The fourth, fifth, and sixth sentences suggest a more intense relationship, like that with an ex-wife, than those implied by the other choices.

3. (2) **Analysis (Inference, Conclusions)**
   "Faint guilt" and "bewilderment" are emotions that convey uneasiness.

4. (1) **Comprehension**
   Busy traffic, crowded sidewalks, and blowing car horns are usually associated with a city scene.

Exercise 4, page 56

Valid Conclusions:

4. At first, when she doesn't meet her mother's expectations, the girl feels sad and defeated. As she looks in the mirror, her sadness explodes into rage. Looking at her own reflection, she sees an "angry, powerful" girl.
5. As she senses a newfound strong will, the girl decides that she won't permit her mother to rule over her actions or to change her. She decides to be true to herself.

Exercise 5, page 58

1. d
2. i
3. j
4. b
5. f
6. g
7. c
8. e
9. h
10. a

Exercise 6, page 58

1. L
2. F
3. F
4. L
5. L
6. F
7. F
8. F
9. L
10. L

Exercise 7, pages 60–61

1. *Icicles* are compared to a *monster's teeth.*
   Interpretation: The comparison explains how the icicles looked—long and sharp.
2. A *character's feelings* are compared to a *tight-rope walker* whose rope is breaking.
   Interpretation: The comparison explains the character's feelings—fear and nervousness.
3. The *eyelid* is compared to a *window shade.*
   Interpretation: The comparison illustrates the movement of the eye lid—up and down.

4. The *sun* is compared to a *club.*
   Interpretation: The comparison illustrates the force of the sun's rays—heavy and strong.
5. *Lucy's look* is compared to a *general inspecting troops.*
   Interpretation: The comparison explains the manner of Lucy's actions—military-like.
6. *Fog* is compared to *grey flannel.*
   Interpretation: The comparison illustrates the density and feel of the fog.

Exercise 8, page 64

1. conversational
2. conversational
3. formal
4. informal
5. formal
6. informal
7. informal
8. informal

Exercise 9, page 65

1. informal
2. conversational
3. formal
4. conversational
5. informal

GED PRACTICE
Exercise 10, page 67

1. (4) **Comprehension**
   The second sentence states, "I built emotional bridges in the imagination to link me to the world and to other people."
2. (1) **Analysis (Diction)**
   The central theme is that, as a child, Paz could stretch his imagination to transform time and space to connect to the past or the future.
3. (1) **Comprehension**
   In the fifth sentence Paz states, "The garden soon became the center of my world."

Exercise 11, pages 70–71

1. (1) Given the frightening content of the speaker's statement, it's reasonable to infer that he would adopt a threatening tone.

2. (3) Statements such as "what a weird age to be male" and "well, things tend to be less than perfect" indicate that the tone is funny.

3. (1) A somber tone would he appropriate in describing the depressing weather and sad situation.

4. (4) It's likely that a speaker would sound intimidating when describing the tortures of the damned.

Exercise 12, pages 75–76

Numbers should be listed in the following order: 5, 3, 8, 1, 9, 2, 4, 7, 6.

Exercise 13, pages 79–80

1. d
2. f
3. b
4. g
5. e
6. a
7. c

Exercise 14, page 82

Answers may vary. Possible answers include:

On the job: avoid losing business; have instant access to clients, suppliers, etc.; and give clients the attention they want

For the family: be in contact with the school, keep in touch with the children, and order food or household necessities as needed

GED PRACTICE
Chapter Review, pages 83–88

1. (4) **Comprehension**
   In lines 11–13 Huck says, "I didn't need anybody to tell me that [killing a spider] was an awful bad sign and would fetch me some bad luck. . . . "

2. (4) **Comprehension**
   In lines 14–15, Huck says, "I was scared and most shook the clothes off of me."

3. (3) **Analysis**
   The article is meant to be funny.

4. (5) **Application**
   The author's conversational writing style would also be appropriate for a script of a TV comedy series.

5. (1) **Analysis (Structure)**
   The author explains a process—how to kick a machine.

6. (2) **Analysis (Style)**
   A conversation is the author's primary method for revealing the people's reactions to the coffee machine.

7. (3) **Comprehension**
   Downsizing is the euphemism (pleasant-sounding substitute) big companies use for *layoffs* and *firings*.

8. (2) **Analysis (Structure)**
   The first two paragraphs state the main idea—that word watchers have compiled a list of "misused, overused and useless" words.

9. (4) **Analysis (Tone)**
   The writer's tone is informal and light hearted. The excerpt plays with words to make fun of how they are used.

10. (2) **Analysis (Structure)**
    The first sentence of the paragraph describes the rules governing haiku; the second sentence suggests the desire of the haiku writer to pack multiple meanings into a short poem.

11. (5) **Analysis (Tone, Inference)**
    Earlier in the passage, Rosie mentions that she did not completely understand the poem, and later, she states that it is easier just to say "yes" than to reveal her true feelings.

12. (3) **Comprehension**
    Paragraphs 1, 4, and 5 all discuss Rosie's inability to understand Japanese and her lack of interest in improving her understanding.

CHAPTER 4

Exercise 1, page 91

1. The purpose of this passage is to compare and contrast TV shows with the real world.

2. In paragraph 3 a TV cabdriver is compared and contrasted with a real cabdriver.

3. In paragraph 5 an emergency ward on TV is compared with an emergency ward in a real hospital.

4. According to Dr. Applebaum, television shows present children with an inaccurate picture of real-life situations.

Exercise 2, pages 92–93

1. Ernest Hemingway's work is contrasted with his life.
2. Contrasts include the fact that his prose was simple but his character was complex; he was an excellent writer who became a less-than-excellent human being; he was a writer who started performing instead of observing.
3. (a) paragraph 2, sentence 2
   (b) paragraph 1, sentence 1
   (c) paragraph 1, sentence 2

Exercise 3, pages 94–95

1. The grandmother is contrasted with her daughter-in-law.
2. The grandmother is conservative and old-fashioned in her attire and her behavior; her daughter-in-law is casually dressed and does not seem to respect convention or traditions.
3. (3) The grandmother sees herself as respecting traditional values, whereas her daughter-in-law indulges her children and teaches them to disregard certain traditions. The grandmother believes this indulgence is the cause of their lack of respect for her traditions.

Exercise 4, page 97

1. O
2. I
3. I
4. O
5. O

GED PRACTICE
Exercise 5, page 98

1. (1) **Analysis**
   The speaker mentions his own personal qualities, implying that he will play a role in the story.
2. (5) **Comprehension**
   The speaker states that he is inclined to reserve all judgments, and that therefore many people confide in him.

3. (3) **Synthesis**
   The passage has a serious, reflective tone.
4. (3) **Synthesis**
   Because the speaker generally reserves judgment, he would look at all possibilities before making a judgment.

Exercise 6, pages 99–100

1. (3) The narrator is most likely a teenage boy who is experiencing his first romantic crush on a girl.
2. (1) The language of the excerpt suggests that the narrator has matured and now looks back on his childhood experience.
3. (4) In the second paragraph the narrator watches Mangan's sister without being seen; he has never spoken to her, yet her name excites him.

Exercise 7, pages 100–101

1. "From then on they scanned the horizon. . . ." The men looked for a sight of the rescue ships mentioned in the first paragraph.
   "Slowly the night passed. . . ." The wording conveys the passage of time, suggesting that their experience seemed long.
   "The sea was silent too. . . ." In the preceding paragraph, the men grew silent; now, the sea was also silent; this suggests that the men feared rescue wouldn't arrive in time.
2. The men talk of rescue; Bride reveals that three ships are on the way; the Carpathia should reach them by dawn; to encourage one another, the men pass the news around.
3. The men watch for the rescue ships; at times they are cheered by the green flares, which they think must come from the rescuers.
4. At dawn the air became colder, the seas choppy; bitter cold waves caused bodily pain and blinded the eyes; the men watched some roll off the boat and disappear; others focused on staying alive.
5. (5) The last two paragraphs reveal a growing fear of not being rescued in time.

GED PRACTICE
Chapter Review, pages 103–105

1. (1) **Analysis**
Lines 18–20 state that the mother is no longer pretty and that is why she picks on Connie. Therefore, you can infer that she is jealous of Connie's looks. You can assume the mother's remarks stem from her jealousy.

2. (3) **Analysis**
This statement implies Connie's conceit about her appearance. There is not enough information in the passage to support the other conclusions.

3. (5) **Comprehension**
The mother's constant praise and approval suggest that she approves of what June does.

4. (4) **Analysis**
Trash is something that is worthless. The phrase "trashy daydreams" suggests that her mother thinks that Connie's inner thoughts are worthless.

5. (2) **Analysis**
The father does not interact with his family. Since he reads the newspaper during supper, you can assume he isn't talking to his wife or daughters. You also know that he goes to bed after supper.

6. (2) **Application**
A family counselor is trained to analyze the relationships within a family.

7. (3) **Extended Synthesis**
In paragraph 1 Connie is portrayed as a conceited fifteen-year old girl who sees her beauty as privilege. Paragraph 3 reveals that Connie's mind is filled with "trashy daydreams." When the Demon Lover Death appears, Connie finally realizes what her mother now sees, that beauty is only temporary.

8. (4) **Comprehension**
In Paragraph 2 it states that, with her marriage, Edna "felt she would take her place with a certain dignity in the world of reality, closing the portals forever . . . upon the realm of romance and dreams."

9. (2) **Comprehension**
In paragraph 3 the narrator reveals that Edna "grew fond" of her husband. There is no mention of her love for him.

10. (5) **Comprehension**
In Paragraph 3 it says, "It was not long before the tragedian had gone to join the cavalry officer and the engaged young man . . . Edna found herself face to face with the realities." This implies that Edna had crushes on these other men.

11. (1) **Synthesis**
The paragraph expresses that Edna is satisfied that there is no excessive passion in her marriage.

12. (1) **Extended Synthesis**
In paragraph 1 the narrator reveals Edna's independent streak, illustrated by her marriage to Mr. Pontellier over the "violent" objections of her father and sister. Now that she sees herself in a loveless marriage, she is ready to challenge society's expectation that she is her husband's property.

CHAPTER 5

Exercise 1, pages 111–113

Part I
1. (1) F
   (2) F
   (3) O
2. (1) F
   (2) F
   (3) O
3. (1) O
   (2) O
   (3) O
4. (1) F
   (2) F
   (3) O
   (4) O

Part II
1. 3
2. 4
3. 1
4. 3

Exercise 2, pages 114–116

Part I

Your answer should include any four of the following adjectives: *electric, great, spectacular, strongest, most energetic.*

Part II

Your answer should include any four of the following adjectives: *big, brash, strong, mature, tremendous, clear, good.*

Part III

Your answer should include any two of the following adjectives: *readable, wonderful, best.*

Part IV

1. A nuclear power plant releases a radioactive mist that turns some schoolchildren into monsters. The nasty tykes commit such despicable acts as killing their parents with deadly hugs.
2. predictable
3. dreadful

Exercise 3, pages 117–118

1. **MBWA** consists of having managers care enough about what's going on in the organization to walk around and find out from the employees. **TQM** has as its goal instilling pride in getting the best possible job done for the organization.
2. The best techniques for solving employee problems must come from a genuine caring attitude.

Exercise 4, pages 118–120

1. (2) Paragraph 1 states, "No other writer is asked to commit words to paper with such speed, under such pressure." Therefore, you can conclude that the journalist, unlike the novelist or the poet, is pressured to meet strict deadlines.
2. (3) Both Leo Tolstoy and John Ciardi restate the importance of the writing rule "show, don't tell."
3. (1) (b) This sentence specifically states the umpire's decision and shows the coach's angry gestures.
   (2) (a) The verb *arrested* conveys a stronger action than *took into custody. Unregistered handgun* is a more precise image than *illegal weapon. Mayor* is more specific than *man.*

(3) (b) The sentence shows how the woman developed her skills and specifies both the woman's original position and her new position.

GED PRACTICE
Exercise 5, page 121

1. (4) **Comprehension**
   Throughout the excerpt, the writer gives examples of fans and scouts who know everything about Felipe that relates to basketball because they believe he'll be a big star someday.
2. (2) **Analysis**
   "The white men"—meaning scouts and fans—are everywhere, following Felipe and keeping close track of his basketball career.
3. (1) **Comprehension**
   Generally, people like to follow someone who they think is going to be a winner. They're hanging around Felipe because they expect him to be a star player someday.

Exercise 6, pages 122–123

1. (2) Paragraph 1 mentions how the movies "can cross cultures," and paragraph 5 states that the film is one "that resonate(s) through many cultures."
2. (3) The art or style sections of newspapers provide reviews of television shows, cultural events, and movies.
3. (2) Paragraph 4 states that the "pansori" is woven throughout the movies.
4. (1) The reviewer's language praises the film and its director.

GED PRACTICE
Exercise 7, page 124

1. (2) **Comprehension**
   Line 1 says that he is a Detroit area teacher.
2. (3) **Comprehension**
   The story is told to make the point that children have been taught to be unreasonably afraid of adult strangers.
3. (5) **Comprehension**
   Lines 11–12 suggest that only paper cartons "bear the pictures of missing children."

4. (2) **Comprehension**

The author expresses this opinion in the last sentence of the passage.

GED PRACTICE
Exercise 8, pages 125–128

1. (5) **Comprehension**

Although the writer does mention each of the other options, his overall message is one of simple, everyday consideration for people with disabilities.

2. (1) **Analysis**

The writer expects to be treated as a mature, intelligent adult.

3. (3) **Analysis**

The writer points out with irony that even a person who specializes in proper behavior may be insensitive when it comes to dealing with a disabled person.

4. (3) **Synthesis**

In lines 86–87 the author says, "The unifying theme of all the suggestions above is inclusiveness."

5. (2) **Application**

In lines 40–43 the author says, "Those of us who can't stand get tired of talking to belt buckles. Try to park us near chairs. . . . so people speaking with us can be at our level."

6. (2) **Comprehension**

The main idea is stated in the most well-known sentence from this speech: "Ask not what your country can do for you—ask what you can do for your country."

7. (4) **Comprehension**

In lines 3–5, Kennedy states that "each generation of Americans has been summoned to give testimony to its national loyalty."

8. (3) **Analysis**

Kennedy's speech is intended to be an inspirational message to the American people. For example, by appealing to the power of energy, faith, and devotion, he attempts to foster the highest ideals. The speech encourages Americans to involve themselves in achieving the country's goals.

9. (2) **Comprehension**

In lines 22–23 Kennedy states, "I do not shrink from this responsibility—I welcome it."

10. (3) **Synthesis**

The concluding sentence contains religious language such as *blessing* and *God's work.*

Exercise 9, pages 129–130

Answers may vary. Possible answers include the following:

1. It offers the most up-to-date information on the World Wide Web, and provides and maintains web sites for clients.

2. This company provides its clients with the competitive edge to be successful; Their staff is on top of the latest developments in Internet technology.

3. Small businesses, individuals, and organizations would benefit.

4. An employee would be expected to be constantly on top of developments in the Internet and ready to guide clients in making use of it.

GED PRACTICE
Exercise 10, pages 131–132

1. (4) **Comprehension**

The form records any changes in an employee's status.

2. (2) **Comprehension**

There is no mention of training on the form.

3. (5) **Comprehension**

Bcause resignation would have been initiated by the employee, the employee must sign the form.

Exercise 11, pages 132–134

1. (3) The document describes what is expected of an employee and the reason for the hospital's expectations.

2. (3) According to the section "Employment Verification," Employee Records maintains employee information.

3. Employees are expected to dress in a manner that generates confidence and respect for the hospital, is appropriate for the employee's department and duties, and maintains the health and safety of patients.

4. (1) N
   (2) P
   (3) P
   (4) P
   (5) N
   (6) P
   (7) P
   (8) N

Exercise 12, pages 135–136

1. Safe working conditions for these workers are regulated by other federal agencies.
2. Business that is carried on in two or more states or requires the business to cross state lines in order to conduct business is called interstate commerce.
3. (4) The priority of the act is to ensure approved safety plans for workers.
4. (5) An individual with a home-based business would be exempt from the act because the individual would be self-employed.
5. (2) A state plan must be equal to or exceed the federal act.

Exercise 13, pages 137–138

1. Kiowas
2. Answers may vary. Possible answers include the following:
   Sight: "tortoises crawl about on the red earth" "great green and yellow grasshoppers are everywhere in the tall grass" "green belts along the rivers and the creeks"
   Hearing: "grass . . . cracks beneath your feet"
   Touch: "grasshoppers . . . sting the flesh" "grass turns brittle"
3. (1) The author uses figurative language to emphasize the intense summer heat. The plants are not literally on fire.
4. (4) The author vividly describes colors and the scenery. He uses words to paint a picture of the landscape.
5. (1) "Rises out of the plain" is the context clue that supports the answer that a knoll is a hill.

Exercise 14, pages 138–140

1. (4) The purpose of the passage is to describe the Harlem Unit's original production of the play, which was "no ordinary version of Shakespeare" (line 6).

2. Your summary should include these details: Prompted by witches, Macbeth conspires with his wife and murders the king of Scotland.
3. Scotland
4. Haiti
5. "full of voodoo drums and witches' cries" (line 24)
6. (1) F
   (2) F
   (3) O
   (4) O
   (5) F
   (6) F
7. (3) Brooks Atkinson states this opinion in the concluding line of the passage.

GED PRACTICE
Exercise 15, pages 141–142

1. (5) **Comprehension**
   The passage discusses mainly the character of the fictional detective.
2. (2) **Comprehension**
   Lines 4–5 state that the hard-boiled detective "was born in America,"
3. (2) **Comprehension**
   Lines 15–17 state that the origins of the detective were in the lonesome pioneer.
4. (3) **Comprehension**
   Chandler states in lines 35–36 that the fictional American detective is "a relatively poor man."
5. (4) **Comprehension**
   Line 30 states that Philip Marlowe used similes. Similes, a type of figurative language, are direct comparisons using the words *as* or *like*.

Exercise 16, pages 142–144

1. (1) F
   (2) F
   (3) O
   (4) O
   (5) O
   (6) F
   (7) F
   (8) O

2. She melts the witch with a bucket of cleaning water. (lines 27–29)

3. (5) The author uses the introductory sentence of many fairy tales to begin the book review because he is writing about *The Wonderful Wizard of Oz*.

4. (3) Paragraph 2 states the major theme: "The power of Good is greater than the power of Evil." (lines 17–18)

GED PRACTICE
Exercise 17, pages 145–148

1. (5) **Comprehension**
This statement interprets how Emily Dickinson's view of the world is reflected in her poems. The rest of the statements are facts.

2. (2) **Comprehension**
Lines 14–16 state, "She seems to have been, more than other poets, writing just for herself."

3. (2) **Analysis**
The entire paragraph details the way in which Emily Dickinson observed nature, people, and herself.

4. (4) **Comprehension**
You know from the excerpt that Emily Dickinson wrote about death. However, there is not sufficient evidence to support that those poems reflected a morbid fear of death.

5. (3) **Analysis**
Lines 2–4 state that Emily Dickinson "lived a very secluded life. She was alone most of the time; she didn't know other writers." Therefore, you can infer that she was a solitary person.

6. (5) **Extended Synthesis**
The depiction of Death as a friendly neighbor offering a carriage ride is an example of her attitude of familiarity with the most difficult of experiences.

7. (5) **Comprehension**
Classes were taught "by instructors who came from such places as Harvard and Boston universities" (lines 3–4).

8. (1) **Analysis**
The last sentence of the first paragraph indicates that the debates were popular with both the inmate debaters and their audience. The passage also says that well-read inmates among the popular debaters were "almost celebrities" (line 30).

9. (4) **Comprehension**
Lines 25–27 state that "an inmate was smiled upon if he demonstrated an unusually intense interest in books." Therefore, you can infer that the prison officials approved of this activity.

10. (3) **Analysis**
Malcolm X is using this expression figuratively, not literally. He is describing the "well-read inmates."

11. (3) **Comprehension**
Lines 41–43 state, "It always seemed to catch me right in the middle of something engrossing." In other words, the "lights out" rule interrupted Malcolm X's reading.

12. (2) **Synthesis**
Throughout the passage Malcolm X conveys his enthusiasm for "being able to read and *understand*." He also admires the other inmates who show a desire to learn.

13. (3) **Application**
Malcolm X and some of his fellow inmates are examples of individuals who took the initiative to educate themselves. Therefore, you can conclude that if Malcolm X were alive today, he would believe strongly in self-education.

14. (1) **Extended Synthesis**
Malcolm speaks in the third paragraph "of being able to read and *understand*." The additional information emphasizes that the debates provided the inmates with an opportunity to gain more from their readings.

Exercise 18, pages 148–150

1. The sculpture shows the influence of her Indian heritage. Edmonia Lewis's mother belonged to the Chippewa tribe.

2. (1) to learn marble-carving techniques
(2) to pursue her career with greater artistic freedom
(3) to avoid racial discrimination

3. (2) The author states that Indians are often characterized as "brutal and savage."

4. (3) The passage states that the sculpture shows "a moment of quiet reflection being enjoyed by father and daughter." The reviewer says the small size of the sculpture expresses the "intimacy of the moment."

Exercise 19, pages 150–151

1. (3) The introductory sentence states, "Tattoo artists have always felt that their work deserved more acceptance as an art." A museum exhibit of tattoo art replicas would be a form of recognition.

2. (3) The supporting details in the second paragraph summarize the ancient historical background of tattoo art. The authors specify dates and locations.

3. (5) The authors state in lines 3–5, "It is easy to see the craft, the fancy, the individuality, and the art of the practitioner." Therefore, you can conclude that the authors appreciate the artistic qualities of tattooing.

4. (1) I
  (2) V
  (3) I
  (4) I

GED PRACTICE
Exercise 20, pages 152–153

1. (2) **Synthesis**
  The entire passage explains the procedure that Mr. Hagenlocher follows in sketching a suspect.

2. (4) **Comprehension**
  Lines 1–2 state that "Mr. Hagenlocher tries to put witnesses at ease."

3. (2) **Comprehension**
  Lines 15–16 state, "Witnesses are asked to leaf through these [mug shots] to try to find a similar face."

4. (4) **Comprehension**
  According to the passage, Mr. Hagenlocher poses all of the other questions except this one.

5. (5) **Synthesis**
  Quotations from Mr. Hagenlocher explain the process of sketching suspects from his viewpoint.

6. (3) **Application**
  A portrait painter is also skilled in drawing people's faces.

Exercise 21, pages 154–155

1. (2) The author uses this technique to arouse the reader's curiosity about the film. By watching *The 39 Steps*, the reader would discover the answers to those questions.

2. (5) The concluding sentence states that an ordinary man such as Hannay typifies many Hitchcock heroes.

3. The statements should be numbered in this order: 5, 3, 6, 1, 4, 2.

4. (4) The headline describes an average man who apparently finds himself involved in a murder mystery. You can conclude that Hitchcock would find this man's predicament intriguing.

5. (3) The critic states that "this thrilling espionage adventure was the first film to establish Hitchcock as the Master of Suspense" (lines 1–2). There is not enough information to determine whether the critic thinks that *The 39 Steps* was Hitchcock's best work, choice (1).

Exercise 22, pages 156–157

1. They taught themselves.
2. in Harlem
3. (4) Nick Castle, a choreographer, "designed many of the Nicholas Brothers' routines." Therefore, you can infer that a choreographer's job is to create or design dances.
4. (2) Throughout the passage, the author directly quotes Nicholas's comments about the development of his tap-dancing career.

Exercise 23, pages 158–159

1. "The Rickety Wheel Makes the Most Noise"
2. comic, serious, dreamlike
3. Chile
4. (5) Laura Montenegro states in paragraph 4: "What we'd like to accomplish is to make people get a little more insight into our humanness."

5. (4) You can infer from the author's favorable description of the Montenegros' creative ideas that he respects both the artists and their work.

6. (1) I
   (2) V
   (3) V
   (4) I
   (5) I

GED PRACTICE
Chapter Review, pages 160–164

1. (3) **Comprehension**
   A building designed in the shape of a turtle is unique. The other choices describe the center's less-remarkable characteristics.

2. (2) **Comprehension**
   Lines 16–20 state that Dennis Sun Rhodes believed it was important that modern architecture "be adapted to traditional Indian values."

3. (4) **Analysis**
   The second paragraph describes the building's size, rooms, and spatial arrangement.

4. (1) **Analysis**
   Because the author's purpose is to instruct the reader, the tone is informative.

5. (1) **Application**
   Like the Indian Center, churches also show the influence of meaningful cultural symbols. For example, stained-glass windows of biblical scenes, statues of religious figures, and the cross are symbols of Christianity.

6. (4) **Analysis**
   In paragraph 1 the speaker follows *decorum* with the clues "serenity and detachment" and "behave in a civilized manner."

7. (2) **Comprehension**
   Traditional art has changed because computer graphics have given artists new tools to use.

8. (3) **Analysis**
   Paragraph 2 states that art has become two-way, art becomes responsive to the viewer and picks up "gesture[s], provoking changes in the works themselves." In paragraph 4 the viewer picks up a "navigating wand."

9. (2) **Synthesis**
   Paragraph 4 reveals that "For the moment . . . one must go to the [Boston] university's Graphics Laboratory."

10. (4) **Extended Synthesis**
    Although the viewer controls much of the experience, the artist places limits on that experience.

11. (2) **Comprehension**
    Federal discrimination statutes apply to business with specific numbers of employees.

12. (5) **Comprehension**
    Executive Order 11246 requires employers to implement a written affirmative action plan for women and minorities.

13. (3) **Comprehension**
    Legal blindness is a physical disability covered under the act.

14. (1) **Synthesis**
    The first sentence speaks of "employment practices that discriminate."

15. (3) **Comprehension**
    This detail is not found as a basic require ment in any of the statutes.

CHAPTER 6

Exercise 1, page 170

1. (2) The children keep hearing the phrase "There must be more money!"
2. (5) The children are playing in their nursery.
3. (3) The emphasis on money has filled the house with tension.

Exercise 2, page 171

1. (3) References such as "the punishment block (the stone prison inside the camp)," "barbed-wire fence," and "prisoners" support the idea that this is a prison camp.
2. (5) The details describing the environment of the prison camp and the extremely cold weather create an atmosphere of oppression.

---

3. Phrases referring to the weather include:
freezing cold
boots crunching on the snow
the thermometer hung, caked over with ice
freezing weather
frost-covered rail
they all felt cold

4. Words or phrases suggesting Tom's strength and force include:
sturdy
dominance
leaning aggressively forward
enormous power
great pack of muscle
body capable of enormous leverage

5. (2) From the descriptive words in the passage, you can infer that Nick's attitude toward Tom is critical.

GED PRACTICE
Exercise 3, pages 175–176

1. (5) **Comprehension**
Lines 3–5 state, "it symbolized all the misery of the plural South African society."
2. (3) **Comprehension**
Karlie defies the laws of South African society.
3. (2) **Analysis**
Karlie shows courage when he defies South Africa's system of racial discrimination.
4. (5) **Application**
Karlie's actions suggest that he would also support the human rights movement in the United States.

Exercise 4, pages 181–182

Part I
1. Tony grew up in a crowded, poverty-stricken neighborhood.
2. He was sixteen.
3. His friends were juvenile delinquents.
4. He was in a car with boys who robbed a liquor store.
5. Tony would marry Rosa and manage a candy store for her father.

Part II
6. Tony's life was troubled and unfocused, but he had dreams of success.
7. He was pressured into it by his family and neighbors.

Exercise 5, pages 184–185

1. He is wearing riding clothes.
2. **Age:** thirty
Hair color: "straw-haired" or blond
3. "hard mouth"; "arrogant eyes"; "cruel body"

Exercise 6, pages 185–186

1. Pepi
2. one of the men from Detroit
3. Joe Sansone
4. Pepi
5. one of the men from Detroit

Exercise 7, pages 187–190

1. (3) The general topic that the brothers are discussing is Sonny's choice of careers.
2. (1) Sonny's brother says in line 28, "I was furious,"
3. (4) You can conclude from these lines of dialogue that Sonny sincerely wants to become a jazz musician.
4. (1) V
(2) V
(3) I
(4) I
5) I
(6) I
(7) V
(8) V

Exercise 8, pages 191–192

Part I
Numbers should be listed in the following order:
3, 4, 7, 2, 6, 1, 5

Part II
1. F
2. F
3. T
4. T
5. F
6. F
7. T
8. T

Exercise 9, page 195

Interpretations may differ.
1. Hogs are compared to large spotted stones.
   Interpretation: The comparison emphasizes the coloring of the hogs.

2. A man is compared to a crow.
   Interpretation: The man makes birdlike movements.
3. A woman's eyes are compared to chips of green glass.
   Interpretation: The woman has sparkling green eyes.
4. Mrs. Watts's grin is compared to the blade of a sickle.
   Interpretation: The comparison exaggerates the shape of her smile and implies that it is not a kind smile.
5. Windshield wipers are compared to two idiots clapping in church.
   Interpretation: The comparison describes the noise of windshield wipers. The wipers sound like uncontrolled applause.

GED PRACTICE
Exercise 10, page 196

1. (4) **Analysis**
   Painted savages suggest an image of wildness.
2. (1) **Analysis**
   Serpents are usually characterized as evil creatures. The coiled chimney smoke seems wicked.
3. (3) **Analysis**
   The comparison suggests that the steam engine functions like a crazed animal.

4. (2) **Analysis**
   The descriptions of the buildings, the chimney smoke, the river, and the steam engines convey the ugliness of this industrial city.
5. (3) **Synthesis**
   The reference to machinery and tall chimneys refer to the machines that replaced human labor during the Industrial Revolution.

GED PRACTICE
Exercise 11, pages 200–201

1. (5) **Comprehension**
   Paragraph 2 says that the husband's name is on the list of those killed in a "railroad disaster."
2. (1) **Comprehension**
   The second paragraph states that "it was her sister Josephine who told her."
3. (3) **Analysis**
   The story focuses on the woman's thoughts and feelings as she sits alone in her room directly after learning that her husband has died.
4. (3) **Analysis**
   The theme is summed up in the closing lines: "But she saw beyond that bitter moment [when she saw her husband in his casket] a long procession of years to come that would belong to her absolutely. And she opened and spread her arms out to them in welcome."
5. (4) **Analysis**
   The description of new life and hope in paragraphs 5 and 6 foreshadows, or hints at, the woman's feelings about life without her husband.
6. (2) **Synthesis**
   Since the story is about a wife's struggle for personal freedom from control by her husband, it is likely that the author would agree that women should lead their own lives.

Exercise 12, pages 202–211

1. Georgiana Carpenter
2. Georgiana's nephew, Clark
3. Boston
4. The main character left Boston and her musical career to elope with Howard Carpenter.
5. The six events are in the following sequence: 6,1,5,4,2,3
6. Answers will vary.
7. Any three of the following:
   The nephew remembers her teaching him music, Latin, and Shakespeare.
   When he sees her misshapen form, he looks at her with feelings of awe and respect.
   Clark says he owed "to this woman most of the good that came my way in boyhood."
   The aunt would comfort him after his uncle had scolded him.
   Clark says, "I . . . had a reverential affection for her."
   He arranges for the two of them to attend the concert as a way of saying thanks.
8. (4) When Georgiana arrives at Mrs. Springer's, she is covered with dust from her trip, and she is wearing a dress made by a country dressmaker.
9. (4) Georgiana fell in love with Howard Carpenter, who was 9 years younger than she, and they eloped.
10. (5) Georgiana sacrificed her pursuit and love of music in Boston to join Howard on his prairie homestead.
11. (1)
12. (3) Throughout the story the author suggests that the hardships of living on the prairie had stooped Georgiana.

GED PRACTICE
Chapter Review, pages 212–215
1. (5) **Comprehension**
   The fact that an arrested person was treated violently is supported by the description that away from the crowd, the police "whaled him with their clubs" (line 20).

2. (2) **Analysis**
   The second and third paragraphs describe the scene from Tod's point of view.

3. (4) **Comprehension**
   Lines 24–25 state that Tod "began to get frightened."
4. (4) **Analysis**
   The author compares speaking in a "rapid, hysterical voice" to a revivalist preacher to create an image of someone speaking in an agitated manner.
5. (2) **Analysis**
   References such as "They had enough to do without chasing him" and "he began to get frightened" indicate that the story is being told by a narrator acting as an outside, all-knowing reporter. Not involved in the action himself, the narrator relates the events and the thoughts and feelings of the characters.
6. (2) **Analysis**
   The author reveals this theme by describing the crowd's behavior as if it were one personality. The crowd is portrayed as a mob out of control. As a result, individual personalities do not seem to exist.
7. (2) **Application**
   Newspapers frequently report similar mob scenes at rock concerts.
8. (3) **Analysis**
   Miss Havisham is surrounded by clothing and jewelry. Since she appears to he in the middle of dressing, you can infer that the scene takes place in her bedroom.
9. (3) **Analysis**
   You learn about Miss Havisham's character from her physical appearance and the condition of her surroundings.
10. (1) **Analysis**
    Clues supporting the inference that she is wealthy include rich materials and the sparkling jewels around Miss Havisham's neck and on the table.
11. (1) **Analysis**
    The phrases *faded and yellow* and *withered like the dress* suggest decay.
12. (4) **Extended Synthesis**
    The introduction reveals that Miss Havisham had been abandoned by her lover before her wedding day. It is likely that being jilted by her fiancé would cause Miss Havisham emotional distress.

13. (1) **Comprehension**

    The purpose of this comparison is to show how the author presents the action-filled plot.

14. (3) **Analysis**

    Lines 17–19 support the response that the author tells the novel from Bigger's point of view.

15. (3) **Analysis**

    References such as "building of a well-constructed book," "I told of Bigger's life in close-up, slow-motion," and "I restricted the novel" imply that the author deliberately constructed the novel to achieve a certain effect.

16. (2) **Comprehension**

    The author uses the comparison to illustrate how he wants the reader to experience the story. The reader should feel that he is a special audience watching Bigger's drama unfold.

17. (3) **Comprehension**

    The focus of this passage is to show the techniques of writing a novel. The author discusses methods of presenting plot, characterization, and point of view.

18. (3) **Application**

    It is a journalist's job to report on factual events.

CHAPTER 7

Exercise 1, pages 220–221

1. Lines 2 and 4: *play, today*
   Lines 6 and 8: *wild, child*
   Lines 10 and 12: *me, free*
   Lines 14 and 16: *fire, choir*
   Lines 18 and 20: *sweet, feet*
   Lines 22 and 24: *place, face*
   Lines 26 and 28: *wild, child*
   Lines 30 and 32: *shoe, you*

2. (1) "For the dogs are fierce and wild, / And clubs and hoses, guns and jail / Aren't good for a little child." (lines 6–8)
   "For I fear those guns will fire." (line 14)
   (2) "Her eyes grew wet and wild." (line 26)

(3) "She clawed through bits of glass and brick," (line 29)
(4) "O here's the shoe my baby wore, / But, baby, where are you?" (lines 31–32)

3. (1) F
   (2) T
   (3) T
   (4) T

Exercise 2, pages 223–225

1. (3) The title of the poem ("Tribal Cemetery"), the description of the tombstone (first stanza), and line 13 support this response.

2. (2) The pronoun *I* refers to the father's daughter—the speaker of the poem.

3. (2) The repetition of *English words* emphasizes that English was an alien language for the father, a Native American, to learn.

4. (1) The daughter's tone of respect for her father and his culture reveals her pride.

5. (1) **I**—The father was a veteran in World War I. However, no additional details are given to suggest that he was awarded medals for bravery.
   (2) **V**—The father went to the Mission School when he was twelve. He was apparently forced to learn white America's social customs and language. You can conclude that this education gradually removed him from his original heritage.
   (3) **I**—The father learned "to pray to the Catholic God" (line 26) when he attended the Mission School. Therefore, he did not practice only his native religion during his life.
   (4) **V**—In the concluding lines of the poem, the speaker states that she and her children know only English words. Because they don't understand her father's language, you can infer that they are disconnected from an important part of their Native American roots.
   (5) **V**—You can assume that before the father attended the Mission School, he was probably accustomed to going barefoot, eating without silverware, practicing his tribe's religion, and speaking his tribe's language. The training at the Mission School was evidently designed to make him

conform to white American culture and
"white ways of thinking."

(6) **V**—Because of their different language and
culture, non-English-speaking immigrants are
often alienated from mainstream American
society.

Exercise 3, page 229

1. The number on the fire engine. The title of the
   poem, "The Great Figure," provides an
   important clue.
2. The observation occurred in a rainy, dark city.
3. (2) The words *moving/tense* immediately follow
   the word *firetruck*.
4. **Descriptions of sound:** "gong clangs," "siren
   howls," "wheels rumbling"

GED PRACTICE
Exercise 4, pages 233–237

1. (2) **Analysis**
   The title of the poem, "I Wandered Lonely as
   a Cloud," supports this response.
2. (1) **Comprehension**
   Lines 7–9 compare the arrangement of
   daffodils with the stars in the Milky Way, the
   galaxy in which our solar system is located.
3. (5) **Analysis**
   The poet compares the motion of the
   flowers to the motion of dancers.
4. (3) **Comprehension**
   Watching the flowers changes the speaker's
   mood to happy.

Exercise 5, pages 237–238

1. two sisters, a father, a mother, and a stepmother
2. The speaker compares her mother's figure to a
   rag bag.
3. The speaker compares her mother's figure to a
   mattress.
4. The speaker notices a wedding ring on her
   father's finger in the picture. You know from lines
   11–12 that he did not wear a wedding ring
   during his marriage to the speaker's mother. In
   addition, you know that the speaker's father left
   her mother to marry the second wife (lines
   16–17). These clues, along with the legend on
   the photo (lines 13–15), imply that his second
   marriage meant more to him than his first.

5. Your summary should include the following
   information: Two sisters are looking at an old
   photograph of their father. The mother, a woman
   who apparently looks worn out and haggard, is
   also present. One of the sisters mistakenly
   assumes that the photo was originally given to
   her mother. The sister then realizes that the
   photo belonged to her father's second wife. The
   father divorced her mother to marry this woman.

Exercise 6, pages 239–240

1. The woman is in the living room.
2. Scattered around are record albums.
3. He emphasizes how much he is intrigued by the
   dimples on the woman's cheeks, arms, and legs.
   The repetition also produces a musical effect.
4. The woman "loves" Johnny Mathis's music and
   his looks.
5. (4) *Dances* and *whirls* emphasize the rhythmic
   quality of Mathis's voice. *Windblown snow*
   suggests softness. The entire description
   uses figurative language to show the beauty
   of Mathis's voice, as well as its age and
   variety.

Exercise 7, pages 240–241

1. 8:00 A.M., lunchtime
2. "*splintery* redwood rafters"; "*Itch* of haydust in
   the / *sweaty* shirt and shoes"
3. "Grasshoppers *crackling* in the weeds"
4. 17, 68
5. He said that he would hate to buck hay all his
   life.

GED PRACTICE
Chapter Review, pages 243–247

1. (5) **Comprehension**
   Lines 15–16 support this response: "He
   never learned a trade; he just sells gas, /
   Checks oil, and changes flats."
2. (2) **Analysis**
   The poet is using personification to show the
   physical appearance of the gas pumps. He
   implies that they resemble human beings.
   Specifically, the hoses seem to be "rubber
   elbows."

3. (4) **Comprehension**
The descriptive details relate to Flick's outstanding athletic performance.

4. (5) **Analysis**
This simile reveals Flick's skill in handling the basketball.

5. (2) **Analysis**
From descriptions of Flick's actions at the gas station, you can conclude that he misses playing basketball—"As a gag, he dribbles an inner tube." When the speaker says, "But most of us remember anyway," he is referring to Flick's exciting moments on the basketball court. In contrast, his work at the gas station is dull and unmemorable.

6. (1) **Comprehension**
By comparing and contrasting moments from Flick's past with his present situation, the poem makes a statement about the short-lived fame of high school athletes. The title of the poem, "Ex-Basketball Player," also emphasizes that Flick's sports career is over.

7. (2) **Application**
This magazine is the only one of the choices whose topic is sports and athletes who play or played sports.

8. (3) **Extended Synthesis**
The poem discusses what happened to a star high school athlete after he graduated, and the information provides a similar background on a character from a novel by the same author. Both pieces suggest that both men relived their high school basketball successes but never grew up emotionally.

9. (2) **Comprehension**
These references imply that the speakers are poor and hardworking: "So on we worked, and waited for the light,/And went without the meat, and cursed the bread."

10. (5) **Comprehension**
Richard Cory "put a bullet through his head." In other words, he kills himself.

11. (3) **Analysis**
Most people who commit suicide suffer from serious personal problems. These problems are not apparent to the townspeople.

12. (1) **Analysis**
The word *light* is used figuratively, not literally. The poor townspeople are referring to their desire for brighter, happier days.

13. (4) **Application**
This answer restates the central message of the poem as the title of a magazine article. Richard Cory's wealth does not protect him from the circumstances that lead to his suicide.

14. (1) **Extended Synthesis**
People are usually willing to provide emotional or other help to those who need that help in order to live. Had the townspeople been aware of Cory's self-doubt and unhappiness, they probably would have helped him.

15. (2) **Comprehension**
The title of the poem, "Daybreak," is an important clue. The first stanza uses figurative language to describe the dawn—the time when "the light starts up/In the east."

16. (1) **Analysis**
The break between stanzas is similar to a paragraph break signaling a change in topic.

17. (5) **Comprehension**
The speaker indirectly explains how picking onions causes painful blisters on the farm workers' hands.

18. (3) **Analysis**
The onions lie asleep, or motionless, underground. The word *unplug* is an imaginative way of saying *uproot*.

19. (1) **Analysis**
The speaker is showing the force of the raindrops striking the ground. The impact seems to break the raindrops is compared to the breaking of the fingers of a hand.

20. (4) **Analysis**
The poem details the grueling physical work of onion pickers.

CHAPTER 8

Exercise 1, page 253

1. (1) *[Almost in tears.]* (line 22)
   (2) *[Stands up and throws the mouse as far as he can . . .]* (line 27)
   (3) *[GEORGE puts his hand on LENNIE'S shoulder for a moment.]* (lines 33–34)

2. (1) "Blubbering like a baby. Jesus Christ, a big guy like you!" (lines 31–32)

(2) "What, George? I ain't got no mouse." (line 15)

(3) "Don't you think I could see your feet was wet where you went in the water to get it?" (lines 29–31)

3. (1) **I**—When Lennie starts crying, George tries to console him. George says that Lennie can get another mouse.

(2) **I**—Both George and Lennie use conversational language and ungrammatical expressions like *ain't*.

(3) **V**—You can infer that George controls the relationship. He tells Lennie what to do and how to behave.

(4) **V**—Although Lennie is a grown man, he thinks and acts like a child. He cries when George scolds him. Lennie depends on George because Lennie trusts George's judgment.

GED PRACTICE
Exercise 2, page 259

1. (4) **Comprehension**
Oscar states in lines 5–6 that the two men live in "a big eight-room apartment."

2. (3) **Comprehension**
All of the stage directions referring to Felix describe his physical movements and housecleaning.

3. (2) **Comprehension**
Angrily is in italicized print in line 31.

4. (1) **Comprehension**
Felix clears the dishes, glasses, and coasters from the table. He also empties and wipes the ashtrays.

5. (2) **Analysis**
The dialogue between Felix and Oscar clearly reveals their different housekeeping habits. Oscar is annoyed because Felix is always cleaning the apartment.

GED PRACTICE
Exercise 3, pages 261–262

1. (3) **Analysis**
Willa gets exasperated when her husband says "I don't know" in reference to Billy's operation.

2. (4) **Comprehension**
The doctor knows Sheldon does not have a lot of money, but wants to emphasize that Billy must have the operation.

3. (2) **Analysis**
Sheldon finds himself in a difficult situation: he cares about his son, but he doesn't have much money, and Billy's illness will involve expensive medical care.

4. (5) **Comprehension**
The brothers wait in the hallway outside Billy's room while the doctor works on him. They ask their father if they can go in to visit him and how is he doing.

5. (1) **Synthesis**
The family must struggle with doing what's best for Billy and finding a way to pay the medical costs.

Exercise 4, pages 263–266

1. Nora and Helmer are seated at a table.

2. (5) Nora does not mean this statement literally. She is using a financial expression as a figure of speech to imply ending the marriage.

3. (3) Nora is using a figure of speech to describe her roles as wife and daughter. Helmer and her father have both treated Nora like a doll—a plaything, not a person.

4. Nora plays a make-believe role in an unreal home. (Answers may vary slightly.)

5. (1) **F**—Nora says, "I'm saying that we've never sat down seriously together and tried to get to the bottom of anything" (lines 21–22).

(2) **T**—Helmer has no complaints about the marriage and resents Nora's description of their relationship. He asks in line 36, "How can you speak of our marriage like that?"

(3) **T**—Although Helmer declares his love for Nora, she replies, "You never loved me. You've thought it fun to be in love with me, that's all." (lines 28–29).

(4) **F**—Helmer asks, "You mean I should constantly go and involve you in problems you couldn't possibly help me with?" (lines 19–20). This question implies that Helmer considers himself superior to Nora. In line 58 he also speaks of schooling her *and* the children.

(5) **F**—Nora tells Helmer, "you don't understand me" (line 4).

(6) **T**—Nora tells Helmer, "And you've always been so kind to me" (lines 48–49).

6. Answers will vary.

Exercise 5, pages 267–276

1. (2) As the scene opens, Willy says, "Like to have a little talk with you, Howard" (line 7). By playing with the wire recorder, Howard avoids the conversation with Willy.

2. (3) Willy's decision not to travel causes a heated argument between Willy and Howard. Their argument is the central action depicted in this scene.

3. (4) These lines from Willy's speech summarize the main point—the meaning of a sales career when Willy was a young man: "There was respect, and comradeship, and gratitude in it. Today it's all cut and dried . . . " (lines 148–149).

4. He has worked for the firm for thirty-four years.

5. "I don't want you to represent us." (line 200) "I think you need a good long rest, Willy." (line 203)

6. Answers will vary.

7. Three descriptions that apply to Willy are *proud*, *desperate*, and *frustrated*. Willy's long speech (lines 127–151) reveals his pride as a salesman. He also doesn't want his sons to support him financially. The stage directions—"*[desperation is on him now]*" (line 156) and "*[grasping HOWARD'S arm]*" (line 219)—show Willy's desperate reaction to Howard's refusal. Willy's anger reveals his frustration over a no-win situation.

8. Three descriptions that apply to Howard are *insensitive*, *impatient*, and *bored*. Howard is totally insensitive to Willy's emotional and financial needs. Howard also shows no regard for Willy's thirty-four years of service to the firm. The stage directions— "*[barely interested]*" (line 126) and "*[impatiently]*" (line 166)—reveal Howard's boredom and impatience.

9. (2) The essay implies that earlier heroes were individuals of stature—kings, queens, and nobles. However, in modern times there are few royals and nobles, so the common individual who works every day to provide the income for a living is a hero.

GED PRACTICE
Chapter Review, pages 277–281

1. (5) **Analysis**
You can conclude that Eddie's attachment to May is based on jealousy and possessiveness. He threatens to fight her dates and later says, "You'll never escape me either. I'll track you down no matter where you go."

2. (1) **Analysis**
A fifteen-year relationship filled with desperation, misunderstanding, and possessiveness is unhealthy.

3. (2) **Comprehension**
The word *now* is italicized three times in May's dialogue (lines 18–20). According to May's remarks, you can infer that his feelings for her are unpredictable.

4. (4) **Analysis**
You can conclude that her taking a drink and slamming down a bottle demonstrate her anger.

5. (2) **Analysis**
The stage directions state that a *tone of politely feigned interest, masking indifference* (lines 19–20) characterizes Brick's speech with Margaret.

6. (5) **Synthesis**
The children belong to Gooper and Mae. Mae is Brick's sister-in-law (lines 50–51). Therefore, you can infer that Gooper is Brick's brother.

7. (4) **Comprehension**
In line 60, Margaret refers to Big Daddy's birthday.

8. (1) **Comprehension**
Margaret repeatedly calls the children "no-neck monsters" to describe their appearance. She complains about their screaming and table manners.

9. (4) **Application**
Margaret is the only person onstage in this passage. Brick is in the shower. You hear his voice, but he is "unseen." Since Margaret is the center of attention, the camera would focus on her.

10. (3) **Extended Synthesis**
Maggie fights to win Brick's affections to start a family of their own. One reason for her resentment of Gooper and Mae's children is Big Daddy's love of the children and their need to compete for his favor.

11. (2) **Analysis**
Ruth calls Big Walter "a good man," and Mama agrees, "Yes, a fine man." These statements reveal their respect for him.

12. (1) **Comprehension**
Mama says that Big Walter "grieved hisself" over their baby's death.

13. (5) **Analysis**
Although Big Walter could be "hard-headed, mean, kind of wild with women," Mama accepted his faults and sympathized with his problems.

14. (3) **Comprehension**
Mama says in the concluding line of dialogue that Big Walter "just couldn't never catch up with his dreams, that's all."

15. (2) **Analysis**
This gesture emphasizes the thoughtfulness of Ruth's response to Mama: "Yes, life can be a barrel of disappointments, sometimes."

16. (4) **Application**
Big Walter once told Mama, "Seem like God didn't see fit to give the black man nothing but dreams—but He did give us children to make them dreams seem worthwhile." Therefore, you can conclude that if Big Walter were still alive, he would agree that children represent the hopes of the future.

Glossary

A

adjective   a part of speech that describes a person, place, thing, or idea

analysis   breaking something down into its parts and examining each part

application   transferring your understanding of a concept to a different situation

atmosphere   the emotions associated with a story's environment

C

cause   the reason for an action or situation

characterization   the methods an author uses to present characters to the reader

classification   sorting things, people, or ideas into categories

comparison   showing how two or more things are similar

comprehension   understanding what an author tells you directly

conclusion   a judgment made based on a set of facts and opinions

conflict   a struggle that occurs because of different needs or wishes among two or more people or groups, or opposing needs of an individual

context   the phrases and sentences that surround a word

contrast   showing how two or more things are different

D

description   an explanation of someone's or something's physical appearance or an experience

dialogue   a conversation between characters

diction   the words used to express ideas

drama   a written work designed to be acted out on a stage in which the writing consists almost entirely of dialogue between characters

E

effect   the results of a situation or action

example   a model that shows how something should be done

F

fact   a statement that can be proved

fiction   writing about imaginary people and events

figurative language   words that mean something other than their literal definition

I

inference   a conclusion not directly stated but drawn from a set of facts or opinions

M

main idea   the central message of a passage; what the passage is about

main-idea sentence   a sentence that expresses in general terms what a passage is about

metaphor   a comparison that implies that something is something else

N

narrator   the person telling a story

nonfiction   writing about real people, places, events, and social issues

novel   a long story giving a fully-developed portrayal of people, situations, and places

O

opinion   a statement that cannot be proved; a statement that reflects an individual or group's interpretation of something

P

personification   representing a nonliving thing as a human or animal

place   (in fiction) the specific location where a situation or event occurs

plot   the sequence of events in a story

poetry   a form of writing used to convey emotional truths in which the writer uses figurative language and writes in stanzas

point of view   the position from which a person, action, or situation is presented or evaluated

prose   writing in paragraph form

purpose   (in writing) the idea that ties all of the details in a passage together; the reason that the author wrote the passage

R

reasons   statements that answer the question "why?"

S

setting   the place, time, and atmosphere in which a situation occurs

short story   a story focusing on one major event or series of events

simile   a direct comparison using the words *as*, *like*, or *than*

stage directions   directions to actors in a play explaining what their tone of voice, facial expressions, and gestures should be

stanza   in poetry, a group of written lines arranged together

structure   the way an author organizes his or her message

style   the distinguishing characteristics of an artist's performance or work

supporting details   specific statements that give more information about the central message of a passage

synthesis   the integrating of information from different sources to reach a new understanding

T

theme   the underlying meaning of a story

time   (in fiction) the time of day, season, or historical period when an event takes place

tone   an author's attitude toward his or her subject

topic sentence   a sentence that expresses in general terms what a paragraph is about

Index